SLIMMIng
BIBLE

SLIMMING
BIBLE

A Diet for Life

MICHELE SIMMONS

BLOOMSBURY

First published in 1997

Bloomsbury Publishing plc
38 Soho Square
London, W1V 5DF

A copy of the CIP entry for this book is available
from the British Library

ISBN 0 7475 2319 3

10 9 8 7 6 5 4 3 2

Jacket design by Slatter – Anderson
Designed by Neysa Moss Design
Typeset by Hewer Text Composition Services, Edinburgh
Printed in Great Britain by Clays Ltd, St Ives plc.

Contents

Acknowledgements

WHILST WRITING this book I have been struck by the kindness and generosity of all whom I have contacted, in an attempt to provide the most up-to-date and medically correct information. From the BMA to the Department of Health and the Royal College of Physicians – just about everyone I have spoken to has helped me to gain a better understanding of the subject.

Particular thanks go to David Sanders and Sean Larkin of the Health Education Authority; the Dunn Nutrition Centre and The Flour Advisory Bureau for allowing me to use their invaluable Healthy Eating Pyramid.

I am also grateful to cookery whizz Petra Jackson for giving me so much of her time and expertise in helping to devise a healthy and exciting selection of recipes. Her patience and diplomacy were much appreciated! Dr Elizabeth Evans, Scientific Director of Slimming Magazine Clubs was, as ever, generous of her time and knowledge – even to the extent of taking some of my copy home to read at Christmas – just to make sure I was getting things right. Her vast experience and contribution to the whole area of slimming can't be underestimated and she has helped me to focus on the areas that are of concern – not just to self-appointed experts in the field but to those who really matter – anyone who has ever tried, or wanted to lose weight or felt uneasy about their size.

Rowena Gaunt at Bloomsbury has, as always, provided calm and good cheer whenever needed, above and beyond the call of duty – including the so-called time off taken for maternity leave!

However, the two people who deserve the most thanks for patience, support, and humour are Jeff Ostrove and Chris McLaughlin. They have managed to preserve my sanity – if not theirs!

And most importantly, to the late Jenny Glew, whose wisdom, humour and optimism still provide, as ever, a constant source of inspiration.

Introduction

I HAVE SPENT more than a decade writing about health and slimming and, over the years, I have been lucky enough to meet many readers. And all have convinced me that whether or not we think women should lose weight, there's an awful lot of women who want to. And that's not because they want to look like Pamela Anderson, or Cindy Crawford - or even Rosemary Conley. In almost all cases, the women I have spoken to want to lose weight because they want to feel better, move faster and, on occasions, literally breathe more easily.

Of course it's unhealthy to be obsessed about your weight and it's unnatural to try to get down to a weight that leaves you looking scrawny, lacking in energy and having to survive on meagre amounts of food that would barely keep a rabbit alive. But, read some of the diet bashers of today and you could be forgiven for thinking that anyone who writes a word about diets is a morally suspect, money-grabbing opportunist, intent on perverting the eating habits of a generation . . .

In fact, as editor of a top-selling slimming magazine, I was often called upon to defend myself, and my fellow 'corrupters', for promoting such insidious concepts as calorie counting, portion control and artificial sweeteners.

On one occasion, I was even invited onto a popular daily television magazine show to 'debate' the issue. The show was a perfect example of how anything to do with losing weight becomes tarred with the same brush . . . it didn't matter whether you were pushing a tablet that promises to take off pounds or, simply, a healthier approach to eating based on the latest thinking, you were still treated as a latter-day leper - a person to be reviled at all costs.

My hurt pride aside, what I found particularly astounding was that no one - and that included the show's host - was the slightest bit interested in discussing the very real problem that exists today - obesity - and the all too painful reality for many men and women: a constant stream of unsuccessful attempts at losing excess pounds where the self-esteem plummets almost at the same rate as the weight soars. On the one hand as a nation we're getting fatter, but on the other we're shunning any advice on how best to reverse that process. But the big question is – *why*?

This book is an attempt to answer that question and to understand what we, as individuals, should be doing about it. It looks at our relationship with food, and examines the whole question of exactly why we want to lose weight in the first place. It's for anybody who has ever tried to come to terms with their weight – whether they are obese, overweight or just feel uncomfortable with the size they are.

It's my belief that there is an answer – albeit not a simple one. And it all comes down to the way you think. What's important is to find a diet that fits in with your lifestyle and to find a way of eating that revolves around what you can eat – not what you can't. Slimmers and non-slimmers alike eat food – not calories – and should greet meals with relish rather than feeling wracked with guilt.

Women that I've spoken to who had, over the years, grown to obese proportions have talked about how losing weight has, literally, changed their lives. It has given them back their identity, their self-esteem – the power to control their lives again. This book, then, is hopefully about taking control and giving you the power to change. It doesn't matter how small or great that change is. Even if you just end up being aware of what you eat – and why – the change has been significant enough . . . re-think your relationship with food, and you may just end up re-thinking your life.

PART ONE
The Problems

Chapter One

In the Beginning

IN THE BEGINNING there were thin people and not so thin people . . . Not so thin were healthier, fitter and generally richer. A decent amount of padding invariably showed that you could afford to eat well. On the other hand, being thin was a sign of poverty, weakness – even consumption. But years ago people also assumed that getting older meant getting plumper – wasn't everyone's grandmother fat? Fat was something that just happened, particularly to women. No one thought much of it. Probably because women were too busy looking after their families and trying to make ends meet.

So, what happened? Well, fashion and the mass media happened. The rich were tall, elegant but mostly they were slim. Something to aspire to. And the arrival of film and glossy magazines meant we could see how they did it. With the right shade of lipstick, right height of heel and a thick belt, you too could look like . . . Jane Wyman, Jane Russell, Marilyn Monroe. Of course, not everyone wanted to. But for the ones who did, the movies heralded the shape of things to come . . . literally. Hollywood sold us a dream – and with it the dream shape. And so a generation of young women were born who dyed their hair, pushed up their breasts, pulled in their waists and painted their lips red. And if nature wasn't kind enough to supply a decent framework, there were ways to improve on nature. Apart from squeezing yourself into clothes a size too small, you could 'naturally' reduce your size by eating less. *You simply dieted down to your dreams*.

Now before you conclude that times haven't changed much, here's an interesting point to consider. Whilst a significant number of women were – and, there's a case for saying, still are – all but starving themselves slim to look 'right', an even more significant number are eating themselves into obesity. In fact, according to the statisticians, politicians, psychotherapists and self-appointed dieting gurus, the country appears to be split into two: those who eat too much – and those who don't eat enough. We're either obese or anorexic. We're either obsessed with food to such an extent we can hardly bear to eat anything, or we're so gluttonous that we're too busy stuffing ourselves silly to give more than a cursory shrug to the whole question of size.

And whilst the experts fall firmly into two camps - the pro-dieters and the diet bashers - you can be forgiven for wondering whether you should be consulting your inner 'child' rather than confronting your outer fat. All in all, there's an awful lot of silliness written about slimming. Being thin is an extreme as much as being obese. But, between the two is, if you pardon the expression, a world of weight.

NO MIRACLE CURE

The problem is that it's hard to work out the sense from the nonsense. Which is why this is a book about women and food . . . and diets. And, as the song goes, like love and marriage, 'you can't have one without the other'. It's also why this diet book is different from all other diet books. It makes no promises, no claims, and offers no miracle cures. And if it's a miracle cure that you want, I suggest you put the book back on the shelf now! What this book *is*, is an attempt to pull together all the elements that make up the slimming world - and make up the person who wants to slim - YOU.

Having worked in the health and slimming field for years I can say, hand on heart, reams have been written on the subject of diets: how we diet, why we diet, when we diet. Not forgetting of course the 'Big Diet': many a good tree has been sacrificed to provide enough paper to make way for theories on women who spend their lives lurching from the *Hip and Thigh* to the *Hay*, from *The Bank Balance Diet* to *The BBC Diet*. We've gone from *Grapefruit* to *Good Calories*; from *Metabolic Diets* to *Meal Replacements* right through to *You Don't Have to Diet* and *Diets Don't Work*. And then we've had books on some of the people who do diet, some of the people who don't . . . and some of the people who should diet - and some who shouldn't . . .

In fact, when you think about it, what's written about diets has a lot in common with what's written about sex. You could say, in many ways, women and diets *are* like men and sex. Just think: there's an awful lot of rubbish written about sex generally - and about men in particular. And the same is true of diets generally - but about women in particular. Where sex and men are concerned, we're told again and again that men think about sex umpteen times a minute: it's beyond their control and, the conclusion is, generally, that they can't help themselves. It's society's fault, the media's fault, their families' . . . *They have no control*. But the same is often said about women and diets: when it comes to eating, women are often seen as having *no control*. It's society's fault, it's the media's fault. Or – and this is always a good one to lob in – it's their mothers' fault. Of course in some cases any of those factors could play a part. But, if we take the men and sex argument, by allowing them to shield behind a wall of excuses, we're really saying . . . it's okay, carry on the way you are. Which is another way of saying no one really expects you to change, and no one expects you to have control over your life . . .

But I believe we do *have control and we* can *change. And that includes what we eat.*

However, changing is a complicated business but, if you take some time to understand how to take control – and more importantly why you haven't in the past – you're building solid foundations that will give you a much better chance of getting what you set out to achieve. As I hope I'll show, a prescription for healthy eating isn't something that you take, like a course of antibiotics. You don't stick with it for a given period and then say, *I'm okay now*. The problem with many diets is that, as with antibiotics, they often come with a list of dos and don'ts. Let's face it, when we're prescribed antibiotics we're given instructions – anything from 'no alcohol' to 'do not operate machinery'. And, with many diets, it's often the same. Don't eat biscuits, avoid cakes, steer clear of chocolate, pass on the pies . . . you know the type of thing?

Which is why, probably, all those diets you've tried in the past have been, if you're lucky, a short-term success – but a long-term failure. In the same way that a dog isn't just for Christmas, it's for life, the same can be said when it comes to re-thinking about the way we eat . . .

A ROSE BY ANY OTHER NAME . . .

Dieting is, of course, nothing particularly new. Good old Hippocrates, the ancient Greek, was probably the first person who noticed that your size could have a considerable bearing on your health. And the first diet on record was dispensed, in France, a hundred years ago, by a doctor who was convinced that the type, and amount, of food his patient was eating was having an adverse effect on his health. What all this means is that we've actually been dieting for a hundred years . . .

These days, unfortunately, the word diet has been largely hijacked by the anti-dieting lobby. One reason, I think, is to do with money. Slimming has become a money-spinning industry. A fortune is made from slimming foods and the profits from meal replacements – found at any good chemist near you – are phenomenal. Even the humble calorie-counted cook-chill meal is often more expensive than the ordinary version containing the same, or slightly more fat. Let's face it, when money's involved, motives are questioned, people become suspicious. And it isn't helped by the fact that many of the more high-profile authors are not academics or medics. That said, most of the writers' knowledge is culled from years in the business – and, in some cases, years of talking to academics and medics. So, while it's become almost *de rigueur* to attack some of the high priestesses of diets, many have been in the 'business' for years, dealing with slimmers, often on a daily basis, trying to monitor what works – and what doesn't.

Diet, according to the dictionary, can mean anything from 'the food and drink that a person or animal regularly consumes' to 'a specific allowance or selection of food'. But the word diet has come to mean a restrictive way of eating. You can go on a fat-free diet, a sugar-free diet, a detoxification diet, a grapefruit diet. Then there are the diets that appeal to what we might consider to be the less appealing parts of ourselves: the Slob's Diet; The Lazy Girl's Diet, The 5 Minute Diet (five minutes because that's how long the meals take to prepare). In the slimming industry, the key is to come up with 'an angle'. And most exploit the fact that we'd all rather do as little as is humanly possible to ensure that we can take off as much weight as possible – with the minimum of fuss . . . and time. As one nutritionist once said to me, 'There's no such thing as a new diet. The only thing that we change is the way we package it.' That's worth remembering next time *you* may be about to embark on this season's slimming special . . . !

Of course even though there is no such thing as a new diet, the reality is that every year sees new dieters. Statisticians tell us that 70 per cent of women diet at some time in their lives. At any one time nearly 40 per cent of all adults are trying to slim – and over 67 per cent of these are women. But all the evidence shows that there's a lot of people doing something wrong when it comes to trying to take control of their weight. Despite all that dieting, according to the British Medical Association, 38 per cent of women are overweight and 12 per cent are obese. And that figure is increasing. Added to this, a survey at King's College, London, has reported that 98 per cent of diets actually fail. Perhaps this is less surprising when we consider the appalling way dieters are treated.

Within the diet, or should I say anti-diet, industry, there appears to be a type of guerrilla warfare between dieters and the anti-dieters who suggest that admitting you want to lose some weight indicates that you're not only several slices short of a loaf but you're only doing it because 'everyone else' wants you to and you're using it as a diversion tactic to stop you facing the *real* problems in your life – which is that you have a secret desire to look like Kate Moss (does anyone really?) or you're about to enter a period of stuffing and starving that will last at least ten years. But the truth is you don't have to be a dyed-in-the-wool dieter to feel dissatisfied with the way you look. One survey, sponsored by the Butter Council, in 1992, found that 80 per cent of women are dissatisfied with their shape, and 88 per cent of women admitted to avoiding food some days.

Of course losing weight can well mean more than shedding a couple of stone. There could be all sorts of reasons why you put on the weight or, more importantly, why you can't take it off and – perhaps most importantly – why you want to take it off. And while there are undoubtedly an awful lot of influences – many of which we're not even conscious of – that *do* put pressure on us to lose weight, many women who talk about going on a diet want to do it simply for themselves. Not because of an overbearing partner, a dominant parent or a cruelly critical colleague. But simply because *they want to*.

Having spent years not only interviewing past slimmers but also people who have worked with many of these women, I am convinced that there are many women who, as far as the experts are concerned, are either considerably overweight or obese. But, most importantly, many of these women are unhappy about their size. And not because they're obsessed with looking like Kate Moss or any other underweight figures who have become symbols for the anti-diet industry. It is my belief that many women want to lose weight for themselves because they feel unhappy or unhealthy – or both.

A NATIONAL PASTIME?

But what's important is that if you do want to lose weight, you do it for the right reasons, and the right way. And that you're realistic. Ultimately what goes into your mind is as important as what goes into your body, which is why I have devoted so much space to the whole question of what makes us eat. Logically, of course, the answer is hunger. If only it were that simple! Every time you reach for another chocolate bar the chances of it being because you're hungry are pretty far down the list of reasons. Of course, it could be just because you want it. And that's fine. Unless of course ten minutes later you end up hating yourself and feeling as if you have no willpower – and no control over your life. Let's face it, food – like love – is satisfying but what do you do when it's not satisfying you? Go on eating until it does? Or worse, stop eating altogether?

Yet the number of people dieting grows as much as the number of people who are overweight. Whatever way you look at it, clearly dieting is something of a national pastime – if not an obsession. The big question of course is, why?

You may not be surprised to hear that there is a multitude of theories. **Social historians** say . . . it's because our eating habits have changed. **Doctors** say . . . it's down to too much fat and not enough exercise. **Therapists** say . . . it's an expression of some fundamental unhappiness. **Psychologists** say . . . it's to do with deprivation. **Scientists** say . . . it's because we eat too much. **Feminists** say . . . it's another symptom of male oppression. **Diet bashers** say . . . it's the media. **Nutritionists** say . . . it's because we don't understand enough about food. **Women** say . . . 'I'd really like to lose a little weight but don't know how . . .' **The government** says . . . we're getting fatter, let's set a target and that'll be the end to the problem!

You see, in the same way that everyone has their own theory of what makes a successful sex life, there are almost as many people who, ostensibly, have the answer to the nation's weight problems. The problem is they *don't*. The truth is there is no simple answer. Before we even attempt to understand why we want to diet – or why we even put on weight in the first place, we need to understand a bit about our relationship with food. *Why* we eat, *when* we eat – and *how* we eat.

As psychologist Sara Gilbert explains in *Tomorrow I'll be Slim* (Routledge), 'if we can have some understanding of what influences the way we eat, both in the normal course of events and when we are trying to diet, then we stand a better chance of making informed decisions about whether to diet in the first place and of achieving success if we do.' But wanting to lose weight doesn't necessarily indicate some deep psychological problem. No more than being obese suggests a personality disorder. Maybe you want to lose some weight because you feel better when you weigh less, when your clothes aren't tight, when you don't get breathless from walking up a flight of stairs. Maybe you just feel happier with yourself . . . many slimmers complain that being 'large' can mean anything from being ignored to being addressed slowly as well as loudly, to being stared at in disbelief as they attempt to eat a meal in a public place.

Of course this behaviour is wrong and, in an ideal world, people shouldn't be treated differently. But, we live in the real world, not a perfect world and I believe it's patronizing to expect women who, as we've seen, can be perceived as being at a disadvantage, to take on the mantle of idealism. I think that to a certain extent, the whole fat/thin debate has been hijacked by a variety of warring factions which includes both big players like the food industry and the government and smaller ones like the politically correct, as well as opportunists who are only too happy to jump on the weight wagon as soon as a new 'angle' presents itself. But, through the maze of misinformation, the people whom it's easy to forget are the women who actually *do* want to lose some weight. They don't want to look like Twiggy and wouldn't dream of identifying with Kate Moss, Naomi Campbell or Claudia Schiffer. And how many women do any of us know who look like *any* of them?

THERE IS NO SECRET

There are endless theories as to why we put on weight, why we want to lose weight and why we're so bad about doing it - whether that means losing it at all or keeping it off once we have lost it. It seems to be that the problem is that everyone who creates a diet, a theory or a 'programme' presents their information as if it is the one and only solution - the answer to every dieter's prayer. As far as I can see, the real secret is . . . there is no secret. Wanting to lose weight has as much to do with your state of mind as it has to do with the state of your body. The two aren't mutually exclusive. What's more, people who treat them as if they are will spend their lives wanting, trying and failing to be something they're not. It's a bit like being told the answer to a difficult maths problem without anyone explaining how you get the answer. If you don't understand the theory, the practice is not going to make a whole lot of sense. Eating a tub of cottage cheese when your mind is still craving for a chocolate bar is hardly a recipe for success!

What I hope this book attempts to do is to give you the complete picture about slimming. All the whys, wheres and hows. At first you may think I've devoted a large chunk of the book to what getting fat - as well as getting slim - means. I make no apology for this. I fervently believe that the only way we're really going to take control is by understanding how our bodies got like that in the first place. Eating can provide a mental need as much as a physical one - haven't we all, at some time, reached for 'something nice', like chocolate or a packet of sweets, when we're feeling down? The actual act of trying to lift our spirits by filling our stomach is a good example of the part our mind plays in determining what, as well as when and how, we eat.

By looking at why you want to get slim in the first place you may also find that you start to question what you want out of getting slim. Maybe it's a wardrobe of size ten dresses, but maybe what you're also after is the the confidence that you feel goes with being a size ten. Or maybe you just want to change everything and you feel a different body will mean a different life. Let's face it, for women, how we look is mixed up with what we are - in a society that judges people by their appearance, when you move away from this so-called acceptable image, you assume people's perceptions of you change. Just look at the media's obsession with the Duchess of York - from the 'Duchess of Pork' to 'Slimline Fergie', the coverage of the former Sarah Ferguson seems to increase or decrease - depending on the size of her waistline.

So this book is not just about losing weight. It's about being and, if necessary, getting to, a weight that you feel happy about. And it's about arriving at a state of mind that means you feel confident about the way you feel as much as the way you look. It's about discovering why you want to lose weight as much as why you put it on in the first place. There is no doubt that food - whether that involves buying it, preparing it, cooking it or eating it - can cause great concern for a great many people. And it's only by really trying to understand our relationship with food that we can begin to get back in the driving seat, and get back in control. This book is designed to help you gain a better understanding of yourself as well as your body image. It will, hopefully, offer explanations as to why food has, up to now, played an important part in your life - be it consistently or intermittently. Ultimately I hope it will help to change your approach to food - buying it as well as eating it.

Apart from the chapters that explore some of your personal food history, I have included chapters that cover some of the different theories as to why we may have put on weight – and why it can be so hard to take it off. There is also a section on food (eating it rather than avoiding it!), and I've included some up-to-date information on the type of foods that women in particular should be concentrating on: foods to get you healthy and keep you that way. If you want to buy chocolate, then that's fine, but at least you know you're buying something high in fat and sugar. But you might decide to go for one of those fruit pies, stuffed with apples and blackberries, in a wholemeal pastry crust, thinking that's pretty healthy – full of fruit and wholemeal flour – but in fact, some pies can contain as much fat as chocolate does.

And it isn't just the sweet pies – the savoury ones are also loaded with the sort of things that experts are telling us to cut back on. So, while there's nothing wrong with buying a bar of chocolate because you know what is in it, opting for a pie when you think you're getting one thing, but you're actually getting something completely different, is altogether another question. So knowing *what* you're eating can be as important as *why* you're eating it.

For those who prefer a more structured approach I have included a selection of food plans. These are not devised initially as diet sheets: the idea is to give a variety of examples of how easy it is to eat a varied, mixed – and appetizing – diet that doesn't count calories.

There is also a chapter that will guide you through some of the support systems that are on offer – from slimming clubs to calorie-counted meals. Ultimately, what I have tried to do with this book is to provide as much information as possible for readers. Enough for you to make up your own mind about what's right for you. Everyone is unique and everyone has their own reasons for wanting to lose – or for that matter not lose – weight. Even if you are overweight, you still need to eat – and enough to keep your body healthy. Being thin at the expense of your health is being on a hiding to nothing. And if at the end of the day you're too weak and sick to enjoy a slimmer you, what's the point? The answer is to find a weight that suits your body and your mind. You need to feel good about yourself but you also need to feel healthy.

All that I've tried to do is provide enough information for you to be able to decide what's right for you. By making your own decision you can be sure of being in control. And if you do binge, overeat, have that bar of chocolate that's 'had its eye on you for ages' . . .? Remember, it doesn't much matter. Eating a little of what you fancy is no big deal. It's only a problem when what you fancy is high in fat and you don't stop at a little. At the end of the day what's important is the way in which you eat and the way you feel about eating. A healthy attitude is more likely to mean a healthy appetite.

Chapter Two

Fat as a National Issue

IF YOU'RE WORRIED about being fat, you may be interested to know you're not the only one. Last year the *Daily Telegraph* ran a front-page news story, called, 'Alarm over huge rise in obesity'. They had managed to get hold of a government report that predicted 'an explosion in obesity that could lead to a disastrous decline in general health'. This rather sobering fact is something of an embarrassment to a government that merrily announced, three years ago, that their aim was to reduce the numbers of obese men and women aged 16–64, by at least 25 per cent for men and at least 33 per cent for women by the year 2005.

You may think that doctors could provide more support but the scale of the problem clearly overwhelms the resources available to deal with it. In fact the Office of Health Economics estimates that to provide weekly consultations, every GP in England could have their workload increased by as many as 41 obese, or 136 overweight, patients every day. *Clearly the problem is getting out of hand*.

WHAT HISTORY TELLS US

But it wasn't so long ago that one of the major nutritional problems concerning this country was one of *under*nourishment. Ironically, during the first half of the century doses of fish oil were being given out in some areas by the bucket load. The diseases that were food-related tended to be the result of deficiencies – diets that were lacking in essential vitamins, such as cases of rickets caused by lack of vitamin D. There was also a shortage of protein – vital for growth – as well as a lack of food in the first place.

Poorer people were more likely to be shorter, as well as weaker. In the First World War Britain was characterized as having a fairly undernourished army and the image portrayed by the weak and wimpish Baldrick, played wonderfully by Tony Robinson, Rowan Atkinson's sidekick in Blackadder, is an example of how the poorly-fed, conscripted members of the Forces differed from the well-fed, upright and 'strong' members of the Army's élite – such as the objectionable Blackadder himself. In fact the creation of the rather pathetic, pale and unhealthy Baldrick is closer to reality than many Blackadder fans may realize. When conscripts underwent a medical examination at the beginning of the First World War, apparently only three in nine were deemed fully fit. Of the rest, three were completely unfit, two were below average and one was so undernourished they were considered completely unsuitable for service.

Sadly the situation hadn't changed 20 odd years later when the poorly children of the working classes in the inner cities were, whenever possible, sent to the country where they were able to breathe clean air and eat a varied diet, in many cases for the first time. If people were encouraged to eat anything, often it was fat which was able to, literally, fatten them up. Nineteen thirty-four saw the introduction of free milk for schoolchildren, something that remained a right for kids for almost 40 years, right up until a Mrs Margaret Thatcher arrived at the Education Department in the early Seventies. And by the late Thirties, children were receiving free vitamins and cod liver oil as well as concentrated orange juice if they were under five.

The outbreak of the Second World War saw many men enlisting to escape the poverty of the depression and, in many cases, the Army introduced these sheltered young soldiers to a completely different way of life. Unlike these days when we have the television to show us exactly how 'the other half lives', for the generation that came of age in the Thirties and Forties, the Army was an opportunity not only to broaden their horizons, but to broaden their appetites too.

Apart from having a healthy Army, restrictions on food trade and concern over the general health of the nation meant the government knew they needed to devise a food policy, with the emphasis being on healthy eating and the need for exercise. With the outbreak of war, when most people's energies were put to work on the war effort, there was a shortage of food – hence the introduction of rationing, which meant the nation had to depend on the government for advice on what to eat . . . although 'what' tended to depend on what was available. My mother tells me that she never saw a banana or a fresh egg for years and her family, like others, was encouraged to grow what they could and vegetable patches proliferated.

Coming from a time when supermarkets are groaning with food, it's hard to appreciate what it was like to have limitations imposed on what we eat, even though, at the time, the government's Ministry of Food referred to rations as 'the foundation of your fighting diet'. Bearing in mind that getting hold of the food depended on availability, for an adult, per week, these 'foundations' translated into:

- 2oz (55g) butter
- 4oz (100g) margarine
- Between 2–4 oz (50g–100g) cooking fat
- 2oz (55g) cheese
- 2–3 pts (1200ml–1800ml) milk
- 8oz (225g) sugar
- 1lb preserves – every two months
- 12oz (350g) sweets every month
- 4oz (115g) bacon and ham
- 2oz (55g) tea

Meat was linked to price: you were allowed up to the value of the equivalent of 6p today – not a huge amount by anyone's standards!

In Christina Hardyment's *Slice of Life* (published by BBC Books), she explains how the government developed a three-pronged offensive. Apart from making sure that women had the right sort of information to make sure they fed their families well, price control and rationing meant people bought nutrient-dense foods and to make sure that everyone had one substantial, nutritious meal a day, canteens and civic restaurants were established and school dinners introduced. Some of those original ideas remain to this day. The tradition of eating the main meal of the day outside the home continued for many years. In some cases it still continues. School-children in particular have benefited, although the advantages of school dinners are more questionable these days with the government forcing many local authorities to turn to private catering companies where the emphasis is more likely to be on cheaper, faster, fatty foods than more nutritionally balanced meals.

Without doubt making food exciting certainly presented a challenge to people who cooked in the war, but many a nutritionist today would be delighted if we ate as little fat, sugar and meat, and as many vegetables, as was consumed during the war years. And if there were cases of overeating, they tended to occur on special occasions when rations had been saved, begged or borrowed. Rationing went on well after the war when the government did its best to try to build up the country's depleted wealth. While the Forties' diet may not have been exciting, the British left the Forties a fitter, healthier nation than it had been when the decade started. And, with Beveridge's vision of a country of people who would always have access to some of the fundamental rights – food, health, education – from cradle to grave, things looked like they could only get better.

But they didn't. So what happened? Well, quite a lot, actually.

THERE'S SO SUCH MORE CHOICE

With rationing a dim and distant memory, the availability of food no longer depends on seasons or ships arriving from the other side of the world with cargoes of 'fresh' fruit and vegetables. Advances in transportation, as well as in food technology, mean that we can expect to find all manners of exotic fare in the shops – regardless of the time of year. And after years of going without and worrying over whether you were getting enough, you could suddenly base your choice of food on what you wanted, rather than what your body needed or what was available. By the Fifties and Sixties food became steadily more plentiful and people could eat as much as they wanted of sugar, eggs, fat, meat, chocolate and sweets.

If we put this in the context of the Nineties, when packets of biscuits are readily available, we'll gaily chomp our way through a plateful, whereas in World War Two rationing meant that if you had the ingredients to cook a batch of biscuits, you expected them to last. The Sixties saw an explosion of manufactured food. This has often meant that food has become more convenient (it can be stored rather than needing to be eaten immediately) and better preserved. But the disadvantage is that the original foods have undergone so much processing that they may bear little resemblance to their original components in terms of nutritional value.

Supermarkets have increasingly replaced small shops (which means we're faced with a torrent of choice even when we've only popped in for a carton of milk), fast food has arrived from America and food technologists have created a variety of tastes, textures and colours which, in some cases, have little to do with the actual foods that they set out to represent. Who needs strawberries when you can produce strawberry flavour?

Colin Tudge, in *The Food Connection* (BBC Books) compares how differently we select what we eat in the days of plenty, compared to the times when we had to fight and forage for food. In the past, our appetites had a definite role and were determined 'to help us find rare but valuable nutrients, against whatever odds'. Now, of course, this has all changed and, as Tudge wryly remarks, whereas 'our jungle ancestors learned to live with austerity. In our jungle, we must learn to steer a course through abundance'.

FAT CAN BE CHEAPER

How many times have you picked up the packets of reduced fat 'healthy' (interestingly, no one actually refers to the alternative as 'unhealthy') meat, realized that it is about *twice* the price of the family pack, only to find yourself reluctantly putting it back in the freezer cabinet, while you feel you have no alternative but to buy the cheaper, fattier version?

Even when we know the theory of what we should be eating, putting it into practice can be as expensive a business as it is inconvenient. The fact is, ordinary meat is half of the price of healthier cuts and foods like low-fat sausages, beefburgers and reduced-fat cheese are also considerably more expensive. Subsidies from the European Union mean that milk, butter and sugar can be sold particularly cheaply and schools and caterers, who have access to the EU butter mountains, can buy whole milk considerably cheaper than skimmed milk – one of the reasons that full-fat dairy products are cheaper to produce than their reduced-fat alternatives. On the other hand, packets of biscuits and cakes are cheap – and filling – and are made from inexpensive ingredients like fat, sugar and flour. Our diet has increasingly become a more refined one and the more refined our foods, the more likely they are to be stripped of their essential nutrients.

We also eat out more now than ever before. In *Which? Way To A Healthier Diet* (Consumers Association), the authors noted that according to recent studies, men on average now get a third and women at least a quarter of their calories from eating out. Unfortunately though, as the authors discovered, 'food eaten outside the home is more likely to have a high proportion of fat than food cooked at home. Hot dogs, chips and hamburgers topped with hefty dollops of mayonnaise, relish or cheese have helped to see to that.'

With an increasing demand for convenience foods, the manufacturers are obviously under pressure to produce as much as they can, as cheaply as they can. And nothing's much cheaper than fat. So the chances are those plump economy sausages have been bulked out with fat and bread, and the family-value packs of meat contain fat from various parts of the animal's body, including MRM (mechanically, recovered meat), which is basically anything that the food manufacturer's machine can suck off from the animal's carcass, and that invariably includes fat, gristle and muscle. None of which offers much on the 'goodness' front.

OUR FOOD HABITS HAVE CHANGED

Not so long ago eating meat frequently was seen as a sign of affluence. It meant you earned enough to *afford* to eat meat. No one saw too much meat as a bad thing. Meat and meat fat were what we ate. Eating your crackling with your pork was what everyone did, and how many people can remember fighting with their brothers and sisters so that *they* got to eat the crispy skin on the roast? And it was only a few generations ago when almost every family kept a pot of hardened fat from the roast, which was not only used in cooking but often spread on your bread. There's still many a person who, given the right company, will wax lyrical about the joys of bread and dripping!

Food, or to be more precise, eating, also used to be much more of an occasion. As a nation, these days our lives are less dominated by mealtimes. The vast choice of convenience foods has meant it's quite possible for all members of the family to eat something completely different, at different times, with little extra preparation. Women, increasingly, are having to cope with two jobs – one inside and one outside of the home. This means that short cuts like convenience foods and the introduction of cook-chill cabinets have changed the way we eat, as well as cook. Microwaves have also meant that meals can be prepared quickly and simply. And with the plethora of new 'quick' 'convenience' products we are all happily being seduced by convenient, ready-prepared, all-in-one-box-type meals.

Supermarkets even sell jacket potatoes, cleaned and halved, just waiting to be popped in the microwave for a few minutes to complete the 'cooking' process.

The move away from eating together as a family seems to coincide with an increase in take-aways which now account for more than a quarter of the food that we eat. In this country, we manage to get through more than 4,000,000 take-away meals a year. The whole eating experience has become one typified less by enjoyment and more by necessity. We refuel rather than eat, and the quicker and easier the refuelling process is the better.

WE EAT DIFFERENTLY

Snacks are forming a much greater part of our diet than before. For example, by 1990 the total sales of snack foods in the UK reached about £1000 million. Of this £585 million were spent on crisps; £242 million on savoury snacks whilst a staggering £930 million was spent on biscuits. Furthermore, a survey carried out by Taylor Nelson discovered that snacks and light meals accounted for 40 per cent of in-home eating occasions. As social historian Christina Hardyment remarks in her book, *Slice of Life*, 'in this context, food is not so much a source of nutrition as a means of immediate oral gratification, of comfort, even entertainment'.

We've learnt to rely on snack foods to 'fill that gap' and just to make sure we don't have to wait until mealtimes to eat if we don't want to, most stations – not to mention pubs, hospitals, colleges and fast-food centres – provide a variety of machines piled high with snacks, generally all high on fat and low on nutrients. In fact, last year we were told gleefully that Britain is a nation of chocoholics with sales growing to 510,000 tons, as more and more types of chocolate goodies tempt our tastebuds. Apparently nine out of ten people eat chocolate regularly, spending an average of more than £1 a week – twice as much as they did a decade ago.

Cadbury's annual review of the chocolate market in 1993 reported that sales grew 79 per cent to a record £3.1 billion. The confectionery industry now, it seems, is worth more than the tea, coffee, biscuit and crisp markets combined. However, while nutritionists and health educationalists around the country were probably gnashing their teeth in horror, Cadbury's were truly delighted, with their marketing director, Alan Palmer, declaring, 'Chocolate has firmly established itself as a versatile food and as a widely acceptable gift, treat, snack or simple indulgence.' Grazing, it seems, is no longer a term simply reserved for cows . . .

LACK OF KNOWLEDGE

Because we're relying much more on ready-prepared meals – either to save time or simply because it's more convenient – cooking has received something of a bad press. It's become associated with thankless drudgery which takes us away from doing things that are 'much more important' – and this is emphasized all the more by advertising campaigns, designed exclusively to convince potential customers, mainly women, that fast-food products really *will* change their lives. We've almost reached the stage where cooking is perceived as something you do on special occasions or when you're entertaining. The spectacular success of the variety of food programmes that have appeared over the last five years or so bear testament to the fact that cooking food has been elevated from an everyday chore to a special occasion activity.

Whilst Delia Smith offers a weekly step-by-step pot-pourri of tempting delicacies, it has to be said that, generally, most of us don't regularly include such ingredients as champagne vinegar or even cranberries, in our weekly family suppers. Keith Floyd, too, offers a wonderfully entertaining half hour as we watch him slosh – sometimes quite literally – his way through sautéing, braising and pan frying, but there's little that we can take away from the programme and apply to daily cooking. Whilst I accept that this is not necessarily the aim of the 30 minutes of culinary expertise on TV, learning the correct way to poach quails' eggs, or cook grouse, is not quite as handy as being shown how to make, say, a really good vegetable lasagne or a low-fat tart.

Of course cookery programmes are wonderfully inspirational but the majority of recipes we see whizzed up these days bear little resemblance to our day-to-day cookery – as little as Fanny Craddock did, all resplendent in swathes of chiffon, complete with full war paint and the obligatory Sixties nipped-in waist! – as she issued instructions to Johnny. Let's face it, the less we see of people displaying basic cooking skills, the less opportunity there is for us to learn how to cook. The preparation of food simply becomes time-consuming – and boring. And something you only do when you have to.

Delia Smith probably offers the most practical approach, although at times her list of ingredients can make even sophisticated shoppers reel.

Curiously, she has had to endure more criticism than other TV cooks. Whether it's because she's female and prefers to show viewers what to do, rather than show how clever she is, is open to discussion. Interestingly, though, whatever the critics say, her books *walk* off the shelves, which must say something about our need for being shown exactly what to do when it comes to cooking . . .

PEOPLE ARE CONFUSED

In a Mori poll, conducted in 1992, interviewees were questioned on their attitudes towards a healthy diet and whilst 95 per cent believed healthy eating to be important, when questioned in more detail about what constitutes healthy foods, it was discovered that the gap between perceived and real knowledge is surprisingly wide. For example, when asked to describe a healthy diet, 65 per cent focused on eating more or less of one or two specific foods (e.g. fruit and vegetables or red meat) and only 13 per cent were able to describe the need for a balanced diet.

Confusions were highlighted again when respondents were asked to identify particular nutrients that were contained in certain foods. Although 63 per cent of people interviewed knew that one of the important ways to improve our diets – and health – is to increase the amount of fibre we eat, half of them were unaware that fibre is found in pasta and potatoes, while three-quarters didn't know that it was also contained in white bread.

So, while certain foods may be easily identifiable as high fat (chocolate, sweets, biscuits and so on), there's a whole range of foods that contain what is known as hidden fats – the fat from the crusts in meat pies, the fat in burgers or sausages, the pastry in a pie full of only '100 per cent' fruit; the French dressing drizzled prettily over those dainty lettuce leaves . . . And then, of course, there is the whole area of fats themselves – should you go for low fat – or no fat? Polyunsaturates have now swapped their perfect fat persona for a problematic one while saturated *anything* sinks to the bottom of the fat parade. Then there's hard fat and liquid fat. And let's not forget 'liquid gold' . . . the so-called oils of health. Should you opt for sunflower, or safflower, olive or virgin? Nut oil or sesame oil? Never mind the cost, think of the coronaries you could be avoiding . . . No wonder we're confused!

And then there's the perplexing question of cheese. Cheese, high in protein, with great dollops of calcium. Like full-cream milk, what could be better? But then nutritionists highlighted the fat content of cheese and this nutrient-dense food became a no-no for many. Dieters in particular treated dairy products as if they had been injected with botulism. Perhaps this is one of the reasons why so many women are suffering from the bone thinning disease, osteoporosis – a condition where one of the primary causes is lack of calcium.

Chapter Twelve discusses hidden fats in more detail and helps to identify some of the less obvious 'offenders', but it's worth noting that in the so-called well-informed Nineties, many people are as confused about what they should be eating as ever.

WE'VE BECOME LESS ACTIVE

Our bodies now need less energy than they used to, for the very simple reason that we do less. Experts are now saying that the relevance of this very simple fact has as much to do with us getting fatter as any changes made in, or to, our diet.

The huge number of labour-saving devices available means that, physically, we rely more on our machines than our bodies. Take washing. While Mrs Bridges, from *Upstairs, Downstairs*, forced her newly hand-washed sheets, towels and assortment of clothes through her washing mangle, nowadays most homes not only have washing machines, but also spin-dryers, which makes even the need for hanging out washing unnecessary. And then there are vacuum cleaners, dish-washers, self-cleaning ovens, heating (no need to collect firewood and stoke a fire!), and fridges and freezers means that we can, largely, rely on one-stop shopping. And when we *do* go to the shops, more often than not it's by car.

I'm not for one minute advocating the return to washing sheets in the kitchen sink, waxing all the floors and walking miles through the pouring rain to get the daily pinta. But, where our bodies are concerned, progress has meant that we're conserving the energy that, in the past, was probably used for everyday tasks. For women in particular, labour-saving devices have been a terrific boon and no one would want to turn that clock back. But it isn't just the nature of housework that has changed. Leisure has become sedentary, too. We tend to travel mostly by car, much leisure time is spent in front of a screen, whether that's a television or, increasingly, a computer screen, and leisure generally these days tends to be much more passive than active.

Work too increasingly makes fewer physical demands. With more reliance on computers, faxes, modems and mobile phones, we hardly ever need to stand up, let alone change locations! Estimates suggest that by the turn of the century even more of us will be working at home, so the trend looks likely to continue – for us as well as our children.

WHAT IS THE GOVERNMENT DOING?

It's disturbing to think that in just a couple of generations we've managed to go from undernourished and underfed to overweight and overfed. But make no mistake, the government are disturbed too and have been for years. Hence a variety of government or professionally funded working parties, committees and reports.

The first people to weigh in were the Royal College of Physicians in 1982 with their report on obesity. They confirmed what many health professionals had long suspected, that 'the problem of overweight is a substantial one in Britain, with about 5–30 per cent at different ages of the adult population and some 5 per cent of children affected'. They then went on to outline all the medical evidence that showed how being overweight increases our health risks. The report painted a dismal picture but the Royal College felt the problem was so severe that they emphasized the need for the government to take action: 'the high prevalence of overweight in the community means that public health measures as well as individual health education and medical advice are needed'. And their recommendations didn't stop there.

The report also stressed the importance of the part that food manufacturers have to play in helping to reduce the weight of the nation. 'Food manufacturers should be encouraged not only to produce special low-energy substitutes for normal food but to reduce the fat and sugar content of a wide range of manufactured foods. This applies particularly to meat products, confectionery and desserts.'

None of this could have come as a complete surprise to the government because in the early Seventies Sir Keith Joseph, who was then Secretary of State for Social Services, had publicly declared that there was an urgent need for 'a point of reference that would provide simple and accurate information on nutrition'. Within five years the National Advisory Committee on Nutrition Education had been set up by the British Nutrition Foundation and the then Health Education Council (now the Health Education Authority) to look at all the links between diet, disease and health by some of the country's top medical and scientific experts.

Eventually, in 1983, their revolutionary document, the NACNE Report was published. Basically it highlighted the need to change our diet and the proportions of food items eaten, and their conclusions formed the basis of what we now term as a healthy diet – i.e. low fat (fat was to be reduced by 25 per cent to provide no more than 30 per cent of the total energy intake – saturated fat to be no more than 10 per cent), low sugar (to be reduced by around 50 per cent) and high fibre (increased by 33 per cent to 30g per head per day). The amount of salt consumed was also to be reduced (by 25 per cent to 9g per day) while no recommendations were made for protein, although the other recommendations would mean that a greater proportion of protein would come from vegetable sources.

However, the publication of the report was not without its hiccups. When the Committee's findings first started to trickle through, there was an uproar in some quarters – mainly the food industry and the farmers (basically all providers of food) who understandably became nervous. Radical changes to the diet would mean radical changes to processing, and rearing, and that costs money. The food industry also believed it would cost jobs – presumably because they felt that cutting back on processed foods that were manufactured would result in a drop in production – and less production means less staff. Whatever the reason, while the NACNE report fuelled much debate and discussion, no official action was actually taken.

Eventually government recommendations came in the form of the COMA Report (Committee on Medical Aspects of Food Policy). Although it made no specific recommendations on the fibre and sugar content of our diet, it did concentrate on the relationship between fat and heart disease and recommended that no more than 35 per cent of our total energy (food) should come from fat with a maximum of 15 per cent coming from saturated fat. The conflict between producing food that is cheap *and* nutritious is clearly not an easy one to resolve.

Since 1984, admittedly, the food industry has attempted to reduce the fat and sugar content in many foods. Nowadays 'old favourites' – from mince and cheddar right through to ice-cream and rice pudding – have low-fat alternatives, although, as we've seen, you often have to pay for it. Whether you feel the food industry is actually doing enough – and certainly some health professionals feel they could be doing more – is another question but consumers' concerns about food have meant that the industry is at least beginning to offer a broader choice of healthy options. But as we have seen, despite the so-called low-fat revolution, as a nation we're still getting fatter. And concern seems to be growing as much as our waistlines.

In 1992, the government's *Health of the Nation*'s White Paper, backed by the World Health Organization, announced yet again that we should be receiving no more than 30 per cent of food energy from fat – even though the average person derives 40 per cent of their food energy from fat. The white Paper also referred to the fact that we were not eating enough fruit, bread, cereal and pasta – as had been suggested in previous reports.

The next bombshell came in the form of the government's Nutrition and Physical Activity Task Force which predicted that by the year 2005 a quarter of British women and 18 per cent of men will be obese. Furthermore, the number of obese people has doubled since 1980 and is likely to rise by another 50 per cent within a decade. Not that any of this could have been a huge surprise for the government. Two months prior to this report being 'leaked', a study 'Fit For The Future', the second progress report on the official *Health of the Nation*'s targets, stated that the number of seriously overweight people had risen in the previous 12 months – a third of all women were classified as being overweight – with one in six women and one in eight men classified as obese.

Clearly things are not getting better. The Eighties saw a significant increase in obesity and by 1993 about half the adult population were either obese or overweight. And that's in a decade marked by a greater choice in low-fat, low-calorie food and an increasing awareness of healthy eating. The extent of the problem can be gauged by the fact that the government actually attempted to delay the release of one of their Task Force studies at the end of 1995 *because* it forecast a worsening of our general health due to the increasing problem of obesity. This, after the government had spent thousands on trying to improve the nation's diet.

In fact the 1995 Task Force report revealed that not only is the number of obese people increasing, but families are eating almost twice the amount of fatty and sugary foods recommended by the government's advisory body COMA. Significantly, though, the majority of that total amount comes from hidden fats and sugars – the ingredients that appear in our pies and pastries, snacks and sweets and packets and cans.

You could be forgiven for thinking that, if our food wasn't full of hidden extras in the first place, we wouldn't be consuming them and therefore there would be no need to diet. The government is, understandably, holding back from issuing an actual food policy although there was a kerfuffle a little while back when officials recommended that our diet should be made up of, among other things, three egg-sized potatoes, four and a half slices of bread and one serving of pasta or rice a day, whilst we cut our cream intake from one to half a tablespoon a week and allow ourselves a maximum of three-quarters of a bar of chocolate and three boiled sweets every seven days. Not surprisingly, these ideas were greeted with a fair amount of derision and accusations of ministers acting like servants of a Nanny State or, even worse, food fascists.

Maybe the answer is not so much to tell people what to eat, but to make sure there's a wide choice, at affordable prices, of the sort of food that, when eaten, provides nourishment *and* enjoyment. Whether that is done by inducements to the food industry, subsidies to manufacturers or money-off coupons to consumers, it is a question of national importance. With the latest figures for obesity horrifying health professionals throughout the country, we need all the help we can get to fight these twentieth-century diseases. And in the words of the Ministry of Food in the Forties, we need to be eating what amounts to 'the foundations of your fighting diet'.

Now there are experts who say that if you are overweight, it's up to you to do something to stop yourself becoming yet another figure on the obesity tables. And that something is to diet. Not that many people need reminding – as a nation our appetite for diets, at times, seems to be as great as our appetite for food. However, there's another load of experts that say the *way* we diet offers as many problems as it does solutions. So, what *do* you do?

Chapter Three

The Problem with Diets

LOSING WEIGHT is a confusing business. On the one hand we've got the national finger wagging at us for having become a nation of fatties, and on the other, we have some experts concerned that we've turned into a nation of diet junkies. Certainly for some of us the obsession to be slim has led us to methods of dieting that can only be referred to as . . . potty.

DIETING DAFTNESS

But you don't have to be crackers to be drawn in to the diet craze. In a world that is full of pressures and a constant feeling of having too much to do in too little time, the idea of a short cut to *anything* is certainly appealing. The problem is that even when the methods aren't dangerous, they are almost always costly so the only pounds you end up losing are the ones in your purse.

Nevertheless, the range of slim-quick choices can be enough to make even the most cynical of slimmers think it's worth having a go . . .

- There are teas to help you slim (although one of the most notorious has now been banned).
- Creams that rub the fat away.
- Patches – a sort of 'stick and slim'!
- Wraps, where an 'expert' coats your body in a coloured goo, then wraps you up in protective material, before attaching electrical pads to your body. The pads are then plugged in and the resulting current causes muscle contractions and propels the ingredients into the skin. Apparently you only feel a slight tingling . . .

- Sprays – this time it's 'sniff and slim': the idea is that the spray contains a scent that stifles hunger pangs and so puts you off your food.
- Soaps – herbal-based, these work, apparently, by sucking the fat away . . .
- Clothes – by donning a different top, some manufacturers claim you can speed up your metabolism and shift weight.
- Fasting – this, its supporters claim, lightens the mind as well as the body, as withholding food supposedly purifies the body. If you're ever tempted, just compare your body to a car, and think how the car copes when no one's filled it up with petrol . . . *exactly*.
- Pills – from ones that increase your urine output to others that are supposed to swell your stomach so that you don't feel hungry. I remember one particular pill, a variation on this theme, that came out ten years ago. At the same time that the product was being advertised in the mail-order sections of magazines and newspapers, the medical press were carrying reports of people who had died because the swellings caused by these particular pills had resulted in an obstruction to the gullet . . .
- Herbs – not the type that you might add to your casseroles (although some, somewhere, are no doubt recommended for weight loss), but in this case particular Chinese herbs. Unfortunately, though, when women started to take them in Belgium in the early Eighties, an outbreak of renal failure occurred amongst some users. Renal damage was also reported, as recently as 1993, in the medical journal *The Lancet*, where the authors warned doctors of the dangers of 'uncontrolled therapy with herbal preparations'. Even *The Times* alerted its readers to the problem, reporting that 'fity-eight women . . . suffered permanent kidney damage after embarking on a slimming programme containing two herbs which are freely available in Chinese pharmacies in Soho, London.'

But you don't have to travel to China to find herbal remedies for 'weight problems'. Some years ago I remember one particular treatment that was readily available in just about all chemists.

- 'Minus-Cal' was a course of pills that, supposedly, made fat disappear – even though you were told you could eat as normal. When the late Professor John Yudkin, Emeritus Professor of

Nutrition at the University of London, analysed the product he discovered that these herbal tablets contained a small amount of laxative, a diuretic and pectin. But were they effective? In Yudkin's view, clearly not. 'These amounts of components were too small to have any measurable effect,' he said at the time.

- Vitamins – I remember, only several years ago, as Editor of a health magazine, turning down an ad for a little-known supplement that, apparently, took years off your age, and pounds off your weight. Call me a cynic, but I thought this sounded like a case of 'too good to be true'. I asked the advertiser in question to send me the 'conclusive' medical evidence that he kept talking about. I'm still waiting . . .

- Pills that make you slim while you sleep – one of my favourite 'potty' ways to diet! This idea has been on the market for a while, although its name changes – presumably depending on who is actually manufacturing the particular pill at the time. The so-called magic ingredients are supposed to be amino acids (the substances that make up the molecules of protein in our body), which, we are told, stimulate the body into increasing the amount of growth hormone that it produces – the idea being that increasing growth hormone boosts the body's ability to burn up excessive fat. But, as Yudkin so eloquently explained, 'leaving aside the fact that this simple story is just not true, the reality is that the proteins in your food give you more than you need of these amino acids, and no one who is overweight is ever short of them.'

- Slim foods – a bit of a misnomer because all foods contain energy, or calories, some just more than others so there's no such thing as a slimming food. In fact in some cases, even though some popular meal-replacement bars are conveniently calorie-counted, there's a chance that they may contain as much energy, or calories, as your favourite *non-slimming* chocolate-bar: which is probably cheaper – and more enjoyable.

- Injections – doctors are working on a jab that can inject your fat away, although it seems we will need to wait some time before the treatment is available – and even then only under medical supervision.

- Spiritual help – last year one popular glossy magazine carried a report on women who have replaced eating with something 'far more wonderful' – God. The women concerned had turned to

God instead of food whilst swapping their calorie books for bibles and turning to prayer to give them the strength to fight the flab.

- And then there are diets promoting the idea that by sticking to one type of food, you'll finally crack the slimming game. From the Grapefruit diet to the liquid diet – there's been no shortage of 'fat busting' ideas.

SLIMMING WITH THE STARS

There has also been no lack of dieting personalities. While some of the above ideas are easy to laugh at, other slimming programmes available seem much more acceptable – simply because there's a familiar face smiling at us from a cover or a packet. But the problem is that the familiar face generally has no connection with nutrition, health – or slimming. Personality endorsements are nothing new but whilst actors appearing in ads that tell us how much they like eating a particular brand of cheese, or type of margarine, is one thing, having them claim that they have discovered the secret to a successful shape – which they feel they have to share with us – is quite another.

Personally I would love to think that if I ate and lived like, say Victoria Principal (her book, *The Diet Principal* was published in 1987), I would look like her, but the truth is that no amount of thrashing around my local gym is going to turn me into the former Dallas star. The cult of the personality, though, means, theoretically, that anyone who has been famous – even as the saying goes, 'famous for five minutes' – can share their diet, health and fitness secrets with you, irrelevant of what they are.

But, what's really interesting about the dieting phenomena is not that there are so many diets around, but that with all the books, programmes, videos, advice and products available, as a nation we're not losing weight, *we're still putting it on*.

DESPERATE TO DIET

According to the figures, half of all women are on a diet at any one time: a staggering 90 per cent of women have been on a diet at some time in their lives. But our concern about our size and shape doesn't stop there. At a recent count there were more than 230 books available on dieting and slimming for the general reader. There are magazines devoted exclusively to the subject of slimming and other magazines which cover diet, although they may be more inclined to label the information 'nutrition', or use phrases like 'eat well', to flag up the fact that the article is about 'good' food.

But just because diets sell magazines, and so many of us are dieting, it doesn't follow that diets actually work. Whatever you may think of the slimming industry as a whole, not all of the diets on offer can be simply designated daft or dangerous. And while it's not exactly difficult to see why some of these diets won't work unless you change your eating habits, there are actually some perfectly acceptable slim-plans, devised, if not overseen, by nutritionists who have had years of experience working with men and women who are considered too heavy for their own good.

Many slimming clubs (see chapter thirteen) also offer eating plans that are devised by experts and include nutritionally balanced meals. For example, every eating plan offered at Slimming Magazine Clubs (and, at the last count they offered at least 17) is devised by the Club's Scientific Director, nutritionist Dr Elizabeth Evans, who also tests all new diets before they are offered to members. Of course whether you agree with the approach that a slimming club offers is a different matter, but dieticians and medical experts would be hard pushed to criticize the majority of diet sheets and eating plans that are offered to their members.

So, if it isn't the advice that's to blame, what is the vital X factor, that missing link, which means that the scales are weighed against you whenever you try to lose weight? The problem with diets, it seems, has as much to do with our state of mind as the contents of our diet sheet. And one of the main problems is to do with how we see the whole idea of losing weight. Being on a diet is often treated like being on a course of antibiotics. It's something we 'go on' for a prescribed length of time. Of course with antibiotics, most of us know that we need to avoid alcohol and, for the necessary six to eight days, that doesn't seem too taxing a task. Then of course, we go back to a glass of wine with our meal, an apéritif before supper – whatever fits in with our lifestyle.

But in the same way we may spend a week avoiding alcohol, when we go on a diet we spend time avoiding what we see as diet 'baddies' – the chocolates, chips, biscuits, cakes, pies. Unfortunately though, once the diet is over, in the same way that alcohol is put back on the menu after you've finished the antibiotics, we all too readily go back to the chocolate and chips – those so-called diet 'baddies'. A diet then, is seen almost as a necessarily evil. We go without the foods we enjoy for a while . . . simply so that we lose enough weight to be able to go back to eating those same foods. Sounds crazy, but isn't it all too familiar?

The point is that thinking of certain foods as baddies causes a tension between us and what we eat . . . or rather don't eat. We stop eating foods and start eating calories. Mealtimes become an exercise in dodging the dieting no-nos. And for many of us the tension is increased when we have to cook for a family – a family who, quite rightly, see no reason why *they* should go without their favourite foods. The result is that we then have to spend time and energy preparing the very food that we're trying to avoid. Like an alcoholic who works in an off-licence, you'd need the restraint of a saint not to feel tempted. And, if you're spending all that time buying, preparing, cooking and serving food, not being able to take part in the eating of it would make anyone feel miserable. Whether we like it or not, separating food from family is nigh on impossible.

The opposite effect

But it isn't as if going without food only makes you *think* that you want to eat more. Evidence shows that denying ourselves food not only increases our interest in eating but it also increases the amount we eat – and the likelihood of us overeating. The very act of having to resist certain foods – a fundamental part of so many diets – means that the foods that have to be avoided somehow become more desirable.

In 1980 an American study set out to explore just what effect putting on our own internal restraints has on our appetite. The researchers took two groups of students – one group worried about their weight and what they ate, the other barely concerned. The students were given milk-shakes, either large or small, and then left in a room to help themselves to snack foods: they could eat as little or as much as they liked. To the researchers' surprise, the group that ate more after drinking the large milkshake than after the small one was made up of the students who were most concerned about their weight – not the other way around. But what was interesting about the two groups, though, was that no one had a weight problem. Both groups were what would be termed as 'normal' weight.

Stress itself seems to have a similar effect. The whole process of 'being on a diet' can increase stress levels to such an extent that it not only makes you think about food more, it's also likely to make you eat more: a real case of dieting makes you fat! Many people also admit to eating more when they are depressed or anxious, and in several research studies, people scoring high on the restraint scale have eaten more, or described themselves as eating more, when depressed than 'unrestrained' eaters. This phenomenon has little to do with the psychology of the slimmer – if such a thing exists. Most people when suddenly denied a food, as long as it is not something they actively dislike, will often find that the craving for that food increases.

Chris, in her forties, was diagnosed as diabetic. She wasn't totally surprised as she knew that diabetes ran in her family, so her chances of developing it were greater than if there were no genetic factor. However, she was a bit miffed because she had never had a sweet tooth, and generally ate a low-fat, high-fibre diet. She reckoned she was maybe a stone heavier than she would have liked to have been, but her weight was certainly never a problem. What was interesting though, was that as soon as she was told that, if she wanted to eat chocolate, she was limited to 'one square' a day, she started not only to think about it more – but actually began to crave it. She was more aware of her craving when she went shopping and when she went over to friends where they had dishes of sweets and chocolates ready for guests to nibble at. A classic case of wanting what you can't have. By designating certain foods as out of bounds, the whole business of eating becomes stressful: foods are suddenly transformed into 'good' and 'bad'.

Some dieting regimes, of course, embrace this philosophy to such an extent that they talk about some foods as being 'illegal' – not to be touched at any cost. While undoubtedly some foods may offer nutritionally more than others, to label some as positively out of bounds can't help but create an unhealthy attitude to eating. Food becomes a forbidden fruit. This of course is nothing new. It was something that the Garden of Eden was full of . . . and we all know the story of Adam and Eve!

As well as affecting the way we eat, eating only according to the rules of our latest diet can badly dent our self-esteem. We find that we're constantly battling to stick to the rules and then when the inevitable happens and we break them, we feel guilty and blame ourselves for having no willpower. Dieting is a way of feeling in control. And when you don't seem to have much control of anything else around you, what you eat seems to be the one area that you should, successfully, be able to do something about. But the opposite of in control is out of control, and when that happens you feel guilty and you get depressed – and it affects your attitude to food.

Fear of Failure

Trying to stick to something, particularly when it's unrealistic and bears no resemblance to your lifestyle, can be an impossibility. And for proof, look no further than your friends – or even yourself. Just how many diets have *you* been on? Anything more than one is proof that it hasn't worked. And the problem is once you've broken one diet, you have no reason to suppose you won't break the next. This sets up what counsellor Genevieve Blais calls 'The Cycle Of Failure'.

As she explains in *Fear of Food* (Bloomsbury), 'you put the weight back on, so you think that you've failed. You didn't fail; the diet failed. But your mind grabs hold of the negative results and plays them back to you over and over again'. This, she says, simply re-inforces a negative self-image which makes you feel even worse. 'You end up feeling that you're incapable of sticking to any diet. But then another diet comes along, you know you won't stick to it, but you think you'll give it a try anyway . . . just in case. You see, the Cycle Of Failure has been set in motion where breaking a diet becomes a self-fulfilling prophecy . . .'

The other problem with expecting to break your diet is that every time you do, you see it as confirmation of your inability to stick to anything and, rather than treat it as a momentary lapse, you treat it as The End. The End of the diet, The End of trying to be slim, The End of taking control of your life. And the result is that, as with all those occasions when we feel our situation is hopeless, we give up. And if you just happen to be sitting with a table of food in front of you that means giving in. After all, it's easy to think . . . *In for a penny and in for a pound . . . give a dog a bad name*. Well let's face it, if you're going to be hanged, as they say, it might as well be for a sheep as a lamb . . .

Clearly trying to restrict something as basic as eating is fraught with problems and psychologists have set up countless research projects to prove it. But, sometimes, without even realizing it, we attach all sorts of symbolic meanings to our dieting disasters. It becomes a metaphor for our life. *Typical*, we say, *I've never been able to stick to anything. I always muck things up*. This cycle of failure can be difficult to break out of. Each failure makes you feel worse and in the end you stop trying to achieve anything, so sure are you that you'll fail. It's no longer the diet that's failed – or even the car, or washing machine. It's YOU. Everything becomes *your* fault and so you live in a constant state of guilt-ridden angst.

You feel guilty when you eat – and when you're not eating you feel guilty because you're *thinking* about eating. Clinical psychologist, Sara Gilbert, believes that failed dieters live continually with guilt. 'For the person who longs to be slim,' she explains, 'who feels that her very happiness depends on it, each guilty relapse episode is just one more proof of failure.' And with magazines and some of the newspapers declaring that this week's diet is the 'ultimate, foolproof way to lose weight', the feelings of guilt are increased as we assume that not only is *everyone* dieting, but with foolproof diets around, they're all dieting successfully. All, of course, except you.

EXCUSES, EXCUSES

Having a shape that is vastly different from what is considered the norm can eventually knock your confidence sideways. Somehow your self-esteem seems to get swallowed up in the cycle of failure. Change is always pretty scary but when you're used to be being judged according to how you look, rather than how you do, it's easy for change to become something you resist, rather than relish.

Sometimes, though, we become so convinced that we'll fail at whatever we do, that it's easier not to try in the first place. We end up hiding behind our fat, using it as an excuse. If you're not convinced, ask yourself – have you ever thought any of the following?

As soon as I've lost weight . . . 'I'll change jobs', 'I'll go for that promotion'; 'I'll go back to work'; 'I'll change partners'.

. . . or maybe less dramatic but nonetheless significant . . . Once I've lost weight . . . 'I'll go on holiday'; 'I'll enrol on a course'; 'I'll learn to drive'.

The possibilities are endless but one thing is for sure. Being bigger than you feel you should be can become a reason for not progressing in your life, and dieting can be used to mask the real problems. We worry about tackling the diet when maybe we should think about our relationship with our partner, or the way we feel about work. It's far easier – and safer – to put your energy into working out what you should and shouldn't be eating, than worrying about the element of your life that you should and shouldn't be changing. By allowing our concerns about food to get the better of us, we also allow food to take the focus away from what really matters in our lives. A diet becomes an avoidance tactic. When I'm slim I'll be able to change things . . . I'll just wait until I've finished this diet tomorrow. The problem is, tomorrow never seems to come . . .

THE DIET TO CHANGE YOUR LIFE!

Another huge problem with diets is that we can put so much energy into them, and invest so much confidence in them, that we end up expecting them to change so much more than just our shapes. Of course, in some cases it does. Everyone has read countless readers' stories of 'What losing ten stone means to me!' High on the feel-good factor, sometimes the stories can mask a multitude of disappointments.

The truth is that you're if unhappy with your life, being thinner isn't going to change how you feel. Unfortunately, whatever we do, we take our emotional baggage with us. As the song goes, 'money can't buy you love', but then neither can thinness. While a slimmer body may transform your looks, it *doesn't* transform your life. If you weren't happy in your job to begin with, being four stone lighter isn't going to make you feel any better about it. And the same is true when it comes to relationships. I have interviewed women who have lost weight simply because they felt it would save their marriage. Maybe they suspected – or even knew – that their husband was having an affair and felt that if they looked different then he wouldn't be interested in other women, or, the husband, or partner, has told the woman that he just couldn't bear to make love to her anymore because she was so fat he no longer found her attractive.

So many women are convinced their husbands won't love them the size they are and that they'll go off and find someone thinner. But the truth is that a diet can't make a bad relationship good. Of course losing weight can give you the confidence to make those changes that you were previously too insecure to even think about seriously. But real problems don't go away – whatever you weigh. If fact, if anything, some experts believe that having unrealistic expectations from a diet can often result in regaining all of the former weight loss, and sometimes even more. Let's face it, losing a huge amount of weight and then discovering that nothing in your life has necessarily changed, except perhaps, some of the items in your wardrobe, can be bitterly disappointing. And if the diet hasn't had the desired effect, what's the point of sticking to it? We end up feeling miserable and depressed – and in need of comfort. And if we don't get comfort from the areas where we'd like them, we might well turn to the one comforter that has never let us down – food.

When dieting disappoints

If losing all that weight can be a fearful disappointment when everything else in your life stays the same, unrealistic expectations can also lead to general feelings of discontent. It's no secret that some marriages have buckled under the strain when one partner has undergone a dramatic weight loss. Sometimes husbands find it difficult to cope with a 'new' woman, and all the attention that she suddenly receives, or all the new confidence that she is suddenly instilled with.

An initial weight loss can result in a honeymoon period. There's a great sense of achievement and a huge boost to morale. But then of course, like all honeymoons, it comes to an end and you have to get back to the day-to-day routine of your life. You find that you still have to go to Sainsbury's, still pick the children up from school, still make supper and do the washing. So what exactly has happened to all those great changes that your diet was supposed to have made? The problem is that you had such high expectations that it all too easily heightens your feelings of discontent. Somehow you no longer feel prepared to put up with your life anymore. You're no longer satisfied with what life has to offer you. Of course for women who use their newly found confidence to make positive, and more importantly, realistic, long-term changes to their lives, a substantial weight loss can be an exhilarating experience. But unrealistic expectations can lead to levels of discontent that can make you act hastily – from walking out of jobs to walking out on marriages.

In an effort to cut the cord between your fat past and your thin present, disassociating yourself from everything that reminds you of that past can have its attractions: suddenly you start anew, people treat you as you are, not as you were . . . no wonder it's an attractive prospect. But it can be a case of throwing the baby out with the bath water and not realizing what you've lost until it's too late. By then of course, you start to feel disappointed and depressed, and guess what's turned to for comfort?

Constantly dieting also means that you miss out on being able to fully join in when it comes to your social life, whether that means going out with friends to eat or having supper at home with the family. Constant concerns over what you're eating spill over to the people you're with. And it can't help but add an undercurrent to the occasion, a tension that people can't help but be aware of – either when you're refusing food or they're consuming it. After all, when everyone around you is eating while you're not, it's likely to produce feelings of self-consciousness, so much so that next time there's a get together, you simply won't be asked. And the other problem, of course, is that you get more and more hungry until eventually you're starving. So, what do you do? More often than not you'll go for anything that requires the minimum of fuss and bother. And that generally means going for packets which, at the very maximum, need to be pulled open: sweets, chocolate bars, crisps, nuts – probably all the foods on that forbidden list.

Whichever way you look at it, hunger will eventually lead to eating and the longer you leave it, the more likely you are to overeat or binge. And, of course, the next day you're wracked with guilt over your uncontrollable greed and you therefore feel obliged to be particularly abstemious when it comes to food. Which you are until hunger sets in, again, and you unleash a ravenous appetite on anything edible that you come into contact with. And then you feel guilty . . . And so the circle goes on.

Slimming As A Sickness

Plenty has been written about eating disorders over the years. In one survey, when some people who were overweight were asked whether they had ever binged, 50 per cent admitted to doing so in the last seven days. A worrying thought, but then it's worth thinking about what bingeing means – everyone has their own definition of the word. In the film *Peter's Friends*, bingeing was exactly what one of the central characters, played by Rita Rudner, did when she was stressed. To her, bingeing was eating everything in the fridge, freezer and larder. Leftover joints of meat, tubs of ice-cream, pies, cake – almost anything that she was able to masticate went into her mouth.

Thankfully, not all binges match that of the bulimic character in Kenneth Branagh's film. For many of us a binge is finishing a dish of chocolates, a packet of biscuits or hoovering up the chocolate mousse and apple crumble left over in the fridge. Everyone has their own idea about what a binge actually is. I remember quite clearly working late one evening when a colleague rushed over to me with a mortified expression on her face. 'I feel terrible. I've had a real binge . . . I've eaten *three* biscuits,' she declared mournfully, rubbing her non-existent stomach in self-disgust. Whichever way you look at it, it has to be said that three biscuits do not constitute a binge.

The number of people who suffer from eating disorders is still relatively low, although experts have pointed out that many bingers are generally of a normal weight and it can be difficult to get accurate figures for something that, quite literally, is done in the privacy of your own home. And, unlike anorexia, the tell-tale signs are not so obvious. However, anorexia nervosa and bulimia nervosa are not primarily slimming diseases. As the Eating Disorders Association explain, these conditions are not 'a way of committing suicide – they are a way of coping with life'. The pursuit of thinness through self-starvation is a symptom of a much greater problem. To quote the EDA again, 'while on the surface eating disorders appear to be about food, they are fundamentally the outward expression of deep psychological and emotional turmoil . . . it's a way of exerting control over one's own body, and life in general, in a situation where the sufferer feels other people are in control'. But that said, eating disorders are an increasing concern and can cause a multitude of problems, in the present and in the future.

A relatively new syndrome that has been identified is 'binge-eating disorder'. Although there are similarities between this and bulimia nervosa, experts recognize distinct symptoms that characterize this condition. These are:

- recurrent episodes of bingeing characterized by eating abnormal amounts of food within a discreet period of time, say two hours.
- lack of control over what or how much you eat.

Binge-eating episodes are also associated with three or four of the following:

- eating more rapidly than normal
- eating until feeling uncomfortably full
- eating large amounts of food but not feeling physically hungry
- eating alone because you're embarrassed by how much you're eating
- feeling disgusted with oneself, distressed, depressed or guilty after overeating
- the binge eating occurs on average for two days a week for six months
- the bingeing is not associated with other compensatory behaviour e.g. fasting, excessive exercise, etc.

Obviously if you feel any of the above may apply to you, it's important you seek medical advice as soon as possible.

OTHER PHYSICAL PROBLEMS . . .

Diets don't just affect your mind, they also have an influence on your body, too. For example:

- One American study discovered that when they looked at a group of men whose weight fluctuated by more than eleven pounds over an 11 to 15 year period, they were more likely to die of a heart attack in the subsequent 12 year period than men who kept their weight steady.
- Another American report, found that a wide range of side effects were associated with diets that contained less than 800 calories a day. Apart from heart problems, other side effects included deterioration of muscles and organs, depression, personality changes, fainting, dizziness, gallstones and hair loss.
- People who repeatedly lose and regain more than 25 pounds (just under two stone), have been shown to have a higher risk of dying prematurely than people who smoke cigarettes.
- Many diets, quite rightly, encourage us to cut down on fat. Unfortunately, though, the message most of us take on board is that 'fat' is a baddie and, in the name of good health, we attempt to erase it from our diet. But this is bad news for our bodies because small amounts of fat are essential.
- American experts have demonstrated that the risk of heart disease and death from all causes was 25 to 100 per cent higher in the group with the most weight fluctuation, regardless of a person's initial weight, and other factors such as blood pressure, smoking and levels of cholesterol and fitness.
- As well as putting a strain on the heart, a constant cycle of weight gain and weight loss, experienced by so many dieters, can also result in episodes of gout and even gallstones.
- More bad news for people who spend their lives putting on and taking off weight. Evidence suggests that the weight lost tends to be muscle whilst the weight gained seems to go straight to fat. So the result is that every time you lose and gain, you're increasing your overall fat content. Interestingly, although much research has centred on people who have lost and regained weight, some experts have pointed out that, in some cases, we don't actually know *why* those people have lost weight. Certainly for some people ill health

following a period of losing and gaining weight may be as much to do with illness or emotional stress, as with dieting. It's just that we assume the weight loss is voluntary i.e. due to slimming.

However, regardless of the ups and downs of the scales, the problems associated with constantly dieting continue to weigh-in.

■ A Consumer's Association report in 1995, based on evidence from two pieces of research, reported that slimming can reduce the number of cells in body systems. This slows down cell renewal and impairs natural body maintenance. All of this means that dieting can have adverse effects the older you get. Apparently, heavier middle-aged patients had better reserves of nutrients which meant they were better able to survive illness or surgery.

■ They can make you depressed. Apart from the obvious misery caused by not being able to eat what you want, researchers have discovered that people who severely restrict what they eat have lower levels of the chemicals that affect our moods – the feel-good chemicals – particularly tryptophan. So, slimmers do actually get more depressed. However, more worrying is that the lowering of levels of particular chemicals can affect the brain functions and this, experts feel, may play a part in some of the psychological consequences of dieting, in particular the development of eating disorders.

■ Extreme dieting can seriously increase your risk of the bone-thinning disease, osteoporosis. This is because a lack of minerals – notably calcium – weakens the bones, making them more susceptible to fractures and breaks. Women are at risk of osteoporosis if they avoid dairy products, lose excessive weight quickly, suffer from anorexia or bulimia, are deficient in Vitamin D, which is needed for the absorption of calcium, and are dieting after pregnancy or are breast-feeding, because a baby can deplete the mother's calcium stores fast. To many people calcium means dairy products, foods with a reputation for being high in fat. However, this is not necessarily the case. These days the option of low-fat dairy products means that you can reduce your fat intake without jeopardizing your calcium levels. But the tendency of some dieters to reduce their intake of calcium means that they are likely to become one of the 50 per cent of women who end up with thin, fragile bones. (*Discover how to protect your bones in chapter Twelve.*)

■ Diets can leave you deficient. Experts believe that while it may be possible to get all the nutrients we need from our food, the less you eat, the less chance there is of meeting all your nutritional needs. Surveys have shown that on some diets, dieters often don't get an adequate intake of all the vitamins and minerals they need. Some experts believe that a lack of B vitamins in particular may be one of the reasons why women give up on a diet because they end up feeling tired all the time.

■ Dieting can effect your brain functions. In a recent study by scientists at Reading's Institute of Food Research, dieters were found to perform worse than non-dieters at tests measuring their mental performance in areas such as memory, problem solving and reaction times. The reason, apparently, is more to do with the fact that dieters are too preoccupied with food rather than, as you'd suspect, that they are not eating enough.

And lastly, one of the major problems with diets is that anyone can go on one. Every month a variety of magazines offer a selection of diets, all quick, easy to use and all but guaranteed to get results – *fast!* Even if you'd never dream of buying a slimming magazine, the mainstream mags offer such a wide choice that you can follow a diet for your skin, your bottom, your health, your vitality . . . and then there's the diets that flatten your stomach, get rid of your toxins and banish your cellulite. We've all bought them. But clever as the titles are, at the end of the day what almost all of them offer is a low-calorie eating plan, showing the reader how to restrict their energy intake, or, if you prefer, how to limit what she eats. Now, if you are overweight reading about alternative ways of eating may do you more good than harm but, if you're not overweight the result is reversed – there's more chance of your doing yourself harm than good.

But if dieting is at best disappointing and at worst downright danger-ous, why do so many women take it up? Sadly it seems that all women – regardless of how big they may or may not be – seem to think they are bigger than they actually are. Proof of this was supplied by one American study which discovered that many people see themselves as overweight, even when they're not, and this particularly applies to women. The doctors involved also noticed that 'many people appear to be using a stricter standard for their own weight than is required for good health'.

Furthermore, the 'standard' used was based on what people felt looked good. Other research has shown that women overestimate their size by up to ten per cent. So, it seems that everyone, with the exception of young boys, feels that the shape they are at the moment is larger than the shape they would like to be. Clearly there's a difference between being fat, and feeling fat, but if so many of us think we're overweight when we're not, just where are we getting this distorted picture from?

Chapter Four

Images of Women

WANTING TO BE THIN – or thinner – is nothing new. Recently, hundreds of column inches have been devoted to how much the Rubenesque women were greatly admired but it's worth reminding ourselves that we're talking about images from the seventeenth century. I daresay flogging was also generally admired then – but, as they say, times have changed. What's more, if an average Rubenesque figure in the Nineties decided to pop along to their doctor, complaining of anything from breathlessness to aching joints, there's a pretty good chance that most GPs would suggest that such complaints may well improve were the person to consider losing a little excess weight.

More recently Twiggy – along with the swinging Sixties – is often blamed for the twentieth-century obsession with thinness. Poor old Twiggy! It may be nice and simple to try to hang our obsession with dieting on a single event, and fixing the blame on, what was, a shapeless, underdeveloped 16-year-old may offer a convenient explanation but it's hardly the whole story. The truth is that women have been trying to re-shape their bodies for centuries.

BODY IMAGE IN PERSPECTIVE

Remember *Gone With the Wind*? One of the most vivid scenes has to be the sight of Scarlet O'Hara being laced into her corset by Big Mammy. She holds onto the bedpost for dear life as her torso is pushed and pummelled until it is compressed just enough to get down to 'the 18 inch waist'. No wonder literature is full of pale women, feeling faint, who always had to sit down. It was a miracle any of them could breathe, let alone carry on a conversation! Of course the corset was not simply designed to squeeze the life out of a woman – all in the name of a tiny waist – it also had the effect of uplifting the breasts, acting like a sort of eighteenth-century Wonderbra. Equally, it successfully emphasized the bottom, with a variety of bustles used to decorate a woman's rear end: the more noticeable, the more appealing – a passing tradition that many women these days who spend time worrying about the all too obvious shape of their bottom, may sadly mourn.

From the nineteenth century where the ideal image was one where everything was pushed in, we eventually moved onto the middle of the twentieth century when everything was pushed up. But not before we flapped our way through the Twenties. As one observer remarked, the women of the period should have more accurately been referred to as flatters because they were flat at the front and flat at the back! In fact, anyone who has ever seen *Bugsy Malone*, starring a very young Jodie Foster, might remember how unnervingly easily the pre-teen actress slipped into the fashion of the day. The more pre-pubescent your shape, the better. All of which hardly portrays a healthy image for women to aspire to.

By the Forties, breasts seemed to develop an unnerving conical shape, almost taking on a life of their own. And while the Hollywood icons of the Forties and Fifties were certainly shapelier than many slender, almost asexual icons of today, it's all too easy to forget that they too were pushed and pulled into clothes that would reflect what was considered the 'right' image for them. Images which, let's face it, on the whole reflected the fantasies of male directors, producers and fashion designers. Women often dressed how they thought men wanted them to dress, rather than for themselves. In a *Good Housekeeping* article from the period, called 'Portrait of a Lady', the readers were told that a lady likes . . '. to please the men. So her aim is to look pretty. Her clothes, her coiffure, her make-up are chosen not to startle but to charm. She knows, however, that masculine eyes soon weary of monotony, so she never permits herself to settle lazily into a stereotyped pattern no matter how much *he* says he likes it.'

This, remember, was the image that was up there on the screen and catwalk for us to aspire to and admire, the image that we were then shown how to achieve through a variety of 'how to' articles in the magazines of the day. Judy Garland's recollections of having to bind her breasts so that she would she still remain 'the little girl' from somewhere over the rainbow, must make every woman wince but, for Judy, becoming a woman wasn't in the film studio's plans and so she was expected to stay a fresh-faced, innocent thirteen-something, for as long as possible. This, all at the time when, on the other side of the Atlantic, Wallis Simpson, the then Duchess of Windsor, did no one any favours when she claimed that 'women can never be too rich, or too thin'. Admittedly never known for her intellectual prowess, Mrs Simpson, nevertheless, reinforced what had become for many women, virtually, an unsaid truism.

From corsets to roll-ons, we now have underwear with 'control' panels to disguise unwanted lumps and bumps and Wonderbras to lift the parts where we didn't realise that there was anything to lift in the first place. In truth, today, our bodies are no nearer the fantasy figures that they are supposed to reflect than they were all those years ago. Of course where you live can affect the way you think about size generally, and yours in particular. In many parts of the world, 'plumpness' is equated with fertility, as well as beauty and if you come from a society riddled with disease and famine, there's nothing to be admired, or envied, about thinness. If anything, if you *are* lucky enough to have a little excess fat on you as opposed to being, literally, skin and bones, your status within the community will be enhanced or, at the very least, envied.

Being a 'good' weight can be a sign of prosperity, as well as health: it's a physical way of showing that you can *afford* to eat well. Not for nothing is AIDS know as 'the wasting disease' in some parts of the globe where thinness has taken on a much more morbid symbolic meaning. Even a flick through the books of Jane Austen and Charlotte Brontë bear testament to the fact that if 'plumpness' represented wealth and good fortune, thinness came to be the description used for those that were pale and sickly; undernourished, underprivileged and under-exposed to lack of 'good, country air'.

WHAT WE SAY ABOUT SIZE

While the associations with being fat or thin have certainly changed over the centuries, these days we seem to have developed very specific ideas about what someone's size says about them. In the same way spots are supposed to shout 'I've eaten too much chocolate', being fat is seen as a sign to the world that you eat too much; you got that way because you're just damned greedy. Time and time again, it's been shown that the bigger a person is, the more likely our perception of them is to be a negative one.

Unfortunately the chances are that if you are overweight, you don't need proof to realize that in many people's minds you often aren't just fat, you're more likely to be 'fat and stupid', 'fat and lazy', or of course, that much used description, 'fat and jolly'. And, of course, if that's how people think of you, their treatment of you will often reflect those perceptions. Whether we like it or not, there's no doubt that, what psychiatrist Dr Judith Rodin describes in *Body Traps* as having the 'right' look matters 'because appearance is extraordinarily important to being successful and being valued in our world today'. Quite why appearance is so directly linked to success is such a vast topic that the subject would easily fill a book by itself, but it's worrying to read all the evidence that shows fairly conclusively that this stereotyping starts young.

Even studies on pre-school children have shown that the children who are considered attractive are the ones who are most popular. When it came to choosing someone to work or play with, the 'attractive' children were picked first and they were the ones that children consistently rated as their closest friends. But perhaps more disturbing was the fact that the researchers also found that *the teachers* rated the more attractive children as the smartest, as well as the most able.

One particularly famous study, often quoted as damning evidence of just how appallingly we treat people who are seen as 'different', involved a group of schoolchildren who were given a selection of photographs, showing other children. Included in the group were pictures of a 'normal' looking child; a child with crutches and a brace on its left leg; a child with a limb missing; a child in a wheelchair with a blanket over its legs; a child with a facial disfigurement and an obese child. The children in the study were then asked to rate the kids in the pictures, according to how likeable they thought they were. And, you guessed it, the photographs that elicited the most negative feelings were those of the fat child, who was easily least liked. Another study that looked at body image and children revealed that when children were shown pictures of other children who were fat, the children in the pictures were immediately labelled with negative adjectives ranging from 'sloppy' and 'stupid' right through to 'dirty', 'naughty' and even 'cheat'.

Bearing in mind that a child's attitude tends to be influenced by their parents' particular prejudices and perspectives, it is not surprising to discover that when a similar study was carried out a year later, by another research group, but this time with adults, the results were unnervingly similar – the least liked picture was the one of the obese child.

Sadly, it's not as if these findings reveal anything new. Many studies have shown the advantages of being physically 'acceptable' - the more attractive you are, the more likely you are not only to get help, but also to find that people will be more co-operative. There was one that even showed that students were actually less likely to be accepted for college if they were obese. As Dr Rodin explains, 'attractive applicants appear to have a better chance of getting a job and they tend to be hired at a better starting salary. Even in the courtroom, attractive people appear to benefit from positive outcomes, and are found guilty less often. They are seen as worthy of milder punishments and awarded favourable judgements'.

Whose fault is it, anyway?

Now whether the illustrations above are all too horribly familiar or, if you're starting to get hot under the collar as, just maybe, you recognize your own prejudices, you may be pleased to know that the way you think isn't just down to you. We subconsciously imbibe all sorts of attitudes and are susceptible to all types of messages, before we've even heard of the word diet. And once again, the process starts early.

In their book, *You Don't Have To Diet*, Dr Tom Sanders and Peter Bazalgette looked at the role models that dolls offered young girls. I know by the time my daughter was two she not only recognized 'Barbie', but was simply *desperate* to have one of her own. And this was a child who had a mother who resolutely refused to buy her dolls, convinced that dollies would open the floodgates to all things 'girlie', the sole function of which is to show girls how to play 'mum'. So we avoided the toy irons and ironing boards, the dolls that said 'mama', the Hoovers, 'little kitchens' - the lot. And guess what? Those are the exact things she wanted! Of course no child is brought up in isolation and they only have to pass by the television during children's TV to be assaulted by images of what constitutes 'male' and 'female' toys: it's easy to tell which is which - the boys' toys are usually in dark colours, make a lot of noise and are accompanied by loud pulsating music, along with a tough, macho voice, almost spitting out the toy's description in short, staccato sentences. And guess what the ads are like for girls toys? In these so-called liberated times, we have images of sweet little girls - often dressed in pink - playing 'mum' as only a Stepford wife would, happily seen changing her little dolly's nappy or brushing her little pony's hair. And in the background the tinkle tinkle of the music can just be heard above the soothing, reassuring, female voice. The result, of course, is the manufacturer gets the sale, the girl gets the doll – and a whole load of stereotypes on which to model her behaviour and attitudes.

When Sanders and Bazalgette looked at the three most popular female dolls – Barbie, Sindy and The Little Mermaid – they discovered that the dolls' dimensions bore little resemblance to a 'real' female's statistics. They measured the dolls, bust, hips, waist and height and then took these measurements and worked out how they compared with a woman of around five foot four inches – which is about average height. They discovered that the dolls all had tiny hips and waists, smaller busts, and exaggerated inside leg measurements, compared to real women.

Personally what I find equally, if not even more, disturbing is that these almost anorexic dolls have *no* hips whatsoever. And then there's the hair – long, glossy locks that look as if they've just stepped out of a *Charlie's Angels* set. Each and every doll is perfectly primed to be squeezed into those tightest jeans and briefest bodies, right down to their pointed feet, shaped so perfectly to fit into those highest of heels.

But you don't need to rely on dolls for proof of the 'shrinking' body. Sara Gilbert in her excellent book, *Tomorrow I'll Be Slim*, believes that the image of women during the twentieth century has become more sylph-like although she says the pressure for women, in particular, to be slim, has increased over the last 25 five years. As an example, she quotes some American research where photographs from *Playboy* were analysed to see if a changing shape of *Playboy*'s pin-ups had emerged. The findings were disturbing because what had been previously considered the ideal shape for women had become increasingly thinner as the years progressed. But, as Sara Gilbert, remarks, 'the proportion of space given to material about diet and slimming in six major women's magazines increased significantly during the ten years between 1969 and 1979 compared with the previous ten years. Yet during the same period, the average weight of women under 30 was consistently several pounds heavier in 1979 than in 1959'.

Bigger or fatter?

Further proof that we're getting bigger came from a somewhat less academic source – a catalogue clothing company. In 1993, the company, JD Williams, carried out a survey that involved a random selection of the company's four million customers. The women involved, who came from all over the country, were invited to a 'measure-in', which involved them having their bodies measured by experts. Their results showed, categorically, that women in the Nineties are bigger than the women 40 years ago. Our arms are fleshier while our necks and shoulders are half an inch bigger; our busts are one and a half inches bigger – and, apparently, significantly lower – whilst our waist is, on average, two inches bigger. It also seems that these days we have a larger abdomen, which makes the upper hip two inches bigger; our legs are a little longer and although the upper thigh has increased slightly, the lower thigh is slightly slimmer. But one of the biggest changes seems to have taken place on our bottoms which, the survey revealed, is now a completely different shape! Flatter and bigger, our bottoms, it appears, now start higher on the hips and end lower on the legs: Barbie manufacturers please take note!

However representative the above research may be, one of the most interesting conclusions must be the realization that, if the survey is correct, the reason that we've grown is, presumably, down to an improved diet as much as an increasingly sedentary lifestyle. When the last national survey that looked at size was carried out we were still in the midst of rationing. Many of the foods that we take for granted today – eggs, cheese, fruit, butter, bread, meat and poultry – were strictly rationed, and that's if they were available at all. And poorly fed adults produced poorly fed babies. The importance of maternal nutrition – how mothers eat when they are carrying a baby – has now been well documented; initiated largely by David Barker's ground-breaking work at Southampton University. The knock-on effect of a 'good' diet means that babies are healthier – and bigger. And a sustained 'healthy' diet ensures healthy growth for a child, resulting in bigger children. In fact research into growth patterns over the years has shown, beyond doubt, that the better the diet, the better the growth of the child. So, getting bigger should be proof that we're eating an improved diet, which should be cause for celebration, rather than concern.

But as with all things there's a down side and while a plentiful diet means an improved choice, it doesn't necessarily mean we always choose the food that is the most nutritionally desirable, as we've seen in the last chapter. And some experts analyzing the results have pointed out that although a larger bust may be put down to the number of women who take the contraceptive pill (the Pill changes the hormonal balance in our bodies and it is not uncommon for women on the Pill to find that their bust has increased by at least half a cup size), the other major reason why we're getting larger is to do with the alarming decrease in our energy levels. Women of the Fifties were a lot more energetic than we are, even if not by choice. As we've already seen in the previous chapter, progress has meant that we do less – and we do it less energetically!

Is society to blame?

Without doubt, our bodies and the image they reflect is of fundamental importance in our society and, as we've seen, the less you conform to what is considered the 'right' image, the more prejudice you're likely to have to deal with in almost all areas of your life. We live in an image-centred society where looks and images are used to sell anything from a stock cube to a lavatory cleaner. But the more luxurious a manufacturer wants us to think a product is, the more attractive and elegant are the images – or people – that are associated with that product. And let's face it, a whole industry, advertising, is based on this premise so we have Elizabeth Hurley wearing Estée Lauder and Naomi Campbell eating Müller Light.

There's no doubt that for many of us our bodies and the way we look are central to how we define ourselves – if you like, our identity. And however much we may, or may not, agree with it, the way we see ourselves forms the basis of how we initially see and judge each other. So, it's no wonder that the way we look ends up being so important. As Dr Judith Rodin says in *Body Traps*: 'appearance will always be important because we are social beings. How we look sends messages, whether we want it to or not, and people respond to us accordingly.'

And, of course, how we think about our bodies deeply affects the way we think about ourselves. And if we're always struggling to change the shape of our bodies we end up not quite knowing who we are. Whether we like it or not, when it comes to first impressions, we are how we look. Often it's women at home who have to bear the brunt of labels, even though we're all susceptible. However, if you have a job, or career, that gives you a label with a more positive meaning, at least it gives you an alternative tag to hang your identity hat on. So, whether you're a teacher, doctor, designer, shop assistant or engineer, you're at least provided with another way to describe yourself. That said, there are few of us that have such terrific levels of self-esteem that we really, truly, don't care what people think of us – and the way we look. Let's face it, we all want to be loved!

Dr Judith Rodin even goes so far as to stress just how normal it is to worry about the way we look, and it's important that our concerns aren't dismissed as vanity, or conceit. Or, as some dieting bashers would have it

- stupidity. 'The body has deep psychological, social and cultural significance,' Dr Rodin explains. 'The problem is that social attitudes have conspired to make how you look too important.'

Having a positive body image, these days, seems rarer and rarer. In fact a survey carried out by MORI for 'The Feel-Good About Food' campaign, in 1993, discovered that 74 per cent of the people interviewed wanted to change their body in some way and that 80 per cent were dissatisfied with at least one physical attribute. One American survey on body image, published in 1987, in *Psychology Today*, revealed that only 12 per cent of people in the survey admitted to having little concern over their appearance and 50 per cent of the women were actually unhappy with their weight. In fact the way we think about our bodies is so fundamental to the way we think, and see, ourselves that psychologists have shown that a distorted and negative body image can cause psychological changes from mood swings to depression.

Of course there are people who feel secure enough within themselves to challenge the prevailing images of 'beauty' and 'attractiveness'. One such person is clearly comedienne, Dawn French, who in 1994, spawned a wealth of articles by columnists in particular, after she appeared on the cover of several magazines, draped in metres of gauze, and was then featured on the *South Bank Show*, waxing lyrical about the joys of being fat. Ms French was attempting to challenge prevailing attitudes to weight and the response was extraordinary. While being brave, her position as Dawn French was bound to gain her a considerable amount of notoriety. She was also out to prove that being overweight doesn't affect your chances of being a cover girl. But, of course, if she *was* simply an 'ordinary' girl - of the same dimensions - plucked from the obscurity of any old High Street, more strength would have been added to the argument. Similarly, if magazine editors had gone for an unknown size 16 plus, they would have been striking a far greater blow for larger women than simply jumping on the bandwagon by featuring one of the most well-known and talented celebrities of the Nineties.

So Ms French got her coverage, but the magazines got an awful lot of 'good' publicity because they were bucking the trend of using the standard, skinny model in favour of one of the most popular - and it has to be said - attractive of women celebrities. Of course the next month it was business as usual and, having made a 'statement' about the validity of bigger women, the magazines could then go back to featuring skinny lizzies of five foot ten with legs that never end.

Having worked in magazines for the best part of 15 years, I can tell you that celebrities on covers sell – regardless of their size. And if, by being a little controversial by moving away from the norm, you attract a not inconsequential amount of media attention, then so much the better. What was more interesting was the coverage that surrounded the stunt. While editors may have been applauded, there was also an outcry from a variety of self-appointed Nineties commentators. A. A. Gill, for example, writing in *The Times* was clearly horrified and described the photos as showing Dawn 'laid out à la Titian family-sized suckling pig . . . cunningly made to resemble a catering pack of clingfilm'. He believes 'fat is ugly because it is deforming and limiting' and considers that 'making a virtue out of a vice or misfortune has become a late twentieth-century parlour game played by the socially right on'.

Whether you believe A. A. Gill's opinion is extreme and offensive, or that he is simply saying what many people think, unfortunately it is indisputable that thinness is often associated with success, brightness and attractiveness. Which, as we've seen, leaves 'fatness' to be linked to stupidity, failure and unattractiveness . . . the list of negatives goes on. But the question we all need to ask is this: if thinness is just someone's perception of how they *think* we ought to look – whether that someone is actually the fashion or film industry, magazines, manufacturers or advertisers – in real terms, does it *really* matter if you're fat?

Chapter Five

Is Fat A *Fictitious* Issue?

HOWEVER HAPPY YOU may or may not be about your body image, with an estimated 20 million adults in the UK overweight and six million obese (as far as doctors are concerned), if you're over what is considered an acceptable range for your height then you're at increased risk from a whole variety of health problems. Problems that have been shown to *decrease*, once your weight is reduced.

HEALTH PROBLEMS

Your joints

Our bodies are designed to carry a certain amount of weight, and the more we exceed the limit, the more pressure and stress we put our bodies under. When the stress gets too much, the body starts to show the strain and we end up with joint problems like arthritis. Obesity is a major risk factor for osteoarthritis and in a study of 1003 women at St Bartholomew's and St Thomas's hospitals in London, researchers discovered that the risk of osteoarthritis of the knee increased by over a third for every 5kg of weight gain. What's more, they estimated that 63 per cent of the cases in the group that were studied were due to obesity.

Your breathing

Being overweight places pressure on your breathing and, the Royal College of Physicians Report on Obesity - probably one of the most important documents on the subject to be published - reported that one of the most frequent complaints made by people who are obese is that of being breathless, even when they have only slightly increased their level of physical activity; in some cases this may mean simply going up the stairs or walking to the local shops. Obesity often leads to a deterioration in lung function and although extreme respiratory problems tend only to occur when a person is 'markedly' obese, just being overweight can be a risk if you need surgery as there's more chance of a post-operative chest infection developing, caused by breathing difficulties.

Your life expectancy

Fat people are three times more likely to die by the age of 45, a report by the Office of Health Economics warned in 1994. It also reported that if they survive heart disease, stroke or diabetes, they could still suffer crippling arthritis, gout or gall-bladder problems. Although being moderately overweight doesn't carry significant health factors for people over 50, in younger people it is clearly linked with increased mortality. The Royal College's conclusion was 'obesity does limit longevity'. Professor John Garrow, who is recognized as one of the country's leading experts in the field, says if you are overweight in your 20s, you are less likely to survive to 65 than if you become overweight in your 50s.

Your heart

As your weight increases, your heart has to work harder and the more stress it's put under, the more chance there is of it breaking down, which means you can suffer a heart attack. Coronary heart disease is the single biggest killer not only in this country, but in the whole of Western Europe, with Britain (and more specifically Scotland) having the dubious honour of being right at the top of the heart disease league. Generally heart disease is not caused by one single factor but by several different factors, all of which increase your risk. And two major risk factors, blood pressure and cholesterol levels, are both affected when you put on weight. While you have little control over some factors, like your genes, there are others that have more to do with what you do rather than who you are. So smoking is a huge risk factor for heart disease, as is a fatty diet. In fact the Royal College of Physicians reported that throughout the weight range, men who smoke 20 or more cigarettes a day have *double* the risk of non-smokers and a substantial proportion of this extra risk can be ascribed to heart disease. So much so that they felt smoking is the hazard that should be tackled first in an overweight smoking patient because the subsequent weight gain on stopping smoking is a smaller risk than continuing to smoke. A decline in physical activity has also been given as another reason why there is an increasing amount of heart disease and experts believe that exercising when you're overweight can do wonders for your heart. But, the sad truth is, that the larger you are, the less likely you are to want to exercise.

Cancer

The American Cancer Society Study showed that as a woman's weight increases, she shows a progressive increase in the risk of cancer of the breast, uterus and cervix. For men, an increase in weight is associated with a statistically increased risk of colon, rectum and prostate cancer. Nearer home, EPIC, the European Prospective Investigation into Cancer is conducting the world's largest investigation into the link between diet and cancer, which will involve seven European countries and over 25,000 people. Although research is still under way, experts do know that an estimated one third of all cancers are linked to a fatty, low-fibre diet. And by making simple changes to eating patterns, it is possible to substantially reduce our risk of developing some of the commonest cancers. Being overweight raises the risk of endometrial cancer and an overweight older woman has a higher risk of breast cancer. There's also growing evidence that it may also increase the risk of cancer of the large bowel and possibly the breast in even younger women.

Blood pressure

Weight gain in adults is also associated with increased levels of blood pressure. Although there may be other factors that play a part (for example, a family history of high blood pressure) being overweight can increase the risk considerably. And high blood pressure itself increases the risk of illnesses such as thrombosis and stroke.

Diabetes

Obesity not only increases the risk of developing diabetes, but the risk is increased further the longer you stay fat. And there is a progressive risk of diabetes developing as weight increases. Once again the genetic factor has a part to play in whether you will actually develop the condition but research also seems to suggest that even a moderate weight gain can increase the risk. However, once obesity is established there is a much greater risk which increases with age as well as with further weight gain.

Your gall-bladder

There is a significant increase in gall-bladder disease once someone becomes obese. Interestingly, studies have shown that low-carbohydrate diets – much loved and followed in the Seventies – may have played a part in increasing the cases of gall-bladder problems. The reason is that obese patients who eat a low-fibre diet have a tendency to form gallstones, so the relationship between obesity and gall-bladder disease may depend at least in part on the type of diet we eat.

And other aches and pains . . .

The probability of suffering from varicose veins doubles if you're obese and the heavier you are, the more strain it puts on your body – hence backache is also a common complaint. Tiredness can be a problem, largely to do with the excess demands that are being made on your body.

Obviously it is important not to exaggerate the risks of being over-weight – as opposed to being obese – but it is important to recognize that carrying excess weight when there is a history of particular conditions in your family, can increase your risk of developing that condition. As the Royal College concludes, 'weight gain is particularly unwise in those with a personal or family history of coronary heart disease, high blood pressure, or diabetes and there is clear evidence of benefit if weight is reduced'. Whether we like it or not, there is a progressive risk of ill-health with weight gain in adult life. Those individuals with a family history of diabetes, hypertension and heart disease, and those already fat in their 20s, are likely to be particularly susceptible to illness.

So, how fat is fat?

There can be no doubt that obesity presents a health hazard, as we've seen. The actual term obese refers to people who are at least 20 per cent heavier than the top end of the desirable weight range for their height.

Most of us have idled away time, pouring over those 'Right Weight For You' guides that seem to pop up everywhere, from the doctor's surgery to our favourite magazine, and they can give you an idea of what, medically, is considered an acceptable weight for your height. Also, as a range is given, it allows for the fact that we all come in different shapes and sizes. So there's no such thing as an 'ideal' weight – as long as you fall within the appropriate range (usually about a stone), there's no problem. So, if the maximum weight for your height is, say, 11 stone (about 154 lbs or 70 kgs), and you weigh at least 13 stone 2lbs (184 lbs or 83.6 kg), you weigh far too much and you need to take action.

The majority of the information about what is considered a 'normal' weight used to be based on statistics from American insurance companies, amassed from years of weighing and measuring anyone who took out life insurance. Their data revealed who had died prematurely of diseases related to obesity and that information, known as the Metropolitan Life Insurance Tables, played a vital role in helping experts assess what was, and wasn't, an acceptable weight. However, now the current method used by experts is an index called the Body Mass Index.

For women optimal BMIs are between 18.8 to 23.4; for men 19.8 to 24. Below these figures is generally considered underweight, above is overweight, while someone with a BMI of over 30 would be considered obese. To discover your index simply take your weight in kilograms and divide it by your height in metres squared (i.e. your height in metres multiplied by itself). For example, a person who weighs 9 st, 10 lbs (136 lbs or 61.8 kilos) and is 1.68 metres (5ft 6) tall has a BMI of 21.9 – which puts them in the desirable range for their height. Disadvantages to using the BMI are that it makes no variations for the difference in weight that exists in bone, fat, organs and muscles. That said, it certainly can provide a useful indicator as to whether your weight may be affecting your health.

While easy-to-use charts, and even the more sophisticated calculations that give us a BMI will give you an indication of how healthy your weight is, it's important not to be too rigid about how you interpret the information. Some experts believe that many of the height and weight charts recommend weights that are far too low for certain heights. For example, if you have short legs and a long trunk, allow yourself a few pounds grace because, as bone is lighter than body tissue, this can have a bearing on what might be considered to be your optimum weight. If you're the athletic sort and you have muscles where others might have fat, you may also get an inaccurate reading over how 'appropriate' your weight is because muscle weighs more than fat. So, although you can be heavy without being fat, the charts won't recognize this fact.

Of course another much easier, but altogether less scientific way of seeing whether you're overweight, is to, literally, pinch an inch. You simply pinch at a particularly fleshy part of your body, like your waist or the flesh under the top of your arms. Then measure the distance between the inner edges of your thumb and forefinger. According to the experts, if the measurement is over 15 mm, (12mm for men), you're overweight.

However, a less scientific approach is simply to see if you're able to grab a good handful of fat – if you can, it's time to take action!

Research has also shown that a more accurate indication of how our weight affects our health depends increasingly on *where* we store our fat. If you're an 'apple', which means you have a more central fat distribution and store your weight around your tummy, you're more susceptible to problems than a 'pear', someone who stores their fat around the hip and thighs. You won't be surprised to hear that 'apples' tend to be male and excellent examples of this are men with beer bellies! Women generally store their fat round their hips and thighs, although after the menopause they develop a shape similar to men. It's also worth remembering that women have more fat than men, with a healthy woman's body containing 20 to 25 per cent fat, while men have between 15 and 20 per cent fat.

Are you at risk?

Whatever the statistics say, there are certainly people walking around who have had long, healthy lives but are clearly obese. But, in the same way, most of us can name at least one person who smokes like a trooper but has lived happily until they're 90 and then died from old age rather than from the ravages of lung cancer, one exception doesn't make the rule. The truth is, if you are carrying around a considerable amount of excess weight, you're not as fit, agile or likely to be in as good health as someone whose weight doesn't tip into the morbidly obese category.

So, when does being overweight become a problem? Sara Gilbert in *Tomorrow I'll be Slim* writes that there is a case for saying that even to be mildly overweight is of some importance 'if only because the risks begin to increase with even a small increase in weight above the upper limits of the range'. However, she also admits that it would be ludicrous for doctors to insist that anyone just over the 'acceptable range of BMI, 20-25, should immediately go on a diet.' Clearly, though, there are many of us who don't need tables or tape measures to tell us whether we weigh more than we would like. But the key is to know whether your weight should be giving you cause for concern. So how do you do so?

Firstly, you need to look at your personal history – and habits. So, if the tables said that you are on the upper limits of the weight range, and you smoked, you'd need to think about giving up smoking because, as we've seen, smoking presents more of a health risk than excess weight, but put the two together and the risks are greatly increased.

The next step is to look at your family's history of disease.

■ Has anyone in your family had a heart attack under 40?
■ Is there heart disease generally in your family?
■ Or high blood pressure?
■ Or diabetes?
■ Or arthritis?
■ Gall-bladder problems?
■ Chest problems?
■ Breast cancer?

If the answer is yes to any of these then it's worth remembering that your risk of developing one of the above conditions is greater if you are overweight. So, if you were to think of your body as a gun, although your genes provide ammunition, it's actually down to you to decide whether or not to pull the trigger. As well as your mortality risk returning to normal, losing weight offers other less life-threatening but equally dramatic changes for the better. Sara Gilbert points to the 'increased ability to take exercise, in itself vital for maintaining health, increased self-esteem, and all the emotional and psychological advantages of reducing one's level of 'disability' compared to other people . . . there is no doubt that any degree of fatness carries with it all the pain, and the stigma, of major disability.' But whether you think of being fat as a disability, or just a plain nuisance, before you can decide what you want to do about it, you need to understand how we get fat in the first place.

WHY FAT IS A COMPLICATED ISSUE . . .

The traditional view that fat people got that way because they eat too much and exercise too little is no longer taken as a universal truth, even though evidence suggests that those who initially have a lower energy need (in other words lead a relatively inactive life and so need less calories to keep them going) are more likely to gain weight and become obese than those who are more active and consequently have a higher energy requirement. So, some people can eat up to twice as much more than others, but without putting on weight. However, it's certainly true that some people seem to have more of a tendency to gain weight than others. The six-million dollar question is *why*. Scientifically, there's a variety of explanations. So, what do the experts say? Prepare to be confused . . .

The fatostat theory

Scientists from Rockefeller University, in New York, studied two groups of people, one obese and one of normal weight. Their observations led them to the conclusion that fatness is controlled by a regulator in the brain which affects the amount of fat on the body, in the same way that a thermostat on your heating controls its temperature.

This regulator, which is known as an 'adipostat', mainly because of the effect it has on the adipose (another word for fat) tissue, adjusts the body's output of energy until weight returns to its pre-set level. Unfortunately there is no *British Standard* that the level has to adhere to, unlike real thermostats! This means the setting can vary tremendously from one person to another which, say the scientists, explains why we're such a motley collection of differing shapes and sizes! So, if you're someone who constantly strives to lose some of your excess weight, it could mean that you're trying to keep to a weight that is lower than the one set by your adipostat.

The genes theory

The evidence shows that obese parents are more likely to produce obese children but studies that have monitored twins and brothers and sisters who have been brought up separately, have revealed that about 25 per cent of obesity is genetically transmitted. That said, there is obviously a link, but this link means that certain people may have a predisposition to becoming fat – it doesn't mean that fatness, or obesity, is inevitable. And whatever genes you've inherited, there's nothing to say that you *have* to reach your genetic potential.

If fatness does run in families this is certainly due, in part, to the fact that parents pass on their eating habits. From an early age the child will 'inherit' not only the parents' idea of what constitutes a 'normal' helping, or portion, but also the family's idea of what an acceptable body shape is. One piece of research that supports this theory that our individual perceptions of what we think is an acceptable shape are purely subjective, published in 1970, showed how obese dog owners are more likely to have obese dogs! So, it seems, anyone is susceptible to dramatic changes in their body composition, regardless of their genes! It's also worth mentioning that, genetically, as a population we haven't changed.

Yet despite this genetic plateau, we're still getting fatter so, clearly, genes can't be held to account for all our weight problems . . .

The metabolism theory

Probably the most well-known of the theories. All the food we consume is either broken down and stored in our body cells or used to give us energy. The process of turning food into energy is called metabolism. The metabolic rate means the overall rate at which food is used up and reflects the total energy needs of the body. The theory is that the more calories you get from food, the faster your metabolic rate, which explains why the metabolic rate of someone who is fat, is around 25 per cent higher than the one of someone who isn't. The fatter you are, the more your energy requirement increases, so weight gain can actually increase your metabolic rate.

The knowing-when-to-stop theory

Some people, researchers say, have an in-built ability to know when to stop eating – or when they've had enough. Professor Barbara Rolls, from America's Penn State University, monitored the eating habits of a group of people and concluded that some of us just don't possess this inborn ability which somehow manages to shut down our appetite as soon as we've had enough to eat. It seems this mechanism may be genetic and is able to regulate an individual's energy intake – what they eat – and also manage to balance it against the energy that they use. By getting the balance right, there's nothing left over which could be used by the body to form fat. If this theory is correct, it may explain why some people never seem to put on weight; but if some of us do have a 'faulty' appetite gauge that fails to let us know when we've had enough, that means some of us really don't know when to stop eating.

The 'you're eating the wrong calories' theory

Research presented at the Association for The Study of Obesity suggests that the calories we get from different foods can have a varying effect on our appetite. Carbohydrates, such as pasta, rice and potatoes it seems, are the most satisfying foods as they manage to suppress the appetite so there's less chance of overeating. Fat, on the other hand, is less satisfying which means you're altogether more likely to overeat. Our body also burns carbohydrates more quickly than fats, which may be another contributory factor. Moreover, fats are more effectively converted by our body into body fat – all of which has an effect on how our bodies deal with food.

In one project, at the Rowett Research Institute in Aberdeen, doctors manipulated the carbohydrate and fat content of meals, unbeknown to their unsuspecting group of volunteers. They discovered that in just one week those who ate a diet containing 60 per cent of fat put on 700g fat, equivalent to one and a half pounds, whereas those who ate a diet with 20 per cent of fat actually lost 200g (about half a pound). These findings certainly reinforce the belief that, if you're on a low-fat diet, it's pretty hard to overeat.

Experts reckon that our bodies need around 9oz (250g) of carbohydrates a day and if we don't get it, our bodies, like Oliver Twist's, are left wanting more. And that's regardless of what else we've eaten. Current guidelines say that we should get at least 50 per cent of our daily calories from carbohydrates.

The 'you've-got-more-fat-cells' theory

We're all born with fat cells in our body – the place where we store our fat – and it's also been established that there are critical periods of our life when we lay down new fat cells, for example when we're pregnant. This theory suggests that people who are fat simply have more fat cells than their leaner counterparts. The theory goes that the more fat cells you possess, the more there are to fill up, which means that your body is more able to store fat, something that it may well do more efficiently than you would want. It may also mean that you require more food in order to 'satisfy' those cells.

The theory was certainly a popular one 20 years ago when experts felt that fat cells were highly relevant in determining someone's size. Some research into this area seems to suggest that there is little you can do about the number of fat cells you are born with. Although their size may decrease, they never disappear. If this is the case, it could well go some way to explaining why so many people, once they have managed to lose weight, find that they end up putting it back on again. This theory has largely been superseded by other theories. However, it's worth mentioning that some experts, including Professor John Garrow, believe that as you get fatter, your fat cells increase in both size and number and if your weight goes down, the opposite happens. Furthermore he is emphatic in his belief that 'it is not true that fat people are born with more fat cells; nor does the number or size of your fat cells cause you to become fat'.

The brown fat/heat theory

Most people give off extra heat immediately after eating through a process known as 'thermogenesis'. Increased heat production is largely limited to certain tissues in the body: these are patches of adipose tissue found in relatively few areas, such as the skin on your back – between the shoulder blades and armpits. This tissue is different from ordinary fat and is referred to as 'brown fat'.

Babies have a lot of brown fat, which is able to release energy to keep them warm. This is obviously crucial for them because they not only lose body heat quickly, they are also unable to shiver, as adults do, when they're cold, which is a physical reaction to the body's need to boost its level of body heat.

Brown fat burns up more energy than white fat which, in theory, means the more brown fat you have, the higher your metabolic rate. The discussion point seems to be over whether some of us are more effective at converting brown fat into energy than others. John Yudkin, in *The Sensible Person's Guide to Weight Control* (Smith Gordon), considered that this variation between individuals in their dietary-induced thermogenesis could be part of the reason why some people are more likely to put on weight than others. To illustrate the point, Yudkin discusses the case of two imaginary men who are the same height, build, age and have about the same activity levels. Both need about 2000 calories a day, an amount that will allow them to gain all their nutritional requirements without putting on any excess weight.

'If they take more calories than this they can dispose of some of the extra calories by thermogenesis. Now suppose that the extent to which they do this is 500 calories a day for *A* and 200 calories for *B*. *A* can therefore increase his daily intake to 2500 calories without putting on weight, while *B* can increase it to only 2200 calories without putting on weight; his weight therefore increases while he is taking 2500 calories. *B* can legitimately claim that he is, as before, still eating no more than *A* is eating, so it is not fair that he should be getting fat. But, unlike many other facts of life that are unfair, he can at least do something to prevent the unpleasant effects of his more limited thermogenesis; he can reduce his weight by eating less, and perhaps drinking less alcohol, than his luckier friend *A*.'

This theory was all the rage in the seventies, but these days experts have concluded that any change caused is so small that it's likely to make little difference to someone's overall body weight. Now, whether you want to follow the late Professor's prescription for correcting the 'heat' balance in your body is up to you, but what the above example shows is that putting on weight is not necessarily as simple as 'enjoying your food too much'.

The 'you-eat-too-much' theory

Admittedly this is not necessarily a new idea but what *is* new is the recent research at one of the leading nutrition centres in the country, the Dunn Clinical Nutrition Centre. The Dunn have probably explored most of the variations on the theme. What is fascinating, though, is that after all the research they have come up with a fairly simple explanation . . . *You eat too much*.

Dr Susan Jebb, one of the Dunn's nutritionists, has stated, unequivocally, 'we have proved once and for all that being overweight is nothing to do with having big bones, food intolerance, enzyme deficiency or with it being in the genes'. And she adds that 'there is no mystery as to why anyone gets fat. Being overweight is simply and solely due to overeating'.

In an experiment, led by Dr Andrew Prentice, a selection of both lean and overweight volunteers were firstly overfed, then underfed. When they ate too much, both groups gained weight at exactly the same rate. Furthermore, both lost at the same rate when they ate too little, proving that weight gain *can't* be blamed on anyone's metabolism.

Of course, this theory has distinct advantages for anyone overweight. It means that by reassessing your diet, it is possible to lose weight, as there are no physiological constraints affecting your weight. It also means you have more control over your weight than you may have originally thought. Clearly the down side of this is that your weight is due purely and simply to the food you eat, as opposed to how your body processes it.

The 'my condition is making me fat' theory

Some people believe that as they eat so little, their diet can't be to blame for their weight . . . so it must caused be something else. That 'something' may be their glands or their hormones. The inner workings of our body have long been used as a reason to explain what we consider to be an unacceptable size. However, all the research into obesity indicates that there are very few cases caused by medical disorders. Thyroid problems, for example, only cause problems with weight in a small proportion of people. And, even in the Royal College of Physicians Report on Obesity, it is acknowledged that even if there is a possibility that a thyroid problem may cause weight problems, 'it is still not certain whether the weight gain depends on an increase in food intake or a decrease in metabolism'. The report also concludes that many of the hormonal changes in obesity seem to be 'secondary effects of increased weight, rather than of primary importance'.

Obviously there will be some people who discover they have a condition that increases the likelihood that they will put on weight, and some forms of medication can also cause a degree of weight gain. However, surplus weight is likely to be one of the least important side effects of a condition that will certainly cause other symptoms. Clearly, if you are at all worried that weight gain is a by-product of something totally unrelated, it is important to see a doctor as soon as you can, and sort out the cause of the problem, rather than just dealing with the result.

As you can see, when it comes to agreeing a definite theory as to why some people are obese, and others aren't, the jury is still very much out. There is an awful lot of research going on in the area at present and new ideas are evolving all the time. Various theories have been put out over the years and then abandoned, then researched, then later taken up again. However, the truth is that there is no one answer. What we do know is that simply assessing someone's food intake by dietary record is unreliable – people overestimate their energy expenditure and under-estimate their energy intake – and this is truer of obese people. Recent research has also shown that lifestyle plays an increasingly vital part in determining our weight.

Many of us have become so sedentary that we're simply no longer using up enough energy. One study even showed that there was a link between being overweight and the number of TVs and cars owned: the more cars and TVs, the more likely it is that the family are overweight! Of course experts have known for some time that our lack of exercise is turning us into overweight couch potatoes and, unfortunately, the less we do the less energy we use up, which means that we need less energy, in the shape of food, to keep our bodies going. However, although we're doing less, there's little evidence that we're eating less to compensate for the lack of activity.

All things being equal, when you're considering losing weight, all that you can really do is work on the information that you know to be true. Whether that's to do with what you eat, or don't eat, your attitude towards food and yourself generally. It is also another reason why the area you really need to worry about is YOU. This book is about doing what's right for your body as well as your mind and while theories are certainly a useful indication about how we should and shouldn't behave, they certainly don't tell the whole story, as we'll see in the following chapters.

Chapter Six

What's Eating You?

UP TO NOW, I've concentrated mainly on HOW we've got fat – or at least fatter – but to really reach a point where you're able to discover the ideal weight for you, we need to look at WHY we get fat. The truth is that what goes on in our minds can have as much, if not more, influence on our weight, and eating habits, as what goes on in our bodies. That's not to say that every square of Cadbury's Fruit and Nut you have ever eaten has some deep and meaningful significance (although some psychologist somewhere is sure to have discovered one!). Psychological explanations for our behaviour have become something of a national pastime, and it would be convenient to believe that our behaviour as adults can simply be explained away as something sinister that happened in our youth: sinister being anything from being forced to eat vegetables (and thereby developing a lifelong aversion to all things green), to having to walk to school (thereby justifying a tendency to spending as much time in a horizontal position as possible).

There's no doubt that much of our behaviour is what the psychologists call 'learned behaviour' – in other words we pick up messages about how we *should* behave by seeing what other people do, and copying them – but it can be all too easy to hide behind mistakes of the past; regardless of whether those mistakes were made by you, or your mother for that matter. But by accepting responsibility for our behaviour, we are putting ourselves back in the driving seat of our lives. We're getting back in control.

As with the medical theories as to why we're fat, numerous psychological explanations abound. Of course your personal reasons for getting fat may be very basic – you may have gained more weight than you might have liked simply because you like eating. Obviously it would be much more convenient to have some dark area of our subconscious that years of therapy would eventually reveal but sometimes the explanation is unnervingly simple. As psychologist Jane Ogden says, in *Fat Chance*

(Routledge), 'Why does "fat" have to be anything other than being fat? Why does it have to be indicative of any psychological problem? What is wrong with believing that you are fat because you were born this way? Some fat people have eating problems, and some have psychological problems. But not all, and no more than thin people.'

She has a point. However, eating, and our approach to food, can easily have more significance than we might realize. And before you can successfully deal with the whole question of your weight, or how you may think you *want* to look, you need to understand why you've stayed fat, as well as why you got that size in the first place. Chances are that the reasons are fairly mundane. Certainly slimmers that I have spoken to have given strikingly similar stories when it comes to explaining their weight gain, and research has identified very clear 'danger times', when it seems we are more vulnerable to putting on weight. So what are they?

FAT: THE CIRCUMSTANTIAL EVIDENCE

'Marriage made me fat!'

A fairly common complaint! Women who maybe spent little time thinking about food suddenly find themselves spending hours poring over cookery books working out which are the most impressive recipes to serve their 'other half'. Whether it's a hangover from being told that a 'way to a man's heart is through his stomach', I simply don't know. What I do know, though, is that perfectly sensible women treat 'setting up home' with a man as a reason to lock themselves in the kitchen for hours at a time, to prove to their partner just how versatile and clever a cook they are.

When a couple set up home, suddenly the whole ceremony of eating can take on much more significance. Cooking is still seen as a largely 'female' function (even if the New Man does like the idea of rustling up a little something on a Sunday, when he's relaxed and away from the pressures of his working life), and it's one of those things that we feel, instinctively, we ought to do well, simply because we're female, in the same way that some people seem to expect women to 'instinctively' know how to clean and tidy . . .

The point I'm making is that we feel duty bound to take responsibility for shopping for food, preparing food, as well as cooking food and, whilst we may be happy to change our eating habits, many women complain that their husbands won't be happy unless, 'they had their meat and two veg on a plate at the end of a day'. Cooking for others can, of course, be really enjoyable but when you're cooking to impress, you're more than likely to rustle up a little something that owes its existence to either cordon bleu, nouvelle cuisine or, at the very least, Delia Smith.

'I was pregnant!'

After marriage, the next rite of passage must be giving birth and for many women, pregnancy affects more than just their shape. In a *Which?* survey on slimming, over a third of women slimmers who answered the questionnaire said that having children was one of the factors which 'made them fat' with one fifth saying it was the most important factor.

While some women complain that pregnancy made them feel hungrier, others have commented that they felt so well that all their pleasures were heightened – including their enjoyment of food! For many women, too, who have spent years 'worrying about their weight', pregnancy can be a welcome relief. Just think, it's one of the only times in a woman's life where the physical signs of an increase in weight are positively celebrated by people whom they come into contact with. Well-wishers smile inanely at their spreading midriff while family and friends present them with food, almost wherever they go.

Of course, after the birth, it can be some months before a woman loses any of the excess weight she gained during the pregnancy. And while doctors may advise her to 'watch' her diet and increase the amount of exercise she takes, for many new mums, dieting and exercise are the last things on their minds. The chances are that not only will she have little time and energy for these, but with sleepless nights and baby blues, she's also unlikely to have the inclination. Added to this, many women have admitted that before they have been able to lose the extra weight, they've become pregnant again and all thoughts of 'doing something about it' have been thrown firmly to the wind. Others may go back to their former weight, but only to find that the change in the type of life that they lead, once the baby is born, means they eat more and exercise less. The result? They put on weight.

'I was stuck at home with the kids!'

Being at home for long periods – whether you're used to working or not – can result in food becoming much more of a priority. The day is broken up, at first into feed times, then into mealtimes. As any mother remembers only too well, feed times can be at anything from two-hourly intervals and can last the best part of the hour. Once the baby is fed, tiredness and hunger compete for your attention and what better way to appease these feelings than treating yourself to a little something?

Everything suddenly seems to revolve around feeding, sleeping and nappy changing. All that hanging about in between can mean there's a lot of time for nibbling, where maybe before having 'a little something', whenever you felt like it never occurred to you. And being much more housebound also means that you can eat whatever you want, whenever you want. Many women complain of feeling isolated and lonely at home when they first have a child. Suddenly their lives become very different to that of someone who can come and go as they please with no responsibilities. And eating at least gives you something to do . . .

As babies grow into children, the situation doesn't necessarily improve. 'Dustbin syndrome', where you hoover up the leftover contents from your child's plate, is a common condition that will be recognized by many mothers! It also has to be said that mothering can be a pretty time-consuming job, particularly if you're working outside the home as well. And it can be easier to rely on easy-to-cook fast foods which may be nutritionally less than perfect, but are quick to prepare and won't require unlimited threats to the offspring before you can induce them to 'at least try it . . .'

Food can so easily turn into a battleground when you have children and anyone who has ever spent longer than two hours with a child – from toddler to teenager – will know that food quickly takes centre stage. And no trip is complete without periodic stops for the three 'T's – toilets, tuck and trinkets. The built-in breaks can be all part of an outing's charm for the children but for the adults, it ain't necessarily so.

'We ended up at a fast-food place – I can't stand the food there myself but it's so easy with the kids because they love it . . .' is probably one of the most commonly mumbled sentences in the English language. We've all said it – and all done it. Not that there's anything *wrong* with eating at a burger/pizza/fried chicken place, but if, given the option, you'd rather opt for something that's low in fat, low in sugar, high in fibre – and tastes pretty good too – let's face it, a fast-food restaurant is hardly going to be your first choice. And if like the kids you've been trekking around for hours, the chances are that anywhere that offers sustenance and a chance to sit down is better than nothing.

The truth is that for women, when they no longer have just themselves to think about, it's all too easy for food to become a compromise. I've yet to meet a child that responds to the sight of steamed fish and sprouts with an enthusiastic 'yum-yum'. Based on an admittedly wholly unscientific survey, taken from the sample of children that have come back with my children for lunch, tea or supper, few desire more than fish fingers, chicken nuggets or sausages served with potato waffles, chips, croquette potatoes – and variations on the theme.

I'm afraid, whichever way you look at it, food takes on a much greater importance when you have children. Apart from nuggets, bites and waffles, our cupboards are full of crisps, snacks, sweet cereal and sugary biscuits. Whether you think food manufacturers should be providing us with what's good for us, rather than what we end up buying is an altogether different issue but the situation is that children have some pretty suspect things thrust on them – be they highly coloured, heavily sweetened, greatly flavoured or simply high in fat.

Food is often central to being a mother and the options for food geared towards kids do not necessarily offer optimum nutrition. And as that's the majority of food that we end up having in our cupboards, it's no wonder that some of it is going to provide part of our diet, too.

'I went on the Pill!'

When the Pill first became widely prescribed, in the early Sixties, the accepted wisdom of the time was that it made you put on weight. And there was certainly something in that belief because most of the Pills available, all of which were in their infancy, tended to contain high levels of the hormone oestrogen, which *can* have an effect on your weight. In fact, experts at the time reckoned that women could put on up to 5 lbs (2.25kg) within a couple of months of taking the Pill, with one study revealing that fat distribution of women on the Combined Pill, in the Seventies, shifted from the arms and legs to the waist, hips and thighs. However, interestingly, the study also found that the percentage of body fat in the women hadn't changed, which meant that the gain was likely to be due to fluid retention.

These days the Combined Pill contains much less oestrogen, so fluid retention, as well as any other type of weight gain, is less likely. Obviously if you have felt, at any time, that the Pill has left you heavier, or feeling more bloated, than you'd like, you need to go back to your doctor and discuss whether it's worth considering another type of Pill, or alternative methods of contraception. However, some experts explain the weight gain as a result of the 'feel-good factor', induced by oestrogen. This, they suggest, can create a general sense of well-being and that, combined with the fact that worries about getting pregnant have been removed, can have an effect on the appetite. But, if you do feel that overeating is a problem and the Pill is to blame, it's worth knowing there is one point all the experts agree on. The Pill cannot cause anyone to put on vast amounts of weight and in the majority of cases the most you're likely to put on is a few pounds.

Middle-age spread

Many people find that as they get older, they seem to put weight on more quickly. Although some experts suggest that some of this may be because our metabolism slows down slightly the older we get, much of the cause is down to the fact that we tend to be less active as we get older. You walk more than you run and are likely to spend more time at home, either entertaining or by yourselves, than being out and about 'doing' things. And if the amount you eat increases, it doesn't have to increase by very much for your weight to increase considerably over the years. As the authors of *Which? Way to Slim* commented, 'You could store an extra 10 lbs (4.5kgs) of fat in the course of ten years if your daily energy balance were out by no more than 20 calories – one small potato more or a five-minute walk less.'

Clinically, though, there is absolutely no reason why our weight should increase or why we should weigh any more when we're 60 than we did when we were 16. The only change is the way our bodies distribute the fat. When we're younger, we tend to carry extra weight around our hips and thighs but as we get older the fat prefers to make a slightly shorter journey – nestling comfortably around our waist and tummy. So, the good news is that although you may *feel* fatter, you're not!

Giving up smoking

In the Consumer's Association's *Which? Way To Slim* survey, a quarter of the men and one tenth of the women said that they had put on weight when they gave up smoking. Some research actually suggests that there is a physical cause to this weight gain – that smoking can speed up the metabolism, using up to 200 calories more, per day. However, undoubtedly the other reason smokers put on weight is because they are likely to eat more because food is often seen as the most convenient substitute for a cigarette. It gives ex-smokers something to do with their mouths as well as their hands. Evidence also suggests that smokers tend to eat more when they first give up smoking simply because their tastebuds are no longer all 'fogged' up by smoke: food tastes better and many ex-smokers, having re-discovered their tastebuds, find that they actually enjoy eating for the first time in years.

These days there are a variety of nicotine substitutes and 'stop smoking' programmes available: local health centres have details of available help near you. However, gaining weight once you stop smoking is by no means a foregone conclusion, and many people manage to give up without putting on a pound. But, if you – or someone you know – refuses to stop smoking because of a possible weight gain, it's worth remembering, as we've already seen, that smoking carries far greater risks than putting on some weight. And if you're worried that once you stop you won't be able to control your appetite, it's time to find out a little more about exactly why your appetite is out of control – and what you can do about it.

WHEN IT'S YOUR MIND THAT MATTERS . . .

But what happens when the way you eat has more to do with the way you think than the way you live? By actually taking the trouble and time to work out why you gained all that weight in the first place, you put yourself in a position of understanding what's going on in your body, as well as your mind, and the result is that you enormously increase your chances of getting down to – and staying at – a weight that you feel truly happy with.

Clinical psychologist Annie Fursland refers to women as the *seen* sex: we are constantly concerned about how our behaviour appears to others and all too often we are judged by how we look. Certainly the whole beauty industry is based around the fact that women aren't happy with the way they look – and even if they are, the chances are that they'll soon grow out of it once they've been exposed to a hefty dose of advertising offering them the opportunity to look thinner, sexier, prettier, bolder – and altogether more attractive. Many of us react to these messages with a predictable level of insecurity and susceptibility that often results in us running with open purses to the nearest beauty counter, as the messenger intended – one way of coping with a looks-obsessed society. In fact, as far as psychologists are concerned, not doing anything about your weight is as significant as spending your adult years being a dieting junkie, addicted to any diet that may come your way.

In the early Seventies, psychotherapist Susie Orbach, wrote her ground-breaking book, *Fat is a Feminist Issue* (Arrow), which attempted to offer insights into why so many women are overweight. Orbach's experience led her to the conclusion that, for some women, there is an unconscious motivation for their weight gain. For her, compulsive eating can be a response to the position that a woman finds herself in. For many women, she says, who don't want to play the 'game' of taking on the role that they're expected to play, getting fat is a way of opting out. It's a way of saying 'I'm not going to compete' in a society where women are judged by the way they look. Some women have also talked about their size giving them presence and making them feel more assertive. This view was particularly common amongst career women who, it seems, waged a constant battle with their bosses to be taken seriously. Orbach quotes one woman who explained, 'when I'm fat I can hold my own, when I'm thin I'm treated like a little doll'. Other women had remarked how fatness made them feel 'one of the boys'.

If you feel that some of the above theories are more complicated than they need be, it's worth remembering that Orbach's book was written over 20 years ago and, to a certain extent, her ideas are very much of the Seventies. Fewer women worked and fewer women had established positions and careers for themselves at work. Also, she and many of the women that she came into contact with were reflecting the ideas of a relatively newly formed women's movement, committed to the idea that 'a new psychotherapy to deal with compulsive eating has had to evolve within the context of the movement for women's liberation'. Of course you don't have to be a high-achieving career woman to have your own reasons why, subconsciously, you may be in two minds as to whether you really want to lose the weight. Being substantially overweight provides a perfect excuse for all sorts of things.

EXCUSES, EXCUSES

Maybe you're stuck in a job that you've been doing for years and you know you ought to be looking to move on. But you don't. *You think you'd rather wait until you've slimmed down* . . .

Or maybe you've been at home with the kids for years and have often said you want to go back to work. But you haven't. *You'd rather wait until you've lost some weight . . .*

Or, you could find yourself at a loose end socially. Maybe a relationship has recently ended, or most of your friends seem part of a cosy couple. You know you ought to get out and meet some new people, but you don't. *You think you'd rather wait until you've got thinner . . .*

Or you're in a relationship that should have ended years ago. You no longer love your partner, he treats you appallingly and you're unhappy. You know you should leave him. But you don't. *You'd rather wait until you've lost weight . . .*

Sometimes it can seem that the advantages of being overweight outweigh the disadvantages. The fear of the unknown means that changing anything about the way we live our lives can be pretty scary. Even when we think the change may be for the better, there's always the chance that it won't be. And it's that 'chance' that all too often holds us back. After all, it can be far simpler to live our lives based on the theory of 'better the devil you know'. Putting off until tomorrow what you could do today is something most of us do, given half the chance. It also means you avoid putting yourself in a position where you may be rejected. All of us fear failure and it's much easier to deal with when you have an excuse . . . *I didn't get the job, or I didn't make friends because of my size.* Of course, once the weight is actually lost, it's easy to feel our protective coating has been stripped away. Suddenly we are being judged for what we really are, rather than simply how we look.

So, it's far easier to stay how you are. And let's face it, fantasizing about what's going to happen once you've lost the weight is a terrific way to spend your time. You get to be scriptwriter, star, and fortune-teller. Unfortunately, though, the problem with real life is that you can never quite predict the outcome . . . so it is far easier not to put yourself in the position where you have to deal with it. Although putting off reality means you'll never be quite sure what would happen, it does guarantee one thing – you'll never be disappointed.

Of course it's easy to understand why some people worry that losing weight may change their lives – but not necessarily for the better. The idea that fat equals jolly is so embedded in our culture that many overweight women are happy to play the part of someone's 'jolly, fat friend'. Losing the weight could mean you no longer qualify for the 'jolly' role. Or worse, you may no longer be jolly. If you think about it, our behaviour is so wound up in our image that sometimes we even find it difficult to separate the two – readily playing out the part that we've been given. So there's always a fear that when our image changes, our behaviour will too.

The strain on your relationship

Men can also play a part in keeping us fat. Men married to women who may not be viewed as overtly sexual, may feel more secure in their relationship. Fatness is often associated with stability and reliability and so it's easy to think that if anyone is going to run off with someone else, it's more than likely going to be the svelte woman at number 19, who is clearly looking for more out of life . . .

By losing weight, the formerly fat wife seemingly crosses over to 'the other side'. She ceases to be the stable influence in the family and ceases to be reliable. So, she too starts to worry that she may be attracted to other men because suddenly, she finds that men are attracted to her. Certainly for women who prefer not to think of themselves in terms of their sexuality, being fat allows them to dodge the issue nicely. They feel safe. After all, there's no chance that anyone is going to think of them as a sex object. But, of course all that changes when you lose weight. Men start to react to you whilst other women become suspicious of their formerly fat friend, whom they could trust and confide in. Whichever way you look at it, losing weight can rock the boat. If not for you, then certainly for some of the people around you. One of the unspoken truths of the slimming world is that a disproportionate number of marriages break up when one partner loses a significant amount of weight. Not surprisingly, there is little empirical research on the subject – well, helping people to slim their way to divorce is hardly what most diets would want to be remembered for!

Somehow the loss of weight can sometimes affect the balance of the relationship. Whether that's because there was an imbalance to begin with obviously differs from couple to couple. However, it seems that when a slimmer loses a lot of weight, it can put a relationship under considerable pressure. In some cases, the husband becomes possessive, unable to trust his wife, even when she's out for a night with the 'girls', so convinced is he that either she's playing away or that every man within a one-mile radius is intent on making a play for her. The husband finds it impossible to cope with all the attention that his wife, who formerly was only too pleased to stay in the background, seems to be getting. Everyone is saying how wonderful she looks, and how clever she is. Of course, many husbands will share in the reflected glory and nod their heads, enthusiastically agreeing that, yes, isn't she clever and yes, doesn't she look terrific. But, unfortunately, men, like women, also have their streaks of insecurity and low self-esteem – and some simply can't cope. Words like jealous, untrustworthy and possessive become common currency. The marriage is put under huge pressure and, in some cases, crumbles.

Another scenario that is not uncommon is far simpler, if not sadder. The formerly overweight, diffident and self-conscious wife becomes more confident and self-assured with every stone she loses. After years of playing second fiddle to a husband who maybe she'd allowed to become overbearing and dominating, she is transformed into a woman who wants to be in the première division. She wants to be in control. And suddenly she looks at her husband through new eyes and realizes that what she loved was the security he gave her, and the knowledge that someone seemed to care enough to be willing to marry her. Maybe her expectations were low in the first place. After all, if you're not used to getting attention, any attention you do receive is better than nothing. But, having lost weight, she finds her needs have changed. And if there's one thing she has discovered that she doesn't need, it's her husband.

Misery and humiliation

Of course your weight can be used to blame all sorts of things that go wrong in life. In the same way that things may get better when you've slimmed down, until you get to that position your weight provides a reason why things are really rotten at the moment – anything from being badly treated at school, or home, to being dumped on at work. When you're bigger than everyone else, people notice. And people comment. From the first hurtful remarks in the playground to the whispered asides in the office, or outside the school, when you're fat, no one lets you forget it. It knocks your confidence sideways and all but decimates your self-esteem.

In a society where 'politically correct' has become a buzz phrase, it's interesting that while we grapple to avoid commenting directly on someone's disability for fear of causing offence, we don't think twice about commenting on someone's size. Over the years I have interviewed overweight and formerly overweight women who have told me they have 'developed' an instant headache or migraine, rather than have to go to a social event with their husband, or a friend, which would mean they would be introduced to people they have never met before. Or women who have been asked to represent their firm at an external meeting, and have sat there for hours with their coat on, in the hope that it covered up their shapeless body.

Everything seems to conspire against you when you're fat and the longer you've been that way, the deeper the scars. Ask anyone who was labelled a 'fat child' what they remember about their childhood and chances are you'll unleash a torrent of unpleasant recollections. Having to change into a PE kit, and then having to go out into the playground with the rest of the class generally ranks near the top of the humiliation scale. Stories of being left on the sidelines because no one wanted you in their team, or of being laughed at for running and wobbling simulta-neously when you raced your way 'home'. But if children are cruel, at least they've not learnt the art of being patronizing – something that grown-ups can do so well, even unintentionally. In a society that is obsessed with thinness, it shouldn't be a surprise that we treat anyone who doesn't conform to what is considered 'acceptable' as several slices short of a wholemeal loaf.

Studies have shown, time and time again, that thinness is often associated with success, achievement, wit, power – and being in control. So, it's no surprise that fatness is seen as a sign of weakness, failure, laziness, stupidity – and proof that you have no control. Some women I've spoken to have even told me of times, when they've been out shopping, or visited local authority offices, where they were spoken to loudly and slowly, as if being fat meant you obviously had learning difficulties . . .

Anyone who has seen the film *Death Becomes Her*, starring Meryl Streep and Goldie Hawn, will admit that the images of someone who is fat, is hardly a sophisticated one. The film focuses on two power-hungry female characters, played by Streep and Hawn. Hawn is eclipsed, and rejected, by a more cunning and ambitious Streep and her response is to disappear into obscurity. We then get a glimpse into exactly what that obscurity is like . . . the rejection has turned Hawn into an obese lump, a good 150 lbs (or ten and a half stone, if you prefer) heavier, who spends all day, watching 'old movies' made by the Streep character. She is riddled with jealously and hate and only rarely leaves her chair except to waddle over to the fridge to grab another litre tub of ice-cream which, of course, she consumes in one sitting, so desperate to get it into her mouth that we watch as much of it dribbles down her chin. Clearly we are being presented with a slob in action – or, to be more precise, inaction. And isn't the message all too clear? Fatness is equal to lack of motivation, greed, laziness and to general sloth.

One magazine, *Woman's Journal*, once asked one of their writers to don a 'fat suit' for a day, and see if there was any difference in the way people reacted to her. The suit, which made her look five stone heavier, changed the normally elegant size 16 into a shapeless size 24, whose statistics read like measurements from an MFI catalogue: 51- 43.5 -55. The writer reports on the little things, like trying to manoeuvre her bottom onto a bar stool when she meets a friend for lunch – and the embarrass-ment she feels as two men laugh at her quite openly. And then there's the reaction of a friend she's not seen for some months, when she decides to pay her a surprise visit at work. As she makes her way up the rickety staircase, in search of her friend, her body receives some unsolicited attention. 'I glance back,' she recalls, 'to see a young man in the handbag department gawping after me.' But worse is to come. 'I greet my friend enthusiastically but she seems embarrassed . . .'

After a day of being five stone bigger the writer comes to some stark conclusions. 'For me, more shocking than disapproving sidelong glances, was my own readiness to adopt self-imposed limitations . . . the pleasures of eating out and shopping for clothes turned into embarrassing, exhausting experiences. My confidence was the smallest thing about me. I felt like a heap. I hated my slowness and physical discomfort. How can you feel chic when you're hot and dishevelled?'

Of course being 'fat for a day', hardly gives you a deep and meaningful insight into obesity. But it does give a significant glimpse. We expect fat people to have slower minds, as well as slower bodies and we see them as pathetic individuals who are unable to control themselves. And for some reason, we seem to assume that if you're thin, you're bound to be happier and more in control that someone who is fatter. Just witness the way we pillory celebrities who 'allow' themselves to get fat.

Star-gazing

The tabloids regularly reveal how the stars battle over their bulges and we are constantly presented with visual updates of The Duchess of 'Pork', as well as being invited to tut-tut over countless photographs of a 'recently spotted' ballooned Oprah Winfrey or Liz Taylor. Other celebrities we, apparently, love to weight watch include American stars Melanie Griffith, Kathleen Turner and Cybil Shepherd. But you don't have to be American to gain the attention of the British press; *East Enders*' Letitia Dean has been fat watched, as have Emma Thompson, Mavis Nicolson, Nina Myskow, Kenneth Clarke - to name but a few.

If size helps get you noticed, it can also play a part in keeping you noticed. And even if you have the effrontery not to be particularly concerned about your weight, odds are that other people will. Comedienne Jo Brand, for example, has received as much - if not more - attention for her size as she has for her talents as a comic. Male commentators and male comedians, in particular, use her as the butt of their jokes and so-called acerbic comments. They can't criticize her humour, so they go for her size. It's sad, but true, that some less imaginative male comedians still prefer to fall back on going for cheap laughs, based on someone's looks, with that someone generally being female.

Of course if you're famous there are compensations for being criticized. And fame tends to be something enjoyed by people with big personalities - to be anything that involves being in front of the camera generally requires an extrovert, rather than an introvert personality. Also fame increases confidence because the individual concerned often commands respect because of their particular skills. Skills that have been recognized and, by the very nature of that recognition, valued. Unfortunately, we mere mortals who have lesser claims to fame also have less to make us feel good about ourselves. We haven't received nation-wide recognition for our talents. If we are noticed, the most likely reason is because of our size. And unless we too have a big personality and a huge amount of confidence, then being treated as if we have a disability is likely to make us feel as if we really do have one.

'Thin is better'

It's no wonder that our self-esteem plummets along with our confidence and belief in ourselves. One woman who was interviewed for *Options* magazine, in January 1995, said quite candidly, 'I've been fat and I've been thin . . . and thin is better.' She talked about being fat all her life - and miserable with it. From bearing the teasing and taunts at school, her working life began at 17 when, working in a hotel, she was required to wear a uniform. Hers had to be made up specially. 'It was the beginning of years of embarrassment and humiliation,' she remembered. 'I just put up with living in a world geared towards thin people. Because of my lack of confidence, my social life suffered. I gave up eating out because I was so worried that I wouldn't be able to fit into the seat in a restaurant. There was no point in going to the cinema either – it was too uncomfortable. Holidays abroad were out, how could I sit on a plane?' Since those days, Irene Shannon has lost 9 stone – hence her view that 'thin is better'.

Having a low opinion of yourself seems to be an automatic response to a society that is constantly critical of us, simply because of the way we look. If society doesn't seem to value us, what basis do we have to value ourselves? Perhaps what's worth remembering is that if you're over-weight, it could be down to any of the factors that have been discussed so far. So, your size might be explained by something physical, or psycho-logical. Or you might feel the problem has to do with the way other people view you as opposed to the way you view yourself. Or the answer could be down to a little bit of all the different theories. Or none at all. As Jane Ogden says in *Fat Chance*, for some of us, fat has nothing to do with anything other than being fat. Whatever explanation seems to suit you, no book that concerns itself with eating would be complete without turning it's attention to food.

Chapter Seven

Food and You

FOR WOMEN, THE relationship with food has always been a tricky one. On the one hand we spend an awful lot of time thinking about it, shopping for it, cooking it, and serving it; whilst on the other we're constantly worrying about it. It's interesting that we see all the time spent cooking for our family as part of the nurturing role: a way of making sure they eat 'properly' – it's also a way we show our love. But, when it comes to nurturing ourselves, that's a different matter. Food that we implore the rest of the family to eat, we spend much of our time avoiding. And then feel guilty when we're not quite as successful at avoidance as we'd like to be . . .

Of course if you feel quite relaxed around food, it's not a problem. But if you don't, it can be a little like a drug addict taking a job in a pharmacy. So many women's lives revolve around food that it can be difficult for them to be objective about it. And if you don't think about food, you can be forgiven for thinking that maybe you ought to. They used to say sex was the national obsession but nutritionist Tom Sanders claimed that this had been replaced by dieting. Personally, I believe that both dieting and sex have been eclipsed by our obsession with food.

Consumer magazines have also made sure that food, and recipes, provide one of the main ingredients of their publications and under-standably so. Most reader research shows that readers love reading about food: they want to see pictures of it and want to know how to do it. Most magazines have cookery editors (although now increasingly becoming known as food editors), if not whole departments where recipes are devised, tested, finely tuned, re-tested and then delivered to the reader on the magazine's cookery pages. Many mags include information about how much the food costs and how long it will take (preparation time as well as cooking time), and some even provide a 'shopping list' – just to make sure you don't forget anything.

This is not a criticism in any way of publishing policies. I have spent most of my life being addicted to magazines and, over the years, confess to having become something of a magazine junkie. But, whether you enjoy the practical advice and foolproof recipes given in magazines like *Family Circle*; reading and drooling over the tasty treats devised by the wonderful Katie Stewart in *Woman's Journal*, or you prefer to invest in over 100 pages of food with *Good Food*, the idea is always the same - you look . . . and you cook.

Whilst offering fast solutions to the daily dinner problem (*Family Circle* offers a perfect example of this with 'What's For Dinner?', seven menu plans for feeding hungry families), all the food pages are geared towards encouraging us to think about food: how we buy it, cook it, present it and even serve it. The food is seductive and we're all too easily seduced. But then we turn the page - and discover a diet. A diet, presumably, to relieve us of the excess baggage we've accrued by following all those luscious recipes . . . You either get guilty or fat - or both.

But you don't need to buy magazines to learn about the joy of cooking. No television channel these days is complete without a cookery programme. From *Let's Cook* and *Masterchef* to celebrity cooking with Delia Smith, Gary Rhodes or Keith Floyd - the choice seems endless. We even have a comedy series based on the theme with Lenny Henry's *Chef*!

But if food plays such a large part in our lives, it's not always something that we necessarily feel comfortable with. Whereas in prehistoric cultures men were the hunters - hunting out food for their families - women have become the gatherers. We gather recipes, we gather food from the supermarket; . . . and finally we gather the dirty plates once the family has been fed. Far from happily gliding around our kitchens, à la Fanny Craddock, with wooden spoon in one hand and recipe in the other, many of us feel torn between the need to feed our families on the one hand, while resisting the temptation to overfeed ourselves on the other. And let's face it, trying to restrict what you're eating, whilst cooking for your family, makes sticking to any diet difficult.

HABITS OF A LIFETIME

The role that we take on as food maker, starts to take shape when we're young. Psychologist Jane Ogden believes 'Children learn from a very early age that eating their mother's food makes her feel positive and valued. They also learn that to refuse her food is rejecting her love and will make her anxious and upset.' All of which is why, as she explains, 'we think about food in terms way beyond the limitations of feeling hungry and needing sustenance'.

What we actually eat is influenced largely by our culture and where we live. A food's availability can often influence a country's diet. Religion also plays a part, with certain foods 'forbidden'. However, it is as children that we receive the important messages about food. For example, eating up is 'good', while leaving food is 'bad', sometimes regardless of whether or not you've had enough to eat. Even from our earlier days, when we're breast-fed, if the baby takes the feed 'well', mothers treat it as a real achievement and a personal triumph. Conversely when baby doesn't feed well or refuses altogether, we take it as a personal slight against ourselves, which results in much angst-ridden hand wringing, and even phone calls to good friends and 'older relatives' in an attempt to discover what *can* be done.

And haven't we all done it? Food finished is seen as a mark of success. Everyone's eaten 'well', the cook is more than pleased that her culinary delights have been appreciated, and the nurturing circle is complete: we cook to please, they eat to please and so . . . we end up feeling all that cooking has been a job well done. Strong emotions can be aroused by mealtimes too. A rejection of the meal can be seen as a rejection of the cook and the very act of eating can become a power game. You assert your power by insisting the 'ungrateful' offspring eats, the offspring asserts his, or her, power by refusing. 'Eat up your greens!' is a common cry from parents. 'They're good for you and will make you grow,' we're told. And it's a message we've all heard a hundred times before.

But whether we're receiving those messages, or giving them out, the truth is that from very early on we start to divide foods into good and bad; nice and, for want of a better word, necessary. No wonder that as a child, food becomes conditional. 'If you eat up your greens, you can have ice-cream'; 'if you clean your plate, you can have pudding'. Unfortunately these well-meaning remarks can actually pass on the subtle messages about certain foods. For example, as children our preference for a food increases if the food is given as a reward, whereas when children are bribed to eat a particular food, they begin to show a sharp decline in their preference for that food. Sadly this is a very different result from the one desired by the well-meaning parent who assumes that the opportunity to eat ice-cream will increase a child's liking for broccoli or spinach!

In fact, one study, actually showed that by making the consumption of one food conditional on another ('if you eat your fish you can have some cake') we are identifying certain foods as 'rewards'. The researchers discovered that the dislike of the food the child 'had' to eat increased while the desire for the food offered as a reward *increased*. What all this means is that the more you try to coerce little Johnny into eating up his greens, the less likely he is to want to . . .

Another study looked at how easily a child's preference for particular foods can be influenced. Having discovered a selection of snack foods that a group of three to five year-olds neither liked nor disliked, researchers offered those foods either as rewards or, without making any fuss, just as a normal part of a meal, so the child didn't associate the food with a particular type of behaviour. Within a short space of time, the food that the children had come to think of as a reward began to be liked more than it had been at the beginning of the experiment. However, the response to the foods offered more as normal snack-time fare remained unchanged. So, it seems the associations that we place on foods has as an effect on how we feel about them, and to what extent we want to eat them.

The sexing of food

Unfortunately, even when we try not to make an issue out of food, we can still unintentionally pass on subtle messages to our children. And eating, it seems, can become an altogether sexist business as much as anything else.

The Open University's *Guide to Healthy Eating* was published almost 11 years ago, but the observations about how we subconsciously 'sex' our food, still ring true. Research shows that masculine meals contain meat and potatoes, whilst feminine meals are considered to be lighter fare – maybe a little chicken, or quiche, and a side salad: a case of meat for the boys, fish for the girls!

Men and boys are also generally given larger portions than girls and young women in the family and, as the authors noted, 'Girls may be encouraged to eat daintily. This means smaller portions, smaller bites and attention to table manners.' Boys who tuck heartily into their food are referred to as having a healthy appetite: girls, on the other hand, are checked if their enjoyment of the food means that they're eating in an altogether 'unladylike fashion'. Eating habits that are hearty in men, become greedy in women. Boys may tuck in, girls should hold back – satisfying themselves with 'tasters', and the privilege of seeing the males of the family enjoy their food. Even when the daughter is ravenous, she may subconsciously take her cue from the mother, who may not only eat less than the rest of the family, but do it more daintily. For females eating can mean more than just satisfying our hunger. For many of us, from a young age we become involved in the whole business of food preparation. Sometimes because we were co-opted, other times – particularly if we're the only girl – because we enjoy being with 'mum' who helps us put together a picture of what we consider to be a female role model.

As The HEC book says, 'The importance you attach to preparing food and your attitudes to it may have been learned in childhood. Think about how meals were prepared and who prepared them. Whoever did most of the catering in your family when you were a child will have had a powerful effect on you. They will have provided a model. And whether you like it or not, it can affect the way you perform the role yourself – or how you react to another person performing it . . . even when you enjoy cooking you can still have feelings of drudgery.'

Of course most parents try to make sure they are serving up a healthy diet but the problem is that our understanding of what's healthy has changed over the years. We used to think it was 'good' to eat meat every day and we'd often follow a standard meat and two veg meal with a doorstep-size piece of cheese. If fashions for food change, then progress means that the more we discover about what we eat, the more aware we become about the health benefits of particular foods and a particular diet.

The other problem is that as well as being seen as rewards, certain foods are seen as treats. And whereas 50 years ago having a joint of meat may have been seen as 'special', as were sweets, which were a rarity: nowadays everyday treats are often the bars of chocolate and packets of sweets that the kids get in party bags; treats are what grandparents bring out when 'the apples of their eye' visit and treats like tubes of Rolos, mini Mars and bags of jelly babies are what we buy the children when we go out for the day. Treating the people we love to something we know they'll enjoy is nothing new, we have been doing it for generations. However, nowadays – mainly because advances in technology have meant that sugar, which was once an expensive and rare ingredient, is now a relatively cheap, everyday food – we 'treat' ourselves on such a regular basis that the treat has become part of our everyday diet.

Also, the amount of foods like sweets, chocolates and biscuits that are available – and the choice, which we, or to be more specific, our children, are reminded of by a constant stream of adverts that either appear on the TV or in their favourite comic or magazine – makes the products even harder to resist. Whole aisles are given over to packets of biscuits these days while advertisers tell us to 'go on treat yourself' with a bar of this, and 'cheer yourself up' with a bar of that.

FOOD AS COMFORT

Some foods are also treated as pacifiers. A sort of oral plaster for our grazed emotions. 'Don't cry, here's some sweeties to make it better', we say. For many of our kids, while a kiss and a cuddle is nice, a kiss, a cuddle and a bar of chocolate is *even* nicer. But the idea of food providing comfort starts much earlier. A baby cries and we offer him food. The food may satisfy his hunger – if he is, in fact, hungry – but it will also give him comfort and security. So food becomes associated with the ability to soothe and comfort almost from day one. When you think about it, we learn to connect it with almost magical powers – food can impress, take away pain, lift the spirits, relieve boredom, and show how much we love someone. And just to prove it the adverts show us pictures of men leaping off mountains to demonstrate their affection simply because, as they say, 'The Lady Loves Milk Tray'.

The American psychiatrist, Hilde Bruch, believes this type of reaction is the result of 'faulty learning' which we have been taught – albeit unconsciously – from childhood. As psychologist Sara Gilbert explains, 'The child whose mother used food as a "universal pacifier" when all the child needed was a cuddle, or maybe a nappy change, grows up to use food as something to turn to whatever the situation, be it in response to anger, stress, or sadness.'

In fact, I'd hazard a guess that everyone reading this can relate to the idea of turning to food when they're feeling particularly stressed. However, for Sara Gilbert, Hilde Bruch's theory isn't completely water-tight because, as she rightly says, if we turn to food to relieve stress then once the food's been eaten we should feel better. Right? Now while that may happen in the short term, the long-term reaction is usually guilt, expressed in a variety of ways, such as: 'God how could I have eaten so much?', 'I can't believe I ate the whole packet!', 'I just can't seem to control my appetite!'

However, I'd suggest that maybe it's *because* we've mostly experienced faulty learning and mixed messages over food that we don't think in terms of dealing with the cause of our stress – whether it be anger, or disappointment, or fear – preferring to treat the result. So we almost eat to push the problem away. Of course the problem doesn't go away, so we still feel lousy. But then we have to deal with the guilt of overeating as well as the stress of the initial problem! Sounds familiar? If it does, you're not alone and it's not surprising that any of us deal with pressure in our lives this way. We live in a society where all situations call for appropriate behaviour: we're brought up to behave nicely, say please and thank you and generally not complain unless it's really necessary. Put it all down to British reserve and the stiff upper lip if you like, but the result is that we turn our anger on ourselves rather than behave in what is considered to be an inappropriate way.

SO WHY DO WE EAT?

In theory, we eat when we're hungry. But hunger is, in fact, as the late John Yudkin says, 'an unpleasant sensation that you seek to relieve by eating'. He explains that being hungry means not being very selective about what you eat, and the hungrier you are the less selective you become.

Hunger versus appetite

However, many of us don't wait until we're hungry to eat and often our desire for food is triggered by appetite which, as Yudkin says, 'is a pleasant sensation evoked by the sight or smell or even the thought of a particularly attractive food or drink'. It is hunger, and appetite, that initially affect when, what and how much we eat. However, Yudkin believes that 'with extreme hunger you might eat foods that you would ordinarily find not only unappetizing, but quite abhorrent, although you will then eat only as much as will relieve the severity of the hunger. On the other hand, the more appetizing a food is, the more likely you are to take it even if you are not hungry, and even when you find that you have already eaten more than you have intended.'

But what has become increasingly clear is that, when left to our own devices, our bodies seem to automatically opt for a healthier diet. In the Royal College of Physicians Report on Obesity, they note that the learning of food habits can mean that some children actually learn to eat more than their bodies would prefer. As evidence of the fact that we all have an innate ability to regulate what we eat, the report describes a study carried out in 1974 that involved malnourished children in Jamaica who, for the first time, were put in a position where there were no restrictions on what, or how much, they could eat.

To begin with the children had a voracious appetite. They consumed twice as much food as would be considered normal for their size and 'grew at 15 times the normal rate'. Amazingly, this pattern continued until they reached an appropriate weight for their height. At that point, their natural ability to decide what we do, and don't need, seems to have kicked into action. 'The amount of food ingested (eaten) usually fell abruptly within 48 hours to the level expected of a normal child of that size.' So, amazingly, their bodies automatically adjusted the amount of food that was eaten to the amount that was needed.

But if our appetite has an automatic adjustment level when left to its own devices then it's no surprise that, if exposed to the right conditions, the level can be manipulated and our appetites distorted. Experiments with animals have shown that specific animal drives means that the animal will choose food that will give it the right amounts of vitamins, minerals, protein and carbohydrates and an innate mechanism, a sort of built-in automatic set of scales, is able to control the amount that the animal eats, ensuring it doesn't have too much.

One experiment with rats illustrates this very well. Laboratory rats are usually fed a fairly bland diet of pellets containing all the nutrients that a rat is likely to need. However, when these same rats are offered a selection of foods that possess a variety of tastes, the rats not only eat more but they actually become fat. This is not to say that we humans behave like rats when it comes to eating, but there certainly may be a case for saying that we are no longer simply satisfying our needs. For John Yudkin the explanation is simple. It is not hunger but appetite that makes us overeat. And we are no longer eating to satisfy our needs, we're eating to satisfy our wants.

While hunger may be a complicated concept, eating is probably even more so. And it's only by understanding why we're eating that we can make any sense of it, and start trying to base our dietary decisions on needs as much as wants. If hunger is influenced by appetite, then it's worth looking at the sort of things that can increase or decrease our appetite.

Good looks . . .

For John Yudkin, how food *looks* is a major factor. He argued that the availability of a large and increasing range of very attractive foods is the major cause of over-consumption in affluent countries. The appearance of food has become more important and manufacturers have, for years, striven to make their foods more appealing. The way something looks has a direct effect on the way we expect it to taste. Brown wholemeal food may be perceived as healthy but it often gets the thumbs down on the yum-yum scale.

American psychologist, Susan Wooley, looked at how much the way that food looks influences what we eat. In one experiment, thirty-two students – half were obese, the other half were so-called normal weight – were given one of two drinks, followed by sandwiches. One drink was low-calorie while the other was high in calories. However, half the time low-calorie drinks were disguised as high-calorie milkshakes, whilst the other half they looked simply like low-calorie drinks. For the high-calorie drinks the situation was reversed. What was interesting was that the mere *appearance* of the drink influenced how many sandwiches were eaten: when the seemingly rich, high-calorie milkshake was drunk, the students said they were fuller than when they drunk the drink that was intended to look low-calorie, and so ate less. What this proves is what scientists have known for some time – our choices of what to eat, or indeed whether we eat at all, are influenced by an awful lot more than hunger. Eating is clearly a complicated business.

Whilst, as we've seen, some research has taken place that shows our dietary needs *will* adapt if we become nutritionally deficient, clearly we've moved a long way away from the days when we just ate what our bodies told us. Obviously left to our devices, with no cultural or social influences, we might well return to eating what we need, rather than what we want, but in today's society the constant bombardment of messages telling us what food can offer us only serves to confuse our internal message system. After all if eating certain types of chocolates means you get a certain type of man – as we're shown regularly by the adverts on our TV screens – eventually we can't think of one without the other, just as the advertisers hoped.

. . . and taste

Taste, or how we expect a food to taste, can also have a major influence. Our reflexes react automatically to sweetness and sourness and this can be seen even when a baby is still in the mother's womb. In one study, saccharin was injected into a mother's amniotic fluid and was found to actually increase the rate of sucking by the baby.

Considering our tastebuds develop before birth, it's no surprise that soon after we're born we show a preference for sweetness, although many people feel this is due to the sweetness of breast milk. When researchers have studied the expressions of babies they've noticed a definite positive response to anything sweet, whilst a bitter taste is greeted with a negative response, as well as an actual rejection of whatever it is that has produced the bitter taste.

So, clearly the more appetizing a food is, the more likely you are to want to eat it, regardless of whether you're hungry. A good example of this has to be when we go to friends to eat. Often we'll be served a sumptuous three-course meal – the courses only punctuated by cries of 'I couldn't possibly!' or 'I don't know where I'll put it!' But then, quite miraculously, we'll sit drinking cups of coffee, while we nibble at chocolates and selections of after-dinner mints!

Too much choice

So it seems that when we're presented with a wide variety of foods, it's all too easy to overeat. But why? Research suggests that it has a lot to do with choice. We just have too much of it. And the more we see, the more we want. At Oxford University, considerable research has been carried out which has looked at the effect the wide variety of easily available food has on our weight.

One study involved giving a group of students a meal. They were told to eat as much as they liked and then offered an unexpected second course which contained either the same foods as the first course or something different. The researchers, Barbara and Edmunds Rolls and Edward Rowe, found that the students who were given different foods ate significantly more than those students who were given the same food. In fact, those who were given the different food ate virtually the same amount as they had eaten in the first course (98 per cent) as opposed to those who were given the same food who ate around 40 per cent of the amount. So, Rolls and Rowe concluded that if offered more of the *same* food, we will eat less of it. But if we are offered another food, with a different taste and texture, we'll not only eat it, but eat it with relish.

Another study which investigated the impact of variety on eating involved giving a group of subjects different flavoured yoghurts. Once again, it was revealed that more yoghurts were eaten if there was a change in the flavour than if the subjects were simply offered more of the same flavour.

The implication of all this research is that if satiety is specific to a food that has been eaten, and if as we eat a food our preference for it changes, we are more likely to eat a varied diet, and so more likely to eat a sufficient variety of foods to ensure we take in a decent supply of essential nutrients. So, during a meal which is served in distinctive courses, we may, for example, find that we have had all that we want of the main course, but still have an appetite for the dessert. It may also go some way to explain how children push an unfinished plate of food away from them, groaning that they're 'stuffed', only to enquire plain-tively, 'what's for afters?' It's a familiar cry for most parents – and for me it's almost as familiar as the astonishment that 'afters' still manages to be completely consumed in what seems like record time!

Of course 'afters' for children as well as for grown-ups, can often be something light that slips down after a big meal. Ice-cream, perhaps, or crème caramel. Posher alternatives might be crème brulêe or mousse. Light in taste and texture maybe, but not necessarily light in energy. It's a fact that fatty foods *can* slip down a treat because they're less bulky than other foods. So, crème brulêe might seem more manageable than a bowl of fruit compote, or even fresh fruit salad.

But before you start to feel guilty as you remember all those times you popped back to that buffet table to re-fill your plate, take comfort in the fact that if you *were* overindulgent, it means you're just like everyone else! Even controlled studies have shown that when we're exposed to a buffet table we'll eat considerably more of the sausage rolls, egg rolls and pizzas than we would if we were offered any of those foods by themselves. So, it seems, the more choice we're offered, the more we'll eat . . .

Now, as there is no way that we can get all our nutritional require-ments from one food, or one group of foods, you could say that our bodies have an innate ability to limit what we eat of a particular food so that it ensures it gets all the nutrients it needs to keep it in good working order. So when our body's 'enough button' pings, if our minds are still telling us to eat more, we have to turn to another source for satisfaction. In fact it's this principle of self-limitation that drove the spate of one-food wonder diets that seemed to pop up all over the place in the Sixties and Seventies. Whether it was the infamous 'Grapefruit Diet', or diets based on pure protein or piles of pasta, there's a limit to how much of any of those foods you can eat. So, even if for a while some slimmers may have found that they did lose weight, eventually the inevitable happens. Boredom sets in and they go in search of other foods. It may mean they stopped losing weight but I'll guarantee it also meant that they suddenly started to enjoy eating again – and felt an awful lot better for it!

Scientifically, experts have also shown that different types of food have different effects on the level of physical satisfaction we feel once we've eaten. For example, at the University of Leeds, Dr John Blundell and his team have discovered that dietary fat seems to have only a weak effect on appetite control. This means that eating a meal consisting mainly of fatty foods is less likely to leave you feeling full than, say, a meal that is made up of carbohydrates. In fact, when their subjects were given a carbohydrate-rich breakfast, their desire to eat at between one and three hours afterwards was significantly reduced, whereas the drive to eat one to three hours later by a second group which had been given a high-fat breakfast was totally unaffected.

TRIGGER HAPPY?

As we've seen, trying to understand what makes us eat is complicated. While there are obvious reasons, like feeling hungry, that propel us towards the fridge, we're equally capable of searching out food because we're responding to 'triggers' that tell us we should be eating.

One of the obvious triggers is the clock. If it's 12 o'clock, or one o'clock, it's time to eat. And if eating lunch means eating a big, sit-down meal, that's what you're geared up to do, regardless of whether or not you're particularly hungry. The same is true if you were brought up to have supper and a snack at bedtime. If that's what you've been used to, your body clock will start to chime good and loud as the evening wears on and it prepares itself for a little dietary top-up. And the same is true if you're in the habit of nibbling throughout the day. Trying to cut them out, without preparing your body, is bound to lead to between-meal hunger pangs.

Being with other people who are eating can also be a powerful trigger. We've all too readily 'joined' a friend in a cup of tea and a sticky bun, simply because it doesn't feel right to let her eat alone. Also seeing someone eat can actually make you *feel* hungry, whether you are or not. Other triggers can be the smell, as well as the sight of food. Certainly it's a strong woman indeed who can walk past a supermarket's in-house bakery without being tempted by the wonderful smell of freshly baked bread that wafts down the aisle . . .

And then, of course, there are all those ads. And isn't holiday time the worst? Advertisers working on confectionery must surely think that most of the country spend the time between Christmas and New Year eating one chocolate bar after the other. Food generally, and chocolate specifically is portrayed as a perfect gift, invested with sensual qualities that far outweigh our expectations.

An example of how the media influence our appetite is ironically illustrated by some recent American research that looked at the effect that even watching diet commercials can have. The researchers showed two sets of women a sad movie clip interrupted by diet-related commercials, neutral commercials or no commercials. One set were slimmers, who were constantly 'watching' what they ate. The other set were non-slimmers. The researchers assumed that the images of successful slimming would strengthen the slimmers' resolve but, in fact, the opposite was true. Slimmers who saw the diet-related commercials actually ate *more* than other subjects! You can discover some of the ways to deal with the variety of eating triggers that are fired at us every day in Part Two of this book: Solutions.

EMOTIONALLY CHARGED

One MORI poll, commissioned for 'The Feel Good About Food' campaign, revealed that a significant minority of people feel they can't enjoy eating because of worrying about the food that they eat. Not too surprisingly, dissatisfaction with diet is significantly higher amongst those who are dissatisfied with their weight or see themselves as overweight – something that, as we shall see in the next chapter, is not necessarily the same thing.

If, as we've seen, we put our weight gain down to lifestyle changes like pregnancy, giving up smoking or staying at home with the kids, we also need to look at emotional pressures that may make us turn to food. We've seen how easy it is for us to adopt food as a pacifier, particularly as it is offered to us as comfort almost as soon as we come out of the womb. Suggestions on how to cope with emotional pressures can be found in the Solutions section of the book but, as well as realizing that there's nothing in the least bit abnormal about looking for comfort when you're feeling down, or stressed, it's also worth bearing in mind that it is thought that some of the foods we may turn to – like chocolate – may actually help to lift our mood.

Our body's needs can also change and that's particularly true for women, with our hormonal levels changing on a monthly basis. These changes can affect our tastebuds, as they cause our blood-sugar level to fall before a period, which can explain why women complain of cravings for something 'sweet' at particular times of the month. Hormones also affect the production of a chemical in the brain, serotonin, which acts as a sort of natural Prozac, inducing a feeling of well-being. Levels of the chemical drop before a period and some experts think that the increase in appetite that many of us have during this time is our body's attempt at searching out foods that will raise the serotonin level: carbohydrates. To complicate matters though, there are two types of carbohydrates: the stodgy, sticky ones that are used to make cakes and biscuits (these are the refined carbohydrates), or the high-fibre low-fat carbohydrates (the complex carbohydrates) such as wholemeal pasta, brown rice, pulses and so on. But if you are feeling in need of a 'lift', given the choice between boiling up a dish of brown rice, or grabbing a bar of chocolate, is it worth even asking what you'd do?!

Cravings? What cravings?

As with many theories, there are experts who disagree that cravings have anything to do with our body making us eat what it 'needs'. Adam Drewnowski, the Director of the Human Nutrition Program at the University of Michigan, believes, 'There is no evidence that people crave specific foods because of nutritional deficiencies. For example, we don't crave chocolate, which is high in magnesium, because we're low in that mineral.'

Even our own Professor Yudkin, over six years ago, said much the same: 'Mothers will explain that the reason they give their children so many sugary foods and drinks is because their little growing bodies need it, otherwise they would not demand it. If a pregnant woman says she feels she must have fruit, it is suggested that this shows she is running short of vitamin C. If someone is found eating earth, it is supposed to indicate that the person is anaemic and needs iron. If a baby picks pieces of plaster off the wall and puts them in his mouth, it is presumed that this satisfies a need for calcium.' However, Professor Yudkin believed that close analysis of these often quoted examples of how our body makes up for nutritional deficiencies, reveals, shall we say, more fat than fibre . . .

'The pregnant woman who is supposedly short of vitamin C does not demand just fruit; she is likely to insist that she needs peaches out of season, or some exotic fruit like custard apples or kumquats when they are unavailable; she is not at all satisfied when offered a vitamin C-rich orange . . . If the baby eats boot polish rather than bits of plaster are we to assume that he is short of wax or turpentine in his diet? Nevertheless it seems true that from a wide variety of foods, some instinct will see to it that our choice will ensure nutritional adequacy, as it seems to do in other animal species.'

Clearly Professor Yudkin illustrated that we need to be cautious in our attempt at trying to find explanations for what initially appears to be illogical behaviour. And if we go to extremes, it's easy enough to explain away anything. That said, more recently we have acknowledged that weird and wonderful cravings can be triggered by other physiological factors. Adam Drewnowski believes, for example, if you crave chocolate, what you really need is its relaxing effect on your body. As he explains, 'chocolate causes endorphins - the body's natural painkillers - to be released in the brain'.

However, another theory about why chocolate seems to raise our spirits has absolutely nothing to do with chemicals, hormones or any part of our bodies. Dr Peter Rogers, Head of Psychobiology at the Institute of Food Research in Reading, accepts that we eat treats to make us feel better, but he believes this is all down to what our perception of certain foods is. So, chocolate may not contain any magical ingredients but because we think of it as special, we respond to it as a treat or a bit of pampering. And the very act of treating ourselves to something a bit special makes us feel better.

Researchers at the Chicago Medical School actually looked at how emotions can directly affect our appetite. They showed a group of women three film segments - a horror film, a comedy and a travelogue. When shown the first two films, food intake rose amongst the subjects - and the more concerned the women were about their weight, the more they ate. Conversely, in subjects exposed to the travelogue, food intake decreased, even when the subjects were highly diet conscious. This seems to suggest that any heightening of emotions, whether it's the happiness you get from watching something funny or the fear you feel from seeing something that terrifies you, can make you want to eat.

Fighting the Food Trap

While Professor Yudkin may have liked us to return more to an eating-what-you-need basis, rather than eating-what-you-want, unless you have the self-control and discipline of the Amish, and you live in a plastic bubble devoid of any twentieth-century trappings, you're unlikely to be successful in returning to such purist ways. Addressing our needs would be fine if food didn't look so nice, taste so nice or have so much of our emotional and cultural history attached to it. Clearly no one can claim to have a truly natural response to food. We're up against an avalanche of influences that help us decide what to eat, and when, and if you're watching what you eat, it's no surprise that keeping your weight down and trying to control what you eat is so difficult.

On the one hand the messages that we pick up, whether it's through the ads, magazines, television, the supermarkets, or even our families and friends, encourage us to eat. Anyone who is trying to lose, or even maintain their weight, has to learn to recognize their innate responses, their learned eating behaviour, the media influences plus the very nature of food itself. And then when we *do* succumb, we find the messages we pick up are very different. We're told we eat too much, we're fat, we're unhealthy and we need to diet.

So, then we diet, but after a while we find those messages about food get louder and louder. And so we start to take notice, start to eat whatever we want again . . . and then, before we know it, we're trapped in the vicious circle of wanting to eat, but not wanting to eat too much; of being greedy, then getting guilty.

The good news is there is a way out of this dieting trap, but before we look at what you should do, it might help to first look at what you shouldn't. If up to now your only solution has been to go on a diet, you might find that you've ended up feeling a complete failure because it didn't work. But, if that's a familiar feeling, you might be interested to hear that you're not alone, and the good news is, you can do something about it. So if the whole question of food ties you up in knots, you need to have a strategy to understand how to untangle this complicated business and how to start eating properly – for life.

PART TWO

Solutions

Chapter Eight

Preparing For Change

AS WE'VE SEEN in part one, the process of working out why you've 'put on, kept on, been unable to take off' your excess weight is a complicated business. And it probably doesn't help that the whole question of whether or not you're actually fat is such a thorny one - especially with studies showing that some women who are dieting aren't even overweight in the first place. Hopefully the section in chapter five will help you assess whether you should be thinking of trying to lose some weight and it's certainly true that for many women the psychological damage of being overweight far exceeds the benefits of getting down to a weight that you feel happy and healthy about.

More importantly, anyone can re-think their attitude towards food – you don't need to think in terms of weight reduction to cast a critical eye on the way, or what, you eat. After all, coronary heart disease, some cancers, diabetes and high blood pressure - to name but a few - are risks to us all and, as we've seen, if you are overweight and/or smoke, those risks get greater.

One of the first steps that we all need to take is to develop a more positive attitude towards food. For some that can be too big a step to take alone and if your concerns about your weight really are clouding everything else in your life, a trip to your GP wouldn't go amiss. Doctors often have dieticians and practice nurses attached to their clinics, many with years of experience in the whole area of weight control. Also, if you have a substantial amount of weight to lose, it's important to discuss how you're going to tackle it with your doctor as he, or she, will have the advantage of knowing your medical history which means advice can be geared specifically towards you and your lifestyle.

In chapter Three, we looked closely at the problems caused by going on a diet. Obviously anyone who has had a history of eating disorders should only consider changing how they eat after receiving medical advice. However, you don't have to have been clinically diagnosed as having an eating problem to benefit from some of the practical suggestions on how to develop a positive attitude to food and eating. None of us eat in isolation and there are all sorts of influences that affect the way we eat – from our childhood, to our self-esteem, right through to how much money we've got to spend on feeding a whole family as well as ourselves.

WHEN IT'S NOT SAFE TO DIET

No matter how much weight you think you may have to lose, there are some groups of people who should never think about restricting what they eat without being under medical supervision. For example:

- *If you're pregnant* – or for that matter thinking of getting pregnant. Research has shown that dietary deficiencies of the mother can affect the unborn child. Also, the less 'goodness' in your body, the less likely you are to cope with the unborn child's demands on you. Obviously it's important not to overeat when you're pregnant and experts now believe that there is need for minimal weight gain in the first six months of pregnancy. But a disproportionate weight gain in the last trimester can be due to pregnancy problems such as fluid retention or pre-eclampsia – conditions that need immediate attention. Hence the importance of discussing your diet with your doctor before you make any changes to how you eat.
- *If you're breast-feeding* – lactating mothers have specific nutritional requirements so, once again, any change of diet needs to be discussed with the doctor or health visitor.
- *If you feel that your concern about food, or slimming, is getting out of proportion* – we all have times when we worry about what we're eating but when concerns about food and diet start to take over your life, it may be necessary to seek help, particularly if your present weight is not vastly different from the weight suggested on those all too familiar height and weight charts. That's not to say that wanting to lose a few pounds means you're heading for

anorexia. However, eating disorders don't suddenly appear overnight, they develop over a period of time and if all your friends are starting to tell you that you really shouldn't be losing weight, getting an independent opinion from your doctor will put their minds at rest, as well as yours.

- *If you're on medication* – some pills can cause a temporary weight gain. However, this can be due to fluid retention and it's important that you don't restrict what you eat unnecessarily because you could deprive yourself of essential nutrients that your body needs. And if you are diagnosed as having a particular condition, you need to be boosting your body's immunity rather than depleting it. If, however, you find that weight gain is more than a temporary blip, have a word with your doctor to see whether there is any alternative medication that won't cause an increase in your weight.

- *Children* – all children need food for growth and having a child that has 'hollow leg syndrome' – when there seems to be no limit to what they eat – is a familiar experience for most mothers! For children weight gain is more complicated than for adults as it is related to height, as well as to how active the child is. Obviously someone who swims, plays tennis or football and goes mountain bike riding is going to need a lot more to eat than a child who spends their free time in front of a computer. There is also thought to be a link between anorexia in girls and the general attitude to food in the home and a seemingly innocuous comment may cause more damage than you think. Consequently, if you are concerned about your child's diet, it's important to have a word with your doctor before doing anything.

We've seen how much our idea of what we should look like is shaped by all those images of women that we're surrounded by and while we may like the idea of looking like Christie Brinkley, we realize that there's little chance that we actually will. But, that said, even when we come to accept the difference between the fantasy and reality we still need to learn how to feel comfortable with ourselves – and that involves feeling happy with who, and what, we are. Of course if you are overweight but feel happy within yourself, then there's no problem. No one has the right to tell you to be something you don't want to be. But if you're not happy with the way you look, it is possible to do something about it. The secret is to be honest with yourself and realistic in what you're trying to achieve. Your aim is to be healthy and get your weight down to an amount that is right for you.

THE AIM IS FOR YOU TO FEEL GOOD

A common complaint of some ex-slimmers is that they had achieved a goal weight that left them feeling weak and irritable and looking gaunt. The result? They abandoned their rigid eating programme in favour of their old habits because at least that way they felt well. Unfortunately, all their diet showed them was how to deprive their body of energy until they reached their given target. Then, like the long-distance runner, when the goal is achieved, they collapse in a heap, exhausted and hungry, until they have gathered up enough strength to go in search of sustenance.

'I feel so much better when I'm that half stone heavier,' is a common cry. If that's the case then that half stone isn't a half stone too much, it's actually a sign that you've reached the right weight for you. Height and weight tables offer a range of weights that the experts feel are acceptable for your given height but unfortunately we life in a goal-orientated society. We like to have something to aim for, a target, so that when we reach it, we have confirmation that we have achieved. We've done it right, we've done what we've been told – and didn't we do well?

But the point is that getting to a weight that makes you feel good about yourself mentally and physically is an amazing achievement. It means that you've learnt to understand your body's needs and that food is no longer a source of tension in your life. Having to buy a size 14 rather than a 12 is not a sign of failure. If anything, it's a sign that you're part of the majority as, contrary to popular belief, there are more size 14s and 16s sold than any other size! Perhaps, though, you prefer to work towards a goal because it gives you a structure – something to aim for. If so, that's fine. Everyone has different ways of approaching problems and the most effective way of finding solutions is by finding the best methods for YOU of dealing with them.

But if what's going on in your mind is as important as what's happening to your body, firstly you need to change your thinking before you see any changes to your body.

So far we've concentrated on how and why people put on weight. Now it's time to shift the emphasis – on to YOU. Generalizations about how we got fat in the first place are all too easy to make. 'I was at home with the kids', 'I do realize how much I'm eating', 'my mum also served big portions': you know the type of thing. However, it's not until you work out exactly what pushes your eating button that you can actually do anything about it. And your starting point is to accept that there is not necessarily one explanation and while some answers may explain a tendency to overeat on one occasion, another time the reason could be totally unrelated. After all, for all the occasions that you've eaten out of sheer anger, there must be dozens of other times when, although steaming over some 'incident', the last thing you thought of was food. So, what exactly is it that presses your grazing button? Remember, making long-term changes to your attitude to food and eating is no simple process. You may need to do a bit of digging.

Sometimes it will be because of how you feel, other times it may depend on where you are. As we've seen, all sorts of events trigger a desire to eat and on many occasions, hunger is the least likely cause. And if we've grown up being given food as a reward, either for good behaviour, to make a bad leg better or simply to cheer us up, it's no wonder that as we get older, we turn to food for the same reasons – to bring back the feel-good factor into our lives; to make us feel better.

At times most of us indulge in a little comfort eating. However, if your weight is a concern and you feel food occupies a disproportionately high place in your life, then you need to work out why. There's certainly no problem in the general idea of turning to food for comfort, it just depends on how often you find you need comforting! Constantly eating for the sake of it stops you enjoying food because the actual process of eating becomes meaningless. And, the more you eat, the bigger the problem gets – unless you start to re-think your relationship with food.

However, the good news is that our attitude towards food and eating isn't innate – it's not a 'natural' reaction. It's learned behaviour and learned behaviour can be 'unlearnt'. Studies have shown that many people have successfully changed the way they eat by 'un-learning' what are likely to be *their* habits of a lifetime. But firstly you need to work out *where* you eat and *when* you eat, then ask yourself *why* and, finally, organize yourself in such a way that you reduce the risk of being in those situations when temptation may get the better of you.

FINDING YOUR TRIGGER

Obviously we turn to food for different reasons. Sometimes it will be because of how you feel, other times it may depend on where you are. So, the triggers can be internal, external or even biological. External triggers are the ones that are generally influenced by where you are and, even, who you're with. On the other hand, internal triggers are more to do with how you're feeling, rather than what you're doing.

Whether you're an external or internal foodie, the answer is to try and devise tactics that will not only make you more aware of when you're eating, but also help you to do something about it, as you'll discover in the next chapter. Most of us are probably a mixture of both internal and external and while there are days that a bitter disappointment will set you off in the direction of the nearest sweet shop, there are other occasions when the very act of just *being* in the kitchen means you end up devouring at least one packet of chocolate biscuits.

The Three Steps to a healthier approach to food

Step one

While it's possible to suggest all sorts of situations where you might turn to food, the only way to understand the way you eat is to work out some of the triggers that affect you. The best way to do that is by using a simple but familiar device – a good old-fashioned diary.

But, although most people who have dieted for any length of time may well be familiar with keeping a record of what they eat, for the purposes of this diary you keep an 'emotional' as well as 'dietary' checklist. So, you monitor not only what you eat, but when you eat it, where you eat it and what was happening just before you ate.

You also need to jot down how you were feeling – before as well as after the food. And, if you feel it's significant, add how long it took you to actually finish the food – and whether you were hungry. To begin with you may feel there's no apparent reason that you eat for the sake of it but the truth is there is always a reason even if it isn't at first obvious.

But, please remember, the point of this exercise is not to make you obsessed with what you do eat. The diary is not meant to play the role of 'food-and-thought police' – a little voice that goes off in your head every time your hand reaches out for anything with a brightly coloured wrapper. The whole idea of a mood-food is to simply make you aware of those times when food seems to pass through your mouth and into your digestive system in record time, neatly avoiding the tastebuds.

Big binges can lead to big bodies and unless you learn how to eat what you really want, when you want to, you're never going to be happy with the way you look or feel. Overeating can also lead to feeling out of control, which in turn leads to guilt, then a period of eating very little to compensate for the blow-out, which is then followed by another bout of overeating – because by that time you've deprived yourself of food for so long your hunger feels as if it's completely out of control. What's more, the longer this circle of guilt continues, the less chance there is of you getting to grips with what you would like to eat because you're too concerned with what you *shouldn't* be eating.

So, how does the diary work? Here's an example of what it could look like:

MONDAY – JANUARY, 15TH

I ate .... *6 slices of ginger cake*
Time....................... *11 o'clock in the morning*
Where? .... *In the kitchen*
How?....................... *Standing by the sink*
Hungry? .... *Not really, I'd only had breakfast an hour before*
How long it took .... *Probably no more than five minutes*
What happened? ..... *I had just had a row at the chemists'*
How I felt, before ... *Angry*
How I felt, after...... *Less angry, more guilty for being such a pig*

Obviously filling in how much you ate, and the time, is the easy bit. When it comes to where, it could be: *in the kitchen, at the bus stop, by the school gate, by the photocopier, on the train, in the lounge, in the hall* and so on. The 'How' refers to what you were doing at the time, and the idea is to see how aware you actually are of eating. So, maybe you were: *on the phone, sitting watching TV, making the kids tea, reading, listening to the radio, getting lunch ready, chatting to a friend, driving the car, maybe even just standing in the kitchen staring into the middle distance*.

Next you need to assess 'how hungry' you were, which is probably one of the most difficult bits of the diary because if you feel you eat too much, and too often, you may have long since forgotten how to recognize whether or not you're hungry. Also, hunger is relative so if you felt peckish, rather than hungry, or even not hungry at all, jot it down.

'How long it took' will give you an indication of the enjoyment you got out of eating. If the food was consumed in about the same time it took to tear open the wrapper, then chances are that it bypassed your tastebuds completely.

'What happened' requires you to think about what has been happening to you. Maybe you had a heated exchange of words with a neighbour or it was simply that you are missing your 'baby' who has just started school.

'How you felt before' you ate may have more to do with a long-term problem than something that has just happened. Maybe financially things aren't going too well and you've just opened a bill which has reminded you of all the other financial commitments you have. So don't necessarily peg your feelings on an event that has just occurred. If our eating patterns, or any other behaviour patterns for that matter, could always be linked to the last event that happened in our lives, our problems would be so much easier to solve!

'How I felt after' is there just to see whether you felt any different after eating, and to discover whether the food really had provided the comfort that you were looking for.

By keeping a record for a week or two, at first, a picture will start to build up of the triggers that seem to launch you headlong into the kitchen or sweet shop. Don't expect the reasons, or your feelings, always to be the same. What you're trying to do is build up a picture of just what makes you turn to food. Keeping this sort of diary can also throw up a number of surprises. We all think we have a rough idea of what we might consume in a day but research has revealed that our estimates can be wildly inaccurate. Referred to by some experts as the 'eye-mouth' gap, in one American study the subjects involved not only under-reported what they ate, but the more they ate, the more they under-estimated. So while they remembered exactly how many biscuits they ate because they had only eaten one or two, they under-estimated by half the actual number of raisins, nuts and sweets that they had consumed.

In all cases though, the inaccuracies were unconscious. In other words, when we try to remember exactly what we've eaten, it's easier than we think to get it wrong. Just think of the last time you got a packet of raisins out of the cupboard to add to a cake or stewed fruit. You weigh out the required amount in handfuls . . . but whereas one handful goes in the cake, how many go in your mouth? Haven't we all sat in front of the TV and easily munched our way through nibbles – only really thinking about it once there's nothing left to nibble? And isn't it all too easy to open the fridge for one thing, only to discover something else that you can graze on while you're looking? By writing it down, though, you'll get a clearer picture of what you eat, as well as how.

Analysing the diary . . .
After a week or so you should find that a pattern starts to emerge. Maybe you're more likely to overeat in the evenings, or in the afternoons while you're waiting for the kids to come home from school. Maybe you just like nibbling or you've just got into the habit of eating whenever you pass an open pack of biscuits, a dish of sweets or nuts.

Whatever it is that gets your salivary glands going, once you've established what it is that's making you overeat, you're in the position to do something about it. It's also worth remembering that while certain situations can make us more vulnerable to outbreaks of overeating, there are going to be times when we're in exactly the same situation but food is the last thing on our mind. So, see if your diary can help you discover to what extent your feelings affect your appetite. Remember, eating is a complicated business. Much depends on the foods you're used to eating as well as the habits you've learnt as a child. And don't forget our mood can play a big part in determining not only what we eat, but how *much* we eat.

Once you've been able to identify the situations that are more likely to make you turn to food, you're in the best position to do something about it. That something could be simply to think before you eat, or it could mean changing your environment so that you're no longer faced with any dilemmas. So, if your diary revealed that you accompanied your mid-afternoon cuppa with a crumpet and a doughnut, you might want to ask yourself whether you could do without one of them . . . Once you're aware of the unconscious eating you're doing, you may find there are things that you could consciously go without – and wouldn't even notice. As well as discovering the obvious triggers you'll also be able to identify other influences that make you vulnerable, like particular times of the day or evening. And once you have that information at hand, you're then in the position to do something about it.

Step two

Right, now you've kept a food diary long enough to see a picture emerge. Can you identify the occasions when you're most likely to turn to food? Is it:

- When you're angry?
- When you're disappointed?
- When you're at home with the kids?
- When you're pleased with yourself?
- When you're feeling miserable?
- When you're lonely?
- When you're anxious?
- When you're under pressure?

If you've eaten for any of the above reasons then you're clearly a comfort eater who keeps returning to food for comfort in the same way that a baby turns to his pacifier. The reasons can be specific – someone's made you angry or let you down – or a general feeling of being emotionally vulnerable; maybe a relationship has broken down, or you've suffered an unexpected disappointment. For many of us turning to food provides an emotional prop, in the same way that smokers light up every time they feel under pressure. It doesn't matter whether the 'prop' is seen to provide comfort for a traumatic event in your life, or some niggling irritation. If you're used to seeking solace in food, that's exactly what you'll turn to when you're feeling emotionally stressed.

Food is so central to our lives though, that if you do feel there are times when you simply eat for the sake of it, it's important that you work out whether you're feeding your emotions or your hunger. For Susie Orbach, this means learning to recognize the difference between stomach hunger – or real hunger – and psychological hunger. Something, she accepts, that is not that easy, particularly for women who have often been brought up to think of others' needs rather than theirs. After all, when it's mealtime, who gets served first? And if your partner arrives home after you, who rushes to put the kettle on, or maybe rustle him up a little snack to keep him going until supper is ready? The result is that we can be forgiven for sometimes thinking that our needs are firmly kept on the back burner.

Step three

Now you need to try and learn the difference between stomach hunger and psychological hunger. There are various ways of doing this. Simply by recording the way you're feeling when you eat means that, maybe for the first time, you have to identify what's making you eat. And that recognition in itself means you're now in a much stronger position to start thinking about establishing new patterns of behaviour.

For Susie Orbach though, it's essential that you actually learn how to recognize hunger itself. She suggests that the best way to do this is by deliberately going without food for a couple of hours so that you start to experience the sensation of hunger. For some people it might spark off uncomfortable memories – maybe hunger was something you remember experiencing as a child, and it's a feeling you have no desire to experience again. If that's the case, then maybe eating becomes a way of warding off hunger rather than satisfying it. Orbach stresses the importance of finding the roots of your relationship with food and of trying to see whether there is any connection between your relationship with food now and the role it played in your life in the past.

Of course for many of us that's easier said than done. If when you were a child you were always forced to finish every last scrap of food on your plate, it is possible to see that you may feel obliged to continue doing so – even if you did leave home 20 years ago. And it's also perfectly possible to understand why someone who, as a child, came from a family whose cupboards were often empty, would want to make sure that their cupboards were brimming with goodies that, in the past, they could never afford. Eating those goodies is a type of confirmation that you can afford to eat what you want, whenever you want and it's a way of distancing yourself from a past that rekindles painful memories.

But – and this is a big but – it has to be said that eating two chocolate bars and a large packet of peanuts in one go doesn't automatically reveal a past filled with deprivation. When it comes to food, we live in a country of plenty. And for many of us the reason for overeating may simply be because *it's there*. Food is everywhere and long gone are the days when our food-buying habits were confined to supermarkets and restaurants. Even the smallest petrol station comes with a ready-made sweet counter and when there's no room for display, there's always the machines. As a nation we stuff ourselves with sweets, chomp our way through chocolate, nibble on nuts and generally graze our way through most of the food that is put in front of us.

Eating has become a national pastime, and none of us any longer need an excuse to have 'a little something'. Mealtimes may come and go but snacktimes can stay all day. With so much food everywhere, it's surprising that any of us recognize real hunger!

But for Susie Orbach, it's only when you start to experience the sensation of hunger that you can then put your mind to the question of how best to satisfy it. So, don't just reach for the nearest bar or packet. Think about what you'd really like. As a guide, try asking yourself the following questions.

- Are you hungry – or thirsty?
- Are you peckish – or ravenous?
- Is it something sweet you're after – or something savoury?

How to discover what you really want

In *Fat is A Feminist Issue*, Orbach suggests a two-minute 'fantasy' exercise to help determine what you *really* want. Before you start, make yourself comfortable – either sitting or lying, whatever suits you best – then close your eyes and try to *think* your way through the options: 'What kind of physical sensation do I have and how can I best satisfy it? Do I want something crunchy, salty, chewy, moist, sweet? Okay, I want some potato chips. Let me imagine myself eating some. No, that's not it. How about some plain chocolate . . . ?'

By imagining how the food will actually taste you will be able to decide what you'd really like to eat; the food that matches your mood. If you don't get a strong feeling over what you want, then maybe you don't actually want to eat much at all, in which case stick to small amounts of whatever you decide to eat until you can identify what you actually want more clearly. By stopping to consider what you might eat, rather than just consuming it, this exercise also gives you the opportunity to think about whether it's really food that you're after at all. And if you're not sure what you're after, why not delay eating for maybe ten minutes or so? Then think about it again, until you have a definite idea about what you would like. Don't worry if you have to have several gos before you get a clear picture.

People who have done this exercise in the past have found that not only is it difficult to actually visualize 'tasting' the food, but the more they thought about it, the more they realized that they didn't really want to eat at all. As Susie Orbach explains, the reason could well have been that they needed to 'feed' themselves more appropriately: comfort doesn't only come from food. Whatever you are hungry for, if it isn't for food, then whatever you eat isn't going to give you the satisfaction that you're looking for – regardless of how much you end up eating.

The more often you do this exercise, the quicker you'll learn to recognize that food is simply a short-term remedy for a longer-term problem. And while eating may initially deflect from the problem, it isn't going to go any way to solving it. Also, once you realize that food isn't going to take away your 'hunger', you start to look elsewhere for ways to satisfy yourself and eating returns to something that, on most occasions, you do when you want to.

By distinguishing between emotional and physical hunger, food is no longer something that creates tension in your life. It ceases to be something that tests your self-control each time you're presented with it. Mealtimes will no longer be an occasion to get through: a hurdle of 'will I or won't I be able to say no?' You start to learn how to give your body what it wants. In an ideal world eating should be enjoyed, something to savour. Of course it doesn't always work out like that because if you're in a hurry, food will be rushed so that you can leave home in time to get the train, the bus, or get the kids to school. And a sandwich grabbed in the middle of a busy day is never going to be enjoyed as much as a plate of pasta with a good friend.

For a while you're obviously going to need to think about what you're eating – which you can do with the help of the 'food and mood' diary. It's then you're in a position to identify what your needs are – and a good reminder is the Five Step Hunger Test.

All you need to do is simply:

Stop . . . before you eat

Look . . . at what you're about to eat

Listen . . . to your hunger – is it emotional or is it physical?

Think . . . about what you really want. And if you're not sure, try to put off the decision to eat until you are.

Do . . . something else. Something that will take your mind off food. Have a bath, phone a friend, curl up with a book, or magazine . . . it doesn't matter what it is as long as it's something YOU want to do.

By learning to turn to food when you actually want it, you are starting to respond to a physical hunger rather than an emotional one. That doesn't mean that there won't be days when you eat more than you want, or would have liked, but at least when you do, you'll be in control. As Sara Gilbert says in *Tomorrow I'll Be Slim*, the people who fare best in dieting are those who are able to make permanent changes in their eating habits and people who are able to find satisfaction in their lives in other things than food.

However, as we've seen, you don't have to have a psychological problem to qualify for a re-think when it comes to the part food plays in your life. And having a weakness for Monster Munch, Mars bars and marshmallows isn't a sign that you used to spend mealtimes locked in the understairs cupboard. Often we eat simply because it's there – out of habit as much as anything else. But, the good news is that there are plenty of ways to break the habit and change your pattern of eating into a healthier and happier one. Now we've discovered how to recognize our emotional triggers, the next step is to look at tackling the temptations that we come up against all of the time.

Chapter Nine

Comfort Without The Calories

HAVING MADE THE decision that you want to lose weight, and are prepared to re-think the way you eat, as well as what you eat, the good news is that you now fall into the category of people who are most likely to succeed! Experts have shown that positive thinking is a key factor in determining who is successful at not only losing weight, but keeping it off too.

Positive Proof

Wanting to do something about your weight has much more bearing on the results than being told that you *should* do something. Think positively and believe in yourself and you're much more likely to be successful. But thinking positively is also about understanding that things don't always go your way – sometimes through no fault of your own.

But how can you tell whether you're a positive or negative thinker? It's actually quite easy . . .

Negative thinkers say . . . I never stick to anything

Positive thinkers say . . . This time I'm really going to stick with it!

Negative thinkers say . . . I shouldn't have had the chocolate pudding

Positive thinkers say . . . Next time I'll go for fruit

Negative thinkers say . . . I'll never lose weight

Positive thinkers say . . . I'm going to lose weight

Negative thinkers say . . . I can't say no

Positive thinkers . . . Do say no

Positive thinkers believe in their ability to influence what happens to them, negative thinkers think they have no control. Thinking positively also helps keep you motivated when you come up against problems. To the positive thinker, problems are seen as inconveniences which can be overcome rather than obstacles which will always stop you getting what you want. If you feel you *can* do something once you've put your mind to it, you're also less likely to see setbacks as catastrophes that mark the beginning of the end.

You may not think of yourself as someone with a natural inclination for thinking positively, but by trying to replace negative feelings with positive ones, you'll start to realize that you have as much right to achieve what you want as anyone else. Start replacing expressions that make you feel out of control with ones that put YOU firmly in the driving seat. So, instead of 'I *should* change the way I eat', begin to think in terms of 'I *could* change the way I eat'.

Part of thinking positively is doing things for yourself – and no one else. If you have decided you're unhappy with your weight and are determined to do something about it, it's important that the decision is yours. Expressions like, 'well, I'm not too bothered, but my husband feels I should lose some weight', is something that many a failed slimmer has said at some time. Other favourites are 'my mum says I'm too fat', or 'some friends have roped me into going to a club with them, but I'm not really interested'. What these expressions really reveal is how we all go along with things, even though we've given up on them before we've even begun.

Dieting, slimming, rationalizing, downsizing, reducing . . . whatever you want to call the decision to do something about your weight, if you don't actually want it to work in the first place, you can be pretty sure that it won't. The maximum you'll achieve is a short-term loss. But all the evidence suggests that the loss, plus more, will be quickly regained.

But if you have decided that you want to lose weight, it's important to see weight loss for what it is. However much you lose, it's not going to change *who* you are. As we've seen, being thinner doesn't make that job you've been wanting suddenly yours; or your husband more attentive; your social life better; or the boredom factor in your life disappear. And it's the people who *do* think that who put the weight back on. They're the ones who, having invested so much time and effort into sticking to their diet, can't believe that they're not getting anything in return, that emotionally life is very much the same. The diet, they feel, has been a waste of time because it didn't achieve the new, exciting, fulfilled life that was wanted. And so, the disappointed slimmer goes back to her old ways . . .

But losing weight isn't necessarily a waste of time – particularly when you clearly weigh too much for your own good. But you need to be realistic about what you're going to get out of the weight loss. You'll certainly feel healthier, and the healthier you are, the more likely you are to experience a feeling of general well-being. And it's when you start to feel good about yourself that you can really start planning for change in your life, because then you're in the best position to tackle problems in your relationship, or work – or your life generally.

PLANNING FOR CHANGE

Positive thinkers refuse to let their past drag them down. As one of the most popular greeting card phrases never ceases to stop telling us: *today is the beginning of the rest of your life* . . . Spending time worrying about 'if only', or 'what might have been' keeps us wallowing in the past, rather than putting our energies into planning for the future. You have to face the fact that you can't do much about what's already happened – although you can learn from the experience. However, you still have an awful lot of control over the present, and the future. Of course no one knows exactly what's going to happen, but the more you plan for what you want to happen, the more likely that it will.

Positive thinking shouldn't be confused with flights of fantasy. Positive thinkers are realists, not idealists. They know that trying to change anything in their life is never easy, particularly when the changes aimed at are permanent ones. Being realistic also means preparing yourself for the way ahead – and that means working out the type of problems you're likely to come across and devising simple and effective ways to deal with them. In the last chapter we saw how we can turn to food when someone, or something, presses our internal or external appetite button. And numerous studies have been carried out that confirm what anyone who has ever tried to lose weight already knows – people often eat more when they are depressed, worried or lonely, but less when they are busy and have plenty to do.

Our lack of success in trying to 'watch what we eat' is often put down to a lack of willpower as we decide that we didn't manage to stick to a

diet simply because we weren't determined enough. Obviously deter-
mination, and a belief in yourself, comes into it. But food is a constant
temptation that we have to deal with every day and it's easy to feel that
giving in is the same as giving up. But of course it isn't.

Most of us have had periods of being on the *see-food* diet – that's the
one where you see food and it instantly disappears! Show me a dish of
'nibbles' and I'll show you a group of nibblers. We eat to be sociable, to be
friendly – we even eat so that we don't offend. 'Do try a slice of cake, it's
my special recipe and I baked it just for you,' our hostess says imploringly.
So how can anyone say no? But even if there are times when we give in,
there are other occasions when our hands go from plate, or packet, to
mouth for no particular reason other than it's there.

So, the first step, as in chapter eight, is to try to identify exactly why
you eat when you're not actually hungry. Once again, you need to
monitor what you eat – and what you're doing while you're eating – for
a short period. Flick back to page 109 to see the sort of questions you
need to ask yourself and how to put together your own mood diary.
Remember, this is not an exercise designed to make you feel guilty
about what you eat, the idea is simply to try and establish what *makes*
you eat. Also, the more conscious you become of what you're doing
when you're eating, the more likely you are to stop. So, by filling in your
diary, if you tend to reach for a bar of chocolate every time there's a
problem at work, by making yourself aware of the fact, next time it
happens you're more likely to think, 'Oh-oh, I'm doing it again! I'm
angry but because I feel I can't say anything, I've got into the habit of
eating instead . . .'

Becoming more aware of how you're feeling allows you to take stock.
Your hand reaches out but your brain says – hang on, what am I doing
here? The few seconds it takes you to think about it may make you realize
that what you really ought to be doing is sorting out your feelings – and
you could find that a welcome side effect of this is that suddenly you
realize you didn't want that bar of chocolate at all. Apart from the
amazing high you'll get from being in control, you'll have proved to
yourself that you *can* say no. And having done it once, you'll feel more
confident about doing it again.

It's worth remembering, though, we all go through stages when we
feel almost an irrational desire for something. Cravings are usually only
considered the privilege of the pregnant – for the peaky looking
convalescent – but actually the truth is we all get them. Why is not

quite so easy to answer. In the last chapter we saw that a compulsion to eat can have psychological roots – we're almost conditioned to crave. But on other occasions we can be spurred on by hormonal changes, as well as psychological difficulties. And sometimes, of course, we keep on eating because we're too busy enjoying ourselves to think of anything else.

Obviously it's vital to understand why we do things but it's equally important to learn to devise ways to deal with the way you eat. By trying to change the way you behave, you may still experience cravings, but it doesn't mean you'll necessarily still give in to them. Which is why it's important to learn the tactics you need to tackle those temptations. You probably won't find them all useful, but sort out the situations that you feel are most appropriate to you – and then get tackling!

Remember, *there's nothing wrong with a little of what you fancy . . .* as long as the little doesn't turn into a lot – and often. There are times when we all eat more than we want, whether it's sitting in front of the TV and aimlessly working our way through a box of chocs or going out for a blow-out meal full of flowing food and wine. But it's when eating has becomes a compulsion, something that you simply can't stop doing, that it's time to take stock. So find out what your danger zones are and you're at least in a position to start to take action.

DISCOVERING YOUR DANGER ZONE

Firstly, it helps to work out what type of eater are you.

Danger zone one
Do you nibble?
Do you find food helps you to concentrate?
Do you finish food left on other people's plates?
If you're standing, or sitting, still for any length of time, do you usually have food nestling by?
Do you 'pinch' food every time you open the fridge?

If you do

If you've said yes to either every or most of the above, you're a confirmed nibbler! Someone who grazes their way through the day without giving much thought to what you're eating – just as long as you're eating. Nibblers are the classic unconscious eaters, the ones who, when you tell them how much they've eaten, just don't believe you!

Tactics

■ Make sure that you stock up on healthy snacks to graze on. See below for some ideas of foods that will fill you up rather than fill you out. The simplest, fastest food is fruit. Experts recommend that we eat up to five pieces a day to help keep us in good health and by aiming for that you're not likely to have that much space left for many other snacks.

■ Keep some munch bowls handy. These are designed for when you get an attack of the 'munchies' and they help to ward off the temptation to eat high fat, sugary snacks. Munch bowls can consist of whatever vegetables you like, but it's useful if they have crunch appeal. They also need to be washed, peeled, diced, sliced – whatever you like – as long as they're all prepared, sitting waiting for you every time you open that fridge or sit down to watch the telly. Try munching on cabbage (red is tasty and has lots of crunch appeal) or sticks of celery, carrots, courgettes or even cucumber. You can also do the same with fruit. Small bite-size pieces are not only more appealing, they also take longer to eat. And your mouth is working so hard that you'll find your appetite will start to wane as your jaw tires because crunching your way through food can be a pretty exhausting experience for most mouths!

■ If you suspect that your unconscious eating more often than not results in unconscious *over*eating, then condition yourself to make a note of everything you *do* eat. Sometimes just seeing what you've eaten can make a difference to what you eat in the future. They say knowledge is power and once you have the knowledge of what you're eating, you're in a much more powerful position to do something about it.

Danger zone two

Do you always finish your plate?

Do you often eat until you're 'bursting'?

Do you feel you haven't eaten properly unless you've had three meals a day?

Does teatime always mean tea and cakes?

Do you always have biscuits with your coffee?

At home, do you have a full biscuit barrel and a tuck box stuffed full to the rim?

If you do

Your eating patterns are based on habit more than anything else. You've probably eaten the same way for years, as has the rest of your family. You need to re-think what are, basically, your habits of a lifetime.

Tactics

- If you've been 'trained' to finish your plate and can't imagine not doing so, try eating off a smaller plate for a while – that way your stomach, as well as your brain, can adapt to smaller portions.
- If you'd really rather not eat biscuits, cakes and sweets – stop buying them. As we've seen high fat sugary foods rarely satisfy the appetite and the chance that they'll satisfy your body's nutritional needs is even slimmer!
- Keep tabs on exactly what you're eating by filling in a food and mood diary. At the end of each day, go back over the diary and decide what you ate out of hunger and what you ate simply because it was there.
- If you're at home, once you've identified when you're full and you get to that point, leave the table. If, for example, you've had your main course and you're full, don't sit there idly waiting for the dessert to be served. And if it's you who usually does the serving, why not ask someone else to dish up for a change?

For some people, it's easier to examine situations that make them feel food-sensitive than sorting out which type of eater they are. So, let's look at the specific scenarios – external ones first:

Danger zone three
Does shopping for food make you hungry?

If it does

For anyone who finds it a strain to be around food, a visit to the supermarket can have the same effect as letting a child loose in a sweet shop. In-store bakeries can just make it worse but shoppers don't just buy to satisfy their immediate hunger – there are so many goodies on show that it's hard not to be tempted to buy a little something for later.

Tactics

- Firstly, be sure never to go shopping when you're hungry. If you go during the day, then make sure it's after breakfast, or lunch. Even those with the strongest willpower will find their resolve turns to sawdust when they're starving.

- Be sure to always take a detailed shopping list with you. Be organized about what you want and don't deviate. If you're tempted by special offers make sure that you only succumb to the products that you would normally buy. However cheap it is to buy three bags of pistachio nuts instead of one, if you don't really want them and don't usually eat them – don't buy them. Many people also complain that they find it impossible to walk down certain aisles in the supermarket without their arms reaching out for packets of biscuits or multi-saver bags of crisps. If that's the case – the answer's simple. Avoid those aisles. If you know your supermarket well enough, it's actually possible to write an aisle by aisle shopping list so that you only need to pass the shelves that have what exactly what you need.

- Don't be drawn unnecessarily into bulk buys. If you know that you'll be the one eating the 'overs', then just buy what you need – whether it's sticky buns, meringues or chocolate slices. None over means no temptation.

- Try to make as few trips to the supermarket as you can – it's easier to resist temptation once a week than it is three times a week.

■ If you find you're an impulse buyer – you pop into a shop for a magazine and end up buying yourself sweeties – have the magazine delivered.

Danger zone four
Do you act like the family dustbin?

If you do

We've all done it – gone to clean away the kids' half empty plates and thought, 'it's a shame to waste it . . .', or 'it's not worth keeping such a small amount . . .' The problem with hoovering up the contents of everyone else's plate is that you lose sight of what you're actually eating. The food on your plate may well have been an example of low-fat virtue but when you add in the finished off chips, beans, fish fingers and Mr Men mousses, it's hardly a sign that you're in control. Preparing food can also be a real temptation – maybe you're cutting up cake and pop the little bit that crumbles off surreptitiously into your mouth. Or you're grating cheese for a sauce and think it's a waste of time to put the bit that's left over back in the fridge . . .

Tactics

■ If the children consistently leave food on their plate, maybe you're giving them too much. Food doesn't have to be hanging off the edge of the plate before it qualifies as 'a good meal'. Try giving them a slightly smaller portion – if they finish that, offer them more. That way they eat what they want – and so do you.

■ Keep a stock of small plastic containers for leftovers. Food not eaten one day can generally be eaten another. Chicken, meat and vegetables can be turned into a stir fry; mince into a shepherd's pie, or moussaka if you prefer, while potatoes can often be reheated or mixed with eggs and onion and turned into a Spanish omelette. Tubs of yoghurt and mousse keep (young children in particular, often can't eat a whole pot in one go) and fruit that's been abandoned after one bite can be turned into fruit salad.

- With food you really can't keep, BIN it. And if you can't do it yourself, get someone else to do it for you. Food should be something you enjoy, not something you consume just because it's there. And the least you deserve is a meal of your own – not someone else's cast-offs.
- Preparing food? Keep a munch bowl handy so you end up snacking on nibbles – not the dinner!

Danger zone five
Is it difficult when the children get home?

If it is

They arrive home starving, with their hyperactive appetites going full throttle! You lovingly prepare plates of sandwiches or a pile of steaming buttery crumpets. Tea for many of us can be an important part of the family day; it's the chance to catch up with the kids, find out what's going on at school and what they've got coming up – and it's easy for the eating to seem as much part of the process as the talking.

Tactics

- Make sure you have a good supply of healthy snacks around, for both you and the kids.
- Put food on a plate for them, rather than in the middle of the table so you're not tempted to dive in whenever you want.
- When they've finished, clear up. If there's anything left, either put it away or put it in the bin.
- Apply the tactics under the nibbling heading to make sure you eat what you want – rather than just what's there.

Danger zone six
Are evenings the problem?

If they are

For many of us it may be the first chance we've had all day to sit down and relax and when we're relaxing with nothing much to do, it's then that our mind turns to food. Whether you're a PM picker or snacker, food eaten at this time of the day, rarely has anything to do with hunger. And if you watch TV and are in the habit of snacking at the same time, the chances are that you're not even aware of *what* you're consuming. Eating when you're doing something else not only means you're likely to eat more than you want but it could also result in you not wanting to eat in the morning because you wake up with a full stomach . . . so you miss breakfast but then find you're starving mid-morning and end up going in search of food to appease your appetite.

Tactics

- When you're not hungry, eating gives you something to do, so you need to keep your hands busy so you can't fill them with food! One tried and tested method that always works is . . . paint your nails! Sounds silly but once you've given yourself a manicure, you'll not be able to eat – even if you want to.
- Try knitting or crocheting: it doesn't have to mean producing a selection of blankets or bobble hats. Look out for patterns in magazines or books and use your evenings to knock yourself up a 'designer' jumper.
- Sort out all those photos still lying around in packets and put them in photo albums. And if you're so organized that you've already put the photos in albums, well done! But you must have something that can be sorted out while the telly is on.

Danger zone seven
Are the hours you work erratic?

If they are

Having to rely on sandwich bars and, or, canteens can be a big problem when you're trying not to overeat. You can be tempted by all sorts of things that you normally won't touch and even when you think you're being sensible by ordering something innocuous like an egg sandwich you may find the bread is plastered with a layer of butter and the eggs are swimming in mayonnaise. And as you go to pay you notice a basket full of chocolate brownies and packs of biscuits . . .

Tactics

- Plan ahead. Take food with you, whether it's home-made sandwiches or a salad. If you don't have time, try to pop into either a supermarket or somewhere like Boots where they stock a huge range of low-calorie sandwiches and snacks.
- Even if you have your own food it doesn't mean you can't go to the canteen with friends. Just take the food with you. But be sure to sit as far away as possible from the food counters. Having to walk a long way back to a serving hatch is a great deterrent!
- There'll be days when it seems your colleagues are grazing their way through the day. If a lot of snacking goes on in your office, take your own snacks with you. That way when everyone is eating you won't start to feel left out but you will get to feel full.

Danger zone eight
Is it awkward when you're eating out?

If it is

For some people eating out can be an important part of their lifestyle but it can increase the temptation to overeat. And your food intake can often be put at the mercy of the restaurant that you end up at. But, whether eating out is reserved for weekends or is part of your working day, there *are* tactics you can employ.

Tactics

- If you can, have soup to start with (although try to steer clear of the fatty 'cream of . . .' variety), which should take the edge off your appetite enough to stop you overeating.
- If the sight of a bread basket in front of you is too much to resist, take a piece of bread and then put it in front of someone else. Or, if no one else wants any, ask the waiter to take it away.
- Check whether the main meal comes with any anything else – often restaurants include chips, roast potatoes and other vegetables as part of the meal. If you have a tendency to clean the plate, make sure you get just what you order, or cherry pick – ask for extra vegetables rather than chips.
- Be firm. If you're asked whether you'd like to see the dessert trolley say 'no' rather than wait to see what's on offer.
- If the food is a 'help yourself type' meal, take just what you want and resist the temptation to pile your plate high with food just because it's there. If you really are hungry once you've got through one plateload, you can always go back for more. Also try to sit away from the food. The nearer you are, the more likely you are to be concentrating on that rather than the conversation that's going on.
- Watch your alcohol intake. Although alcohol contains large amounts of calories, it has almost nil nutritional benefit – hence the expression 'empty calories' when it comes to alcohol. But although it increases your calorie intake, the problem is that it will equally reduce your resolve. After a couple of glasses even the most well-intentioned plans can come to a sticky end. And while that may be fine for the evening, you then have to deal with the reality the morning after . . .
- Stick to your guns! If you really don't want a second helping, another drink or a dessert, say so – and don't be browbeaten by a well-meaning waiter or 'concerned' friend. The only reason a friend should be concerned is if you don't eat anything at all. And turning down an offer of a sweet when you've already had two courses is hardly the behaviour of an anorexic. Say no, don't be afraid to be assertive. It's up to you what you eat – no one else.

A word about kid's restaurants. However good your intentions, if it's Saturday lunchtime and the kids want a hamburger, a hamburger place is where you're likely to end up. If you know that's the case, try to eat before you go. With the best will in the world, if you're starving and the kids are stuffing, you'd need a cast-iron will not to want to join them.

Danger zone nine
Is it difficult when you're waiting for family or friends to arrive?

If it is

Many women say that they find it a real problem when they're waiting for their husbands to get home in the evening. They know he'll be home at, say, around seven but they've been in the kitchen for hours and are just dying to eat something. So, they may have some nuts, or biscuits or bread. The boredom that comes from hanging around is bad news – and it doesn't matter whether you happen to be waiting for dinner or a train. When we get bored we look around for something to fill the time, and food, all to easily, can seem to provide a pretty good stopgap.

Tactics

- When you're at home, try to get out of the kitchen as much as possible. If you need to check food, do what you have to do and then make a swift exit.
- Make sure you have as little time on your hands as possible. Make yourself a list of things to do – short-term and long-term. Then, depending on how much time you have available, start working your way down your list. What you need to do is develop displacement activities – things to do to stop you thinking of food.
- Keep your hands busy. As we've seen in previous chapters, it doesn't much matter what you do with them as long as you do something! So, knitting, sewing, potting plants, sticking photos in an album, manicuring, finger exercises – or anything else you can think of that will stop you eating.
- Organize your day so that you have as little time to spare as possible. If you're bored because you have nothing to do, then join

a society or learn about something that interests you. Whether it's an art appreciation society, an aromatherapy course or French lessons, give your mind a chance to be as active in the future as your appetite is at the present!

■ If you find that you always seem to have a good half hour or so when you're at a loose end, organize your day so that you have something specific that has to be done. Hoovering, cleaning shoes, catching up on correspondence, phoning a friend. It doesn't matter what.

■ Alternatively you could designate that 30 minutes as private time. Have a long soak in the bath, read a book . . . anything, as long as it takes you away from the kitchen.

■ Start preparing dinner later – or earlier enough to allow you time to get involved with something else so that you're only in the kitchen just before you eat.

■ If you start thinking about food well before supper, maybe you're not eating enough lunch. Or you could do with a snack mid-afternoon. Turn to the food section for lots of lunch suggestions but before you eat, decide whether it's what you really want. If you're not sure, put off eating for 15 minutes or so, and go and do something in another room. If you're still hungry, try a piece of fruit which is filling – and nutritious. On the other hand you could find that once the 15 minutes have passed, you've forgotten all about wanting to eat.

There are probably countless other situations that I haven't given specific tactics for but, generally, most situations will fit into the categories mentioned above. But, now we've worked out ways to cope with your environment, the external triggers, the next step is to work out how to deal with your emotions . . .

Chapter Ten

Tactics to Fight Those Triggers

IN THE LAST chapter we looked at how to cope with external triggers – the situations where you turn to food out of boredom or habit. But, as we've seen, what we eat isn't only dependent on where we are and what we're doing. Sometimes it can be as much to do with what we're feeling. Food can be used as a way of distancing yourself from something that's upset you. For example, consider this: imagine you're annoyed with your mother-in-law, but she isn't the sort of person to whom you could say what you think. You'd love to, but well, *you just couldn't*. After a particularly galling phone call, you put the phone down *positively seething. You are so angry!*

What you really want to do is say exactly what's on your mind but you can't. So, instead, you go and make yourself a couple of slices of toast, smothered with butter. Afterwards, you're slightly calmer but still irritated, so you treat yourself to a couple of pieces of chocolate. Then another couple . . . until eventually you feel stuffed – and sick. And, it goes without saying, wracked with guilt.

Now what you should have done is be honest. The truth is, though, while we fantasize about saying what we want to say, it's not that often that we do it. We're constrained by what's expected of us and saying what we believe people want to hear. And the closer our relationships, the more likely we are to conform to expected behaviour. So we look for consolation, which all too often comes in the form of food. The alternative is that we take our anger out on someone who has absolutely nothing to do with the problem. No wonder we're all familiar with venting our spleen on poor, unsuspecting partners!

Now you can try practising being more honest, and saying what you feel rather than what you feel is expected. It may make you feel better and could improve some of your relationships. It can also do wonders for your self-esteem. Stating your case and explaining your real thoughts about a situation boosts your self-image and makes you feel an individual. It's also about being in control and putting enough value on what *you* think to be prepared to say it. But there are times when you can neither say what you want, or get what you want. And accepting that, in some situations you can, as Mick Jagger would say, 'get no satisfaction', you have to start thinking of, as Susie Orbach explains, different ways of 'feeding' your emotional hunger.

IF YOU'RE ANGRY

You can always tell when someone's eating because they're angry. They invariably stab at their food with their cutlery and appear to be on something that resembles a kamikaze-calorie mission – the object being to stuff themselves with as much food as their body can cope with before they feel sick. It's almost as if they're taking out their anger on the food – attacking it the way that they'd like to attack the person who's to blame for the anger in the first place.

When you think about it, it's not all that surprising. As children we're often taught to hide our emotions – not to tell auntie that we're disappointed that she only bought us some pretty hankies when we wanted a dolly; not to show we're angry when cousin Rosie cut the hair off our favourite Barbie. We're told it's not 'nice' to say what we really feel and it doesn't take long before we realize that being truly honest is just not done. Sometimes it's understandable and to make lying a little more acceptable, we have the concept of the 'white lie', where we're taught not to be completely honest in case it hurts someone's feelings. The problem is we get so out of practice with being honest and behaving in what are considered socially unacceptable ways, that on many occasions we don't say what we feel – even when we should. Terms like 'don't rock the boat' or 'don't upset the apple cart' do little to encourage us to be ourselves.

Of course there are times when it's important to consider every one's feelings, not just your own, but equally there are occasions when standing up for yourself wouldn't go amiss. Whether it's a rude and unhelpful shop assistant, a sneaky, ambitious colleague or a ruthless, insensitive boss who works you remorselessly but then takes the credit, the effect is still the same. Rather than say what you really think you often, quite literally, swallow your anger. But anger is one of the most normal emotions - it's healthy too. Apart from giving vent to our emotions, it tells people how far they can go and what they can - and can't - get away with. However, turning your anger in on yourself not only suppresses the way you feel, but allows none of your feelings to be shown to the people around you. So they don't know what you're feeling and don't consider you because you don't allow them to.

Clearly, eating is not the answer to the problem and turning to food when you're angry may offer immediate comfort but, in the long term, it just brings guilt and regret. So next time you're angry, if you feel you're justified (and that's what matters - what *you* feel) try some of the following.

Tactics

- Be honest. Try to say what you really think. That doesn't mean you have to be rude, or even have stand-up rows with people. If you feel you have a case, either against a rude shop assistant or an unreasonable colleague, say what you feel, quietly and firmly outlining what your complaints are in a logical and, if possible, unemotional way. Calmness brings calmness and you'd be amazed how a quiet, thoughtful approach can diffuse the most potentially explosive situation.
- Try to accept that anger can be a positive emotion. Without anger women would never have got the vote, there would have been no such thing as maternity leave . . . and we'd still have the Poll Tax.
- Don't feel guilty about saying what you believe. There's nothing bad about being honest.
- If you're angry, be constructive. Rather than heading for the biscuit barrel, think whether there's anything you can do about your situation. Is there anyone you could talk to? Maybe you need to put your feelings in writing? And maybe you should just tell the person what you think - it could be that they haven't even got a clue.
- If you're not sure whether you can be honest, practise what you want to say on a friend, colleague or partner. Trying out what you want to say is a good way to work out exactly *why* you're so angry as well as helping you to anticipate the other person's reaction.
- Still not sure you have a right to say what you think? Most women have a problem with self-esteem, a feeling of self-worth, so you need to remind yourself that your views count as much as anyone

else's. And prove it to yourself. Make a list of all that you have to offer – whether it's to your job, your husband or even the amount of business you put the way of that shop where you've had to put up with the surly assistant. Certainly when it comes to your job, or home, just consider everything you do – all the work you put in, including the unacknowledged and largely unnoticed activities. Now, don't you deserve better than you're getting – and isn't it about time you told someone?

- Rather than eat when you're angry, if you really feel that there isn't anything you can do about the situation, try using your anger rather than simply feeding it. Exercise is a brilliant way to let off steam. If you play tennis, grab a racquet, if you swim, get your cossie out and if you run, get your trainers on. And if you do none of these things, a brisk walk can work wonders – or try a game of football or tag with the kids.

- Maybe you can't take your anger out on the person who deserves it but rather than turning it in on yourself and ending up with knots in your stomach and cake crumbs on your chin, try talking the incident over with someone. If there's no one nearby, most people are at the end of a phone. And although it's a well-worn phrase, a problem shared can be a problem halved – and you really do feel better for talking to someone.

- If appropriate, write down what you feel in a letter. The process of writing helps concentrate the mind and you may even end up feeling that things aren't quite as bad as you first thought.

IF YOU'RE FEELING MISERABLE

- Pamper yourself! This could mean soaking in a bath full of bubbles, with the radio on and the door firmly locked. Do what you *feel* like doing for a change. Whether that means: curling up in bed with a good book, watching a favourite old movie, getting your hair done or even treating yourself to a new eyeshadow or a trip to town to see an exhibition that you've read about . . . even a trip to Ikea to buy those candlesticks that would go really nicely in the lounge . . . You could go through your address book and arrange to see an old friend whom you have lost contact with. It doesn't matter what you do, as long as it's something you *feel* like doing.

- And if you feel too miserable to indulge yourself, try to break your mood by doing something - for example, calling a friend. If you're disappointed, say, about not getting a job, a promotion, or even a salary increase, try to find out why. Try to turn a negative event into a positive one.
- Get as much information as you can about why you weren't successful. It's easy to be disappointed by events that have nothing to do with us: maybe there was someone else lined up for the job, maybe the budget wasn't big enough for an increase. Maybe you didn't have the right experience.
- Try to rationalise your disappointment rather than wallow in it.
- And then, if you feel like it, have a good cry. It can work wonders.
- Finally, do something you'll enjoy to help you take away the bitter taste of the disappointment. It won't make you forget but it will at least stop you needlessly going over the events in your mind again and again.

Do you use food as a reward?

When you're miserable, it's easy to eat to cheer yourself up and when you've had a lousy day, treating yourself with something special like your favourite chocolate, can seem very appealing. Food can seem to provide compensation for an unreasonable boss, a stroppy bank manager or even an ungrateful husband.

Tactics

- Try speaking up rather than eating up! By being honest and saying what you really feel, there's a good chance you'll be able to sort a situation out rather than just leaving your feelings to fester. Even if things don't end up exactly to your liking at least you've tried. And once you've stood up for yourself once, people may be less likely to take advantage of you in the future. You'll also find that after saying what you really think once, the next time gets easier and easier.
- If you can't, or don't, say what you want to the person concerned, find a colleague or friend to sound off to. Talking a problem through with someone will not only make you feel better, it's also a case of two heads being better than one and you may find all sorts of ways out of the problem - it's just that you haven't thought of them.

- You need to find other ways to comfort yourself besides eating. Maybe a phone call to a good friend or a wander round the shops. Listen to some music or pamper yourself with a bath laced in aromatherapy oils. Go for a walk and find a travel agent and pick up some brochures of weekend breaks, of concerts or shows you'd like to see. If you're at work, can you pop down to see a colleague on another floor, or in another office?
- Look for instant mood-breakers: turn the radio on, put on your favourite tape, look at some old photos, read your favourite magazine, play a game of Hungry Hippos with the kids – or something like Pictionary where you've got to use your hands.
- Realize that 'treating' yourself to food is one of those old habits that you probably learnt as a child. Maybe you were rewarded with sweeties for good behaviour then, or given something to make you forget your sore knee – and that's exactly what you're trying to do here.
- Think before you eat: ask yourself whether you do really want the biscuit/cake/chocolate . . . or whatever. Then put the decision off for 15 minutes to see whether the food is really what you're after.
- And if you still fancy treating yourself, fine. But try to work on the principle of a little of what you fancy does you good. For example, if you can only find one of those huge bars of chocolate, break a few pieces off and put them in a bowl, wrap the remainder up and put it away. Then, sit down, put your feet up and make an occasion of the treat, rather than wolfing it down as you stand there gnashing your teeth and going over the day's events.

IF YOU'RE STRESSED

Stress is bad news whichever way you look at it. It may not do your waistline much good but, for your heart, it can, literally, mean murder. It's important to bring down the stress level in all our lives and the best way of doing it is by identifying what is making you feel stressed in the first place. Then, as with anger, you need to assess whether you can do anything about it.

Tactics

- If, for example, you've been given more work than you can cope with in your job, you need to go and see someone about it. Obviously it's easier said than done but, when coping with anger, sometimes it can help to either write down what you're feeling, or rehearse with a friend the conversation you want to have with a colleague or boss.

- Bringing up kids can be a stressful business, there's so much to do and think about and so much to organize. One survey estimated that a mother bringing up young children suffers as much stress as jet setting company directors, police officers, teachers and even funeral directors – not that many mums need reminding! If this applies to you, see if you can arrange for someone to take the kids off your hands – even if it's just for the afternoon. Being able to have some private time for yourself – to do what you want without having to worry about anything or anybody else – can be an excellent way of recharging your batteries. Maybe you can 'offer' the children to a doting grandparent, or a kindly neighbour? Or try organizing it so they go back to friends after school so you get a whole day to yourself. It really does work wonders – just try it and see!

- Think about doing something physical. As with anger, any exercise from swimming and running to aerobics or walking can calm you down.

- If you've got kids – or can even 'borrow' some from a good friend or a sister or brother – take them to the park, the circus, a museum or a children's play. Being with children can be a great leveller and often you feel you can't help but smile as you get carried away with their excitement.

- Lastly, if you feel you're so stressed you simply feel unable to cope, talk to your doctor about getting some help. It could make all the difference to the way you think and feel – as well as the way you eat.

Other de-stressers

Other comforters include massage, aromatherapy, reflexology, rambling, a visit to the library or a museum or exhibition. Gardening is also an excellent therapy, as is doing something relatively mundane like watching a good film. Weepies are especially good de-stressers as you can bawl your head off from beginning to end, and no one will think any the worse of you!

Other feel-good tricks include writing letters, sorting out drawers (honest! many people recognize the therapeutic value of organizing themselves), phoning a friend, gardening, painting . . . the list goes on. Once again, exercise is a brilliant way of relieving stress. Almost any type that gets your body moving and your heart pumping is good news – although if you're not used to it, get your doctor to check you over first.

The most important factor though is to choose something that you enjoy and is going to make you feel good about yourself. Something that proves once and for all that comfort doesn't only come through food.

IF YOU ARE BORED

For most of us eating is a pleasurable experience and so, when we're at a loose end, it helps us while away some time in a fairly enjoyable manner. The problem is, that if it happens too often, you could find that you're spending more time eating than you'd like. And I'm not talking about eating meals but about the mindless nibbling and unconscious grazing that we all do from time to time. But, when it's what you do, rather than what you don't do, food can end up as the focus of everything. And that's when you need to take action because, before you look round, eating has become a habit.

Tactics

Firstly identify whether your boredom is short term, such as waiting for the kids to get home, or waiting for a train, or long term – something that you feel most of the time. Short-term tactics have been discussed above, and you can opt for the active (a jog or walk) or something more sedentary, such as wallowing in a hot soapy bath. However, if it's long-term solutions you're after, you'll find they require long-term planning. Firstly, ask yourself why you're bored.

- If it's because of work, maybe you need to think about expanding your job. Could you take on more responsibility? Find an area to transfer to that would be more stimulating? Or maybe you need to think about moving jobs altogether? Try to talk to someone that you work with, and see if they can suggest anything.

- Are you bored because you're at home too much with the kids? Maybe you need to think about going back to work, even if it's only part time. Most local boroughs provide lists of registered childminders and some are simply happy to just pick the kids up from school, give them tea and stay with them until you get home. If that doesn't suit you, what about seeing whether you can work something out with a friend? You have their child for some of the week and they do the same for you. Even if you decide not to work, it's still sometimes a good idea to have 'a day off' from the kids - even if it means you spend the time trailing around the shops, going for a haircut or catching up on all those 'little' things that you've been meaning to do for ages. Just a break from the usual routine can be a big boost to flagging spirits.

- Keep a running list of all the things you have to do, as well as want to do. It doesn't matter if it includes mundane tasks like, 'sorting out the undies' drawer' or something a touch more exciting like looking at wallpaper for one of the rooms that is in dire need of decoration. It doesn't matter what it is, as long as it's something that will stop you turning to food, just because you can't think of anything else to do.

IF YOU ARE LONELY

Food can have a lot to offer a lonely person. It provides a structure to an otherwise empty day as mealtimes become pegs to separate out the time: breakfast marks the morning, lunch, the afternoon, while supper signals the end of the day. In fact eating generally provides an activity. It involves planning, shopping, preparing and consuming . . . it's easy to see how food becomes the focus of the day ahead. So, what can you do to break the pattern?

Tactics
- Find something to occupy your mind other than food. Is there something you've always yearned to do, some group that you've always meant to join?

■ If you've got time – exploit it. Many of us wish our lives away, thinking of all the things we'd like to do – if only we had the time. Think about what really interests you. Maybe you'd like to go to art classes, learn pottery, jewellery making, wind surfing . . . it doesn't much matter what it is, as long as it's something that you'd enjoy. The more energy you put into feeding your mind, the more you'll find your body will take care of itself. As with the short-term suggestions, jot down a memo to yourself, including all the things you'd like to do. It doesn't matter whether they're things you'd like to happen in the next week – or the next year. What you're doing is giving yourself a master plan – something to work towards. Once you've got that, you then work through it, trying to see when you can do what.

■ Take yourself off to an exhibition, book tickets for a concert or maybe go to the theatre – or visit a local theatre group. Many community groups are often looking for extra pairs of hands to help with productions and you certainly don't need to be a budding Sarah Bernhardt to be of use. Get yourself a good listings guide so you can find out what's going on in your area: apart from keeping you busy, you may get to meet new people who are only too glad to rope you in with what's going on. You could end up enjoying yourself so much that you find you only just about have time to eat food, let alone think about it!

CRAVINGS

We've looked at all sorts of reasons that make us turn to food but what about all those cravings that are supposed to have a biological, rather than a psychological cause? We've seen in a previous chapter how food can affect our mood, simply because different foods contain different ingredients which have a variety of influences on the brain, some releasing chemicals that can positively improve the 'feel-good' factor.

So when is it your body telling you to eat, rather than your mind? American research has shown that some extreme cravings are caused by a problem with our genetic make-up – they are missing a vital receptor on one of their chromosomes. And some 'sufferers' have admitted to some strange and wonderful cravings – from chalk to frozen peas.

However, for the majority of us, cravings are less extreme or eccentric. Chocolate probably tops most people's lists and is often seen as one of those 'must have' foods that are impossible to resist. Admittedly chocolate does contain caffeine, which is a known stimulant, but you'd have to eat an awful lot of the stuff before it really took a grip on your body. Although different types of chocolate contain varying combinations, an average plain chocolate is likely to contain 30 per cent fat, 5 per cent protein and the remainder is refined carbohydrate – or sugar. The sugar gives the body a sharp injection of energy but, unfortunately, as the sugar is a refined source it is quickly processed by our metabolism and the energy boost we get is followed by a sharp drop – which makes us miserable and sends us searching for comfort. If you *are* looking for a boost, much better to opt for some wholemeal toast, or some fruit, which will release the energy slowly, and so that you get no sharp 'drops' and you feel good for longer.

Some nutritionists claim that an irrational desire for chocolate could also be caused by a chromium deficiency. If that's the case, there is a variety of other foods to try before you reach for your chocolate treats. Besides wholemeal bread, other wholegrain foods would do the trick, as well as cheese, eggs, meat, and – slightly more convenient – bananas.

Anything that contains high levels of sugar is not a good thing for someone who is trying to monitor what they eat. Processed sugar has a profound effect on most people's moods because of the way it changes the blood glucose levels. Too high an intake raises blood levels very quickly and to deal with this, the body releases insulin which in turn causes blood glucose levels to drop significantly – the result is you feel tired as well as miserable.

However, if you find highly sugared products, like chocolate, irresistible, ask yourself why you see chocolate as something special that can, at the very least, change your mood and, at the most, change your life. Advertisements for chocolate are nearly all characterized by beautiful people, living beautiful lives and the message is clear – take a bit of *this* and you could end up like *that*. No wonder the UK has the highest number of chocolate eaters in the world, with a staggering four *billion* pounds a year spent on the stuff. So, even if you reckon you do crave chocolate, just think about whether the craving is down to you or some bright young ad exec who is paid rather a lot of money for making you think just that . . .

And if it isn't necessarily just chocolate you crave but anything sticky, stodgy or sweet, you'll at least now know there's a reason. On a slightly more scientific level, all these refined carbohydrates stimulate the production of a chemical in the brain called serotonin, which acts like a natural Prozac by making you feel good. However, as we've seen, although these foods may have some temporary success in improving your mood, it's only by eating high-fibre, low-fat carbohydrates like brown rice, wholemeal pasta and bread, potatoes, beans and pulses that you end up enjoying a feeling of well-being, and fullness, for longer.

TIME OF THE MONTH TRIGGERS

The link between PMS and cravings is fairly well established. But if your cravings are linked to your menstrual cycle, the good news is there's a lot you can do about it.

NAPs (The National Association for Pre-menstrual Syndrome) have found that a diet that consistently produces the minimum fluctuations in blood glucose levels throughout the month can actually relieve the more severe symptoms of PMS considerably. They stress the importance of healthy eating and recommend a high-fibre, high-carbohydrate, low-sugar, low-fat diet as the keystone for the successful treatment of PMS. However, if you still suffer from PMS symptoms, you may be suffering from a hormone imbalance which requires medical treatment so it's best to discuss this with your doctor.

For further information send a SAE to: NAPs, P.O. Box 72, Sevenoaks, Kent, TN13 1XQ. Or phone their 24-hour information line on 01732 741709.

FINDING THE KEY

As we've seen, the key to changing your weight is to change the way you think – as well as the way you eat. You can discover more about making the right choices about the food we eat in chapter thirteen. However, you may have to accept that for a while it will help if you think about what you're eating – not, I hasten to add, in any judgemental way. What you're trying to do is to identify an eating pattern, which you can do with the help of the 'food and mood' diary. Once you've done that, you can identify what your needs are – remember the Five Step Hunger Test?

What you need to do is simple, just:

Stop . . . before you eat

Look . . . at what you're about to eat

Listen . . . to you hunger – is it emotional or is it physical?

Think . . . about what you really want. And if you're not sure try to put off the decision to eat, until you are.

Do . . . something else. Something that will take your mind off food. Have a bath, phone a friend, curl up with a book, or magazine, strip a wall . . . it doesn't matter what it is as long as it's something YOU want to do.

Chapter Eleven

Winning Support

RIGHT, NOW THAT we've identified what triggers your appetite, and what to do about it, you need to get as much support on your side as possible. Without it you can easily feel isolated and nothing is tougher than trying to 'go-it-alone' when you're trying to change something as radical as the way you eat. Having support means there's someone around to help with the difficult times, as well as being there to share your feelings of success and achievement. Support comes from some surprising quarters, once you tell people what you're doing. Explain that this is not about spending ten days grazing on rabbit food – this is NOT a diet; this is about changing the way you eat – for life. It's about feeling healthier, fitter and altogether better about yourself.

It can be tempting to keep your plans to yourself and certainly if you feel people are likely to hinder rather than help you, it's understandable that you're reluctant to let them know what's going on. However, if you are honest, although you may risk having to put up with wisecracks and so-called 'witty' remarks, there is always the chance that you'll be pleasantly surprised.

You also have to ask yourself whether you have, unintentionally, played a part in being considered 'fair game' by everyone. Let's face it, when we're embarrassed about something one of the oldest ways of coping is to develop a good line in self-deprecation: that way you're sure to get those comments in before anyone else does.

Once you've told people, if their response is positive, talk to them about some of the ways in which they can give you practical support. For example, if you've a friend who regularly pops in for a cup of tea and a chat in the afternoon, but always arrives armed with your favourite cream slice and a box of jam tarts, ask whether she could swap a plate of cakes for a platter of fruit. Or what about a non-food treat, like bubble bath or hand cream?

Everyone needs a little help from their friends and you need to give them credit for wanting to help you. Even if you don't think much of yourself, they clearly disagree with your opinion – otherwise they wouldn't be your friend in the first place! And, as your friend they are likely to be fully aware of the struggle you've had with your weight over the years so the chances are that they will be only too willing to help you do something about it. And, on a practical level, it will also mean that they'll stop baking your 'favourite' pudding or pie when you go round to see them.

If you're serious about changing your eating habits, don't be reluctant about saying so. No one is a mind reader and if friends have grown used to 'treating' you with food because they've always thought that's what you've wanted, if you're not honest you'll find that you're forever looking for excuses to refuse their offerings . . . And there's a limit to the time that *anyone* can suffer from a tummy bug!

Constant refusals can also easily be misinterpreted and before you know it you've unintentionally caused offence. So, try to explain that you want to stop making food the centre of your life and that friends can help by not making food the main focus every time you get together, and not making it central to everything you do. If you find the support you're getting is not enough, you could do with a little extra help. Sometimes enlisting the help of one particular friend can make a difference. It has to be someone that you can be totally honest with and won't be judge-mental – call them your 'Slimming Samaritan' if you like. And in the same way that Alcoholics Anonymous has a system where all members have the phone number of someone they can call whenever they're feeling troubled or vulnerable, the person at the end of your phone number needs to be someone who will be there for *you*.

RELATIVE SUPPORT

Of course the advantage of having a 'Slimming Samaritan' is that it means there's always someone there who's on *your* side. Unfortunately, though, the same can't always be said of other people around you. While some may be out to deliberately wreck your plans, there are many people in our lives who can, quite unintentionally, completely sabotage all good intentions. So, who are these slimming saboteurs?

Your 'better' half

Men can be sensitive souls and you may find that they become genuinely worried that a new slimmer, trimmer you would automatically want a new, slimmer husband, as we discussed before. In the same way that your old, oversized clothes will be duly despatched to the nearest charity shop, a long-standing husband may well worry that a similar fate lies in store for him. After all, we've all heard the expression, 'out with the old, in with the new . . .'

Let's face it, we all get used to our partners – warts and all – and when we think they're going to go through a radical – albeit gradual – change, it can make even the most secure of men worry. Maybe they think your new image means you'll suddenly become interested in other men or, just as hard to cope with, other men will suddenly become more interested in you.

When either partner changes considerably, it can upset the balance in a relationship. Maybe the larger, more self-conscious, self-effacing and seemingly satisfied you has become more confident and more demanding as the pounds have started to slip away. And maybe you've always allowed your husband to take the lead because you've always had so little confidence that you'd rather *anything* than draw attention to yourself. If that's been the case, both of you are going to need a period of readjustment. He has to accept that you have every right to change as much as you have to accept his concerns over how you've changed.

Try explaining how you feel, and get him to realize how important making these changes are to you. You may also have to make him realize that you're making these changes for YOU – not because you want to change your life, or your husband. If he's also feeling insecure, he may too need some reassurance. So make him see the changes in your life could present a challenge for him, rather than a threat. Keep him involved in what you're doing: explain some of the tactics you want to use, and see if he'll help. Having help on the home front is probably the best you can get. And who knows, it may not just be your eating habits that change for the better, it could be his as well. Some husbands may even complain that you're no fun any more because digging into a box of Quality Street is as much a part of their marriage as having breakfast together. If that's the case, *surely* you can think of something else you can do together that would be just as much fun . . .

Watch with mother . . .

Whether you've been married for 20 years, or you're still living at home, changing your attitude to food can have more of an effect on your mother than you'd think.

Firstly, as we've seen, a lot of our eating patterns are habits we've learnt from childhood and when you want to change those habits, you're in effect criticizing the way your mother has brought you up. Although most mothers would readily admit that their child-rearing methods are less than perfect, none of us likes to think we've done a bad job. And when you consider that one of the most fundamental roles of mothering is that of nurturing, or nourishing the child, you're hitting the poor old mother where it hurts.

Perhaps it's also worth bearing in mind that whether you grew up in the Thirties or the Seventies, the way you were fed reflected the perceived wisdom of that time. So if you were told to eat chunks of cheese for protein, or you always had a sandwich before bed to stop you getting hungry at night, or you'll ever remember being reminded to finish your food because children were starving on the other side of the world – whatever you were told, the chances are that so was every other little boy or girl at the time.

It can also be hard for your mother to see *why* you need to change. Chances are she genuinely loves you as you are and can't see why anyone else wouldn't. Also, if you've been big for any length of time, there's a good chance that the rest of your family is too, including your mother. So, saying that you want to do something about your size could be interpreted as a massive hint that she needs to do something about hers.

Our relationship with our mothers tends to be a complicated one – full of emotion and, often, fraught with guilt. On one level you're rejecting the family 'shape' on the other you're rejecting the tokens of her love . . . in other words the food that she has lovingly prepared and cooked for years. You need to be sensitive to those feelings and take the time to explain that what you're doing is for you and has nothing to do with your relationship with her.

On a more maternal note, if a mother sees a child constantly refusing food, it's only natural for her to worry. She thinks you're sick, or starving, or you have an eating disorder. If you don't take the time to explain to her what's going on in your mind, you can hardly blame her for drawing her own conclusions – however off the mark they may be. Make a point of reassuring her that you *are* eating, but you're being selective. Explain about your new eating plan, and tell her about some of the new meals that you've discovered. You may find that she's just as interested in discovering a new approach to eating as you are.

Children's hour . . .

Of course if anyone really has the ability to weaken your willpower it's children – and the smaller they are, the worst it is! Being a mum means having cupboards overfilling with all sorts of weird and wonderful concoctions – from pickled onion Wotsits (maybe not so tempting!) to Curly Wurlys. Even when you're trying to limit the amount of sweets and chocolates they eat, when they're out there on the table, it's hard not to dive in. And of course all children have a habit of not finishing what they've been given so there's always something left on the plate to nibble as you clear the dishes away.

While you can be restrained at home – wrapping the leftovers in a plastic bag and sticking them in a cupboard for another time, you may even throw them away – it's different when you're out. I've lost count of how many times I've been given a half licked ice-cream, a well-dissected bun or a particularly lurid drink. There's no bin in sight, I can't put the offending items in my bag and my hands are already busy holding smaller hands. And there's no prizes for guessing what I do . . .

One answer is not to let the children eat when they're doing something else like, for example, shopping. Apart from anything else, it's easier, cleaner, cheaper and you don't have the problem of sticky leftovers! If the problem is more home-centred you'll find tips in chapter nine to help re-think how you buy and how you store food, but it's worth keeping their goodies separate. Buy individually wrapped items, that way there's less chances of any leftovers. Also when you decide it's tuck time, make sure you've all eaten lunch or supper. Sugary snacks are no substitute for meals and it's as important that you help establish sensible habits for them just as you do for you. Of course there is another suggestion. You could stop buying them sugary treats – it would make the world of difference to their teeth, not to mention their eating habits.

Friendly fire?

Friends can be a great support, but they can also be downright destructive. 'But do have some chocolate cheesecake,' they simper, 'it's your favourite.' You feel yourself sinking under the chair but they remain undeterred. 'Surely one slice won't hurt?' Well, yes, it will if it's not what you want.

Friends may seem like they mean well, but sometimes they can do more harm than good. Be loud and clear with your refusals – if you mean no then say 'no'. And if they still don't want to listen maybe it's time to question how good a friend they are. After all, if you do have 'just one more slice', the only one that may end up feeling bad about it is you. It's worth reminding yourself that friends are people who respect what you say, and what you want. If they simply don't want to listen, maybe it's because they've got their own reasons for not putting your needs first. Maybe they've got used to thinking of you as someone they can always count on to listen to their problems, or who's always there when there's nothing much going on. Just think, if you suddenly develop a life of your own, you can no longer be counted on to be there for them – always at home, always at the end of the phone. And, if in the past friends have always considered you safe – safe to leave with partners, safe to relay messages – the more confident you become, the more chance there is that it could all begin to change . . .

On a slightly more generous note, in the same way that a partner will worry about how this new resolve will change you as a person, so will your friends. For a start you're probably being more assertive, albeit about food, but the fact that you can be strong minded can be difficult for people who are not used to seeing you stand up for yourself. In an ideal world, of course, you want your friends to feel as good about what you're doing as you do. But if they don't, there isn't a lot you can do about it. After all, you're not doing it for *them* – you're doing it for *you*.

Of course some people won't take your protestations of changed eating habits too seriously and, to a certain extent, you're going to have to try and ignore disparaging comments and the doubting Thomases. And to be fair, if they have been through an infinite number of diet plans – each and every one different and each and every one a failure – then you can understand their cynicism. However, you need to explain what's different this time and stress how much you'd welcome their encouragement and positive suggestions, rather than negative criticisms that simply remind you of past failures. For you, the most important word you can say to them is 'no'. And if you find it difficult at first, don't panic, it really is a case of practice makes perfect. Start saying no, and meaning no, and you've taken the first step to being in control and believing in yourself. You've proved that you *can* do it. And the great thing is when you've managed to do it once, saying no in the future is never quite so difficult again.

The friends indeed . . .

There are times when you may find people telling you that you don't need to lose weight. Either because 'you're lovely as you are', or 'you've nothing left to lose'. If the former reason is given then you need to question what basis the friend has for assuming that you won't be just as lovely when you're several stone lighter . . . and anyway, if you don't feel lovely, whatever anyone says won't make much difference.

However, if you consistently have people on at you that you're 'thin enough already', you might need to think about how objective you are being about your size. We've seen in earlier chapters that there are a significant number of women who diet, but have no need to, and it's all too easy to become one of them. If you've felt negative about your body for years, even once you've lost weight, it can take some time to come to terms with the fact that you're, literally, a shadow of your former self.

If you think that there's a chance that the problem is more to do with how you *think* you look, rather than how you *do* actually look, try to get a good friend, or member of the family to be honest with you. Tell them you don't want them to come out with a load of platitudes or feel they should say what they think you want to hear - you want 100 per cent honesty. If you have no one to talk to, it's worth having a chat with your doctor. In truth, if you feel you do have a problem, there's no substitute for expert advice.

GOING FOR GOAL

Although people want to lose weight for different reasons, obviously the most effective one is when you're doing it for yourself. But it's important you have realistic expectations of what a change in your shape will do for you. We've seen in earlier chapters that even if you drop four dress sizes, you'll still be you - even if you are buying smaller-sized clothes. So, while a lighter you won't mend a broken relationship or guarantee a promotion at work, it will make you feel an awful lot fitter, healthier and happier within yourself - which isn't a bad result to get from simply changing your daily menu plans!

But it's also important that you should be realistic in what you're trying to achieve. Weight loss is based on a very simple equation - input and output. Input is what we put into our bodies: that includes all those cups of tea and coffee – plus the biscuits eaten 'to keep the drink company' – all your meals, the food left over from the children's plates and that roast potato – because it seemed a pity to throw it away.

When it comes to the food we eat, our bodies are pretty democratic. Once eaten, food is converted into what is known as energy, and it's then shared out to the appropriate organs – each according to its needs. Obviously we need certain levels of energy to keep our bodies functioning healthily, but if we take in – which means eat – more than we need, the energy left over gets stored. That used to be because it was often needed in times of emergency, but as famines are rare in this part of the world, we have little need to call on those stores – so the stored fat becomes excess weight.

The other side of the equation is to do with the energy we use and this is determined by our output – or how active we are. We all use up a certain amount of energy, even the most sedentary of us, because it takes energy to keep our bodies going and that includes keeping our heart and lungs ticking over. It even takes energy to breathe. But the more energetic we are, the more we use up. So, if you swim three times a week and like to play tennis regularly, you're going to use up an awful lot more energy than someone whose idea of a brisk walk is to stride purposely towards the car which is parked a few houses down the road.

By eating what your body needs your input is constantly balanced by your output – but eat more and do less and all the energy that's left over gets stored – and that, broadly speaking, is when we put on weight. And to lose weight, your output – or the energy you use up – has to be greater than your input – the energy, or food, you consume. But the tricky thing is that you can't simply restrict what you eat until you get down to the weight you want to be . . . firstly you'd be ill and secondly it's a sure route to developing an extremely unhealthy relationship with food.

Even if you are overweight, you still need to eat – and enough to keep your body healthy. Being thin at the expense of being healthy just isn't worth it. And if at the end of the day you're too weak and sick to enjoy a slimmer you, what's the point? The answer is to find a weight that suits your body and your mind. You need to feel good about yourself but you also need to feel healthy.

WHAT YOU SHOULD LOSE

It's fine to have an idea of how much weight you'd like to lose, but it's not fine to get obsessed about getting down to a goal. Far better to say, 'I'd like to lose a stone in the next couple of months' and if you do, fine. Then you're in a position to readjust what you'd like to achieve. It's also important not to try and lose too much too quickly – remember you're not simply trying to achieve a short, sharp weight loss – an amount which may come off quickly but is also likely to go back on twice as fast. What you're looking for is a long-term solution that will last – for good.

Scaling down

Experts recommend a loss of around 2 lbs (900g) a week, although even if you lose less, over the months that loss still mounts up. To begin with you may find you'll lose anything up to 5 lbs (2.25 kg). This is due to the loss of glycogen, a carbohydrate which is stored in the liver and muscle. When this is lost, water is shed – which results in a higher weight loss than normal. That said, it's important not to attach too much importance to the scales. If you want to use them, if only because they can keep tabs on how you're doing, use them as a guide, no more.

Admittedly when the scales register a significant decrease, it can give you a real boost but, conversely it also has the opposite effect when that little arrow indicates no loss – or worse – an actual gain. Being a slave to the scales also means you take no account of hormonal influences on your weight – for example, we can put on up to seven pounds just before a period due to fluid retention. Also, if you've taken up exercise with a vengeance you could be losing fat but putting on muscle – the scales, of course, only reveal the amount you weigh but not where that weight comes from.

What's important is to go by how you feel. I don't believe there's anyone who's reading this who doesn't know when they've lost weight – it's a subject that most women feel too strongly about! And let's face it, we're all aware when our clothes get looser, and we start to find that activities like walking, or running, are less of a trial. No one actually needs a pair of scales to tell them they're feeling better!

Some experts suggest chucking your scales out because they tie you too much to targets which can set you up for disappointment. But the reality is that if you do possess a pair of scales that are nestling happily in your bathroom, you're unlikely to want to part with them and chances are you won't be able to resist hopping on to them from time to time. If that's something you feel happy doing, fine. But, try to:

- not weigh yourself more than once a week – expecting to see a day-to-day difference is like watching paint dry.
- remember everyone's weight fluctuates from time to time and the reasons can have nothing to do with what you've eaten.
- check your scales are relatively reliable. It doesn't matter if they aren't 100 per cent accurate as long as they are consistent.
- make sure the scales are on a flat surface as anything uneven, like a thick carpet, can distort the reading.
- always weigh yourself at the same time of day, in the same state of dress – or undress!

REAL SLIMMERS AREN'T SAINTS!

The *Slimming Bible* is about eating a diet for life. That means finding a style, as well as foods, that suit your tastes as well as your lifestyle. What you need to do is develop a normal pattern of eating regularly, rather than your former, possibly slightly more erratic approach. Food is a central part to all our lives and it's important to bring back the enjoyment of eating. Food should be associated with pleasurable experiences, not fearful ones.

We've seen how certain moods, and foods, can trigger bouts of overeating. However, to bring a normal pattern into the way YOU eat, you need to feel relaxed about food, as well as around food – and that means all food. All the evidence proves that the more we deprive ourselves of something, the more we want it – and you don't need to be a psychologist to know that's true! It's something we've known for centuries – just look what happened in the Garden of Eden when poor Adam was offered the forbidden fruit by Eve . . .

But, if you truly believe there are some foods that you simply can't stop eating, how do you get over the feeling of 'can't live with it; can't live without it'? Well the first step is realizing that the stress caused by not eating what you want is likely to make you eat even more. So, getting het up about whether or not you should eat that Milky Way is counter-productive. On the other hand, eat it without worrying, without feeling guilty and you'll start to realize it's like any other food. If what you can't have, you want, then it's not surprising that what you *can* have, becomes altogether less interesting.

In fact some experts believe that one way of coping with foods that you can't say no to is to make them as available as possible. The idea is that the more accessible they are, and the more you give in to the urge, the less appealing the food becomes. Rather than seeing is as a special food, different from the rest of your diet, it becomes like everything else you eat – ordinary. And the result is you develop a much more balanced attitude towards it. If you can have it whenever you like, then you can just as well eat it tomorrow, or the next day . . . or the next week. Suddenly eating that bar of chocolate becomes less important. Further support for this are the studies that have shown that the more that you eat of something in one sitting, the less moreish it becomes.

In Susie Orbach's *Fat is A Feminist Issue*, she vividly describes how one woman learned to live with ice-cream – something that she 'felt attracted to and scared of'. The woman was persuaded to buy enough ingredients to make up seventy-five ice-cream sundaes – with all the trimmings, which meant sauces, nuts and cream! Not surprisingly the lady in question was horrified at the thought of being surrounded by so much food and was convinced that she'd eat it all – even though it was pointed out that she'd have enough ice-cream to feed a minor army! However, what this exercise did was put the woman in the position of proving to herself that, when it came down to it, she didn't actually want to eat it all at once – which meant she was, in fact, exerting control over what she did – and didn't – eat.

The result? To quote Orbach, 'she learned to love the ice-cream and treat it as a friend to be called on when she wanted it rather than as an enemy to be conquered'. Whether you go along with Orbach's idea of learning to 'love your food' is up to you, but however you describe it, changing the way you think about food can make a huge difference to the way you eat.

Another approach is to simply swap high-sugar, high-fat favourites for something with less calories. So you could swap your cola for the diet variety, butter for low-fat spread and your Cadbury's for a Lo bar. You'll find more suggestions in the next chapter but the point is, there are plenty of alternatives to high-fat fare. However, if you're one of those people who would much rather have the 'real thing' than go for second best, how do you do it but manage to stay in control of your appetite? The answer is to learn when it's time to say 'enough'; you need to limit your treats so that you get the enjoyment out of eating something you like, but without the guilt that comes from overeating.

You can find several exercises in the next chapter which you may find helpful but, whatever approach you feel is best for you, what you're trying to do is get to the point where you feel relaxed enough about food to say thanks, but no thanks, when you've had enough.

Of course this doesn't mean you won't ever binge, or overeat, or give into your cravings . . . or have to undo your button as you leave a restaurant because you've eaten too much! Everyone does it. What's important is that you don't do it often and, just as important, you know what you're doing and feel in control. It's when you don't feel in control that the problem starts.

The only thing now left to work out is the right time to start to re-think the way you eat. Personally, I'm a great believer in 'there's no time like the present'. I also happen to think that if you're reading this, there's a good chance that you're pretty fired up about doing SOMETHING, even if you're not sure what that something is!

That said, if it's a stressful time for you, you may want to wait until things are a little calmer before you make any changes. However, do remember that the changes you are going to make are gradual – no one expects you to open your cupboards and throw the contents in the dustbin. The idea is that you slowly but surely change the way you eat, and the way you think about eating. As you get used to the changes, your tastebuds will become attuned to different tastes and flavours. You might even start to crave new tastes as well as the old ones. But before you get to that stage, remember you may have to accept that for a while you're going to need to think about what you're eating – which you can do with the help of the 'food and mood' diary. It's then you're in a position to identify what your needs are – and a good reminder is the Five Step Hunger Test. Remember, what you need to do is just:

Stop . . . before you eat

Look . . . at what you're about to eat

Listen . . . to your hunger – is it emotional or is it physical?

Think . . . about what you really want. And if you're not sure, try to put off the decision to eat until you are.

Do . . . something else. Something that will take your mind off food. Have a bath, phone a friend, curl up with a book, or magazine, strip a wall . . . it doesn't matter what it is as long as it's something YOU want to do.

Chapter Twelve

Food for thought

IT SEEMS TO ME there are two major obstacles to people developing a healthier approach to eating – how they think and how they shop. We've explored in some detail how our minds can influence our eating patterns but the choices we make when we buy food – either in the shops or in a restaurant – are often based on misinformation and misjudgements as much as gluttony.

So be honest: how much do you really know about what you eat? One MORI poll revealed that although four out of five of the people interviewed claimed that they were informed about diet and healthy eating, when they were asked specific questions about food, their answers suggested there was a lot of confusion about what we think the experts are saying we should and shouldn't be eating. And when you start to think about it, it's hardly surprising.

These days even buying a tub of marge requires a degree in food technology. *'Would madam like butter, margarine or spread? And would that be polyunsaturated, monounsaturated, saturated?'* Actually, you're just looking for something to spread on your bread . . . but the choice is endless. *'We can offer mostly fat, half-fat, low fat, lowish fat, no-fat? Then of course you can choose sunflower, olive oil, soya, dairy free . . .'* I readily admit I don't know much about 'Can't believe it's not butter', but one walk past the chilled cabinet and I, for one, can't believe what's happening!

Of course there is a case for arguing that such a vast choice is great news for the consumer i.e. you and me, because we have so many options but I reckon there's a good case for arguing that so much choice addles the brain. And, a bit like a child in a toy shop – how does anyone choose? Well, because we aren't food technologists or biochemists, we tend to make visual choices or – surprise surprise – be influenced by any number of advertising campaigns that happen to be around at the time. Let's face it, there were a lot of us buying Flora for our men long before we even knew how to spell polyunsaturates . . .

Admittedly there has been an awful lot more information readily available since then – one supermarket chain has even produced a guide to butter, margarines and spreads, subtitled 'Which are right for you?' With all the leaflets and brochures on offer every time you go shopping, supermarkets will soon have to start providing a reading room . . . !

So, when you take away the advertising, the packaging, the strategic aisle positioning as well as those clever marketing ploys of flashing up the words *Health!*, *Slimming!*, *Low Fat!*, *High Fibre!*, *Low Sugar!* or '*Can Be Used as Part of A Calorie-Controlled Diet*' (omitting to mention that a bag of chips and a slice of Sachertorte can be used as a calorie-controlled diet – as long as you know how many calories they contained . . .), what *should* you be trying to eat?

Well, health professionals are so concerned about what we eat, that they have made a number of recommendations that are, thankfully, gloriously unscientific! There have been various ways that this information has been presented but for me, the Healthy Eating Pyramid is the most effective, which is illustrated opposite.

HOW MUCH SHOULD YOU EAT?

The pyramid shows the number of measures from each food group we should eat each day. A measure is not always the same as a portion on the plate. The foods in each group provide similar nutrients and by eating the correct number of measures from every group, we get the right quantities of all nutrients. You need fewer measures if you are older, female, inactive or overweight. You need more if you are younger, male, active or not overweight.

There are five food groups in the pyramid. At the base of the pyramid lies the foods that we should be eating more of, the top contains those we need to eat less of. Even if you need to lose weight, be sure to eat the minimum number of measures from the first four groups – we need all these to get enough minerals and vitamins.

The British Healthy Eating Pyramid

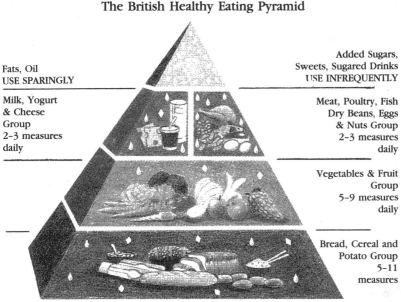

Fats, Oil
USE SPARINGLY

Added Sugars,
Sweets, Sugared Drinks
USE INFREQUENTLY

Milk, Yogurt
& Cheese
Group
2-3 measures
daily

Meat, Poultry, Fish
Dry Beans, Eggs
& Nuts Group
2-3 measures
daily

Vegetables & Fruit
Group
5-9 measures
daily

Bread, Cereal and
Potato Group
5-11
measures

KEY ◖ Fat (naturally occurring and added) ◇ Sugars (added)

These symbols show fats, oils and added sugars in foods.

Produced by the Flour Advisory Bureau/The Dunn Nutrition Centre.

Bread, cereals, rice, pasta and potatoes

These are the foundations of the diet and we should all be building our meals around them; they provide protein, carbohydrate and B vitamins. Aim for between 5-11 measures daily. A measure is: slice of bread/toast; half a bread bun or roll; 3 tbsp breakfast cereal; 1 tbsp cooked rice, pasta or noodles; 3½ oz (100g) boiled potatoes (that's about 2 egg-sized potatoes).

Vegetables and fruit

Excellent for providing vitamins and minerals. Aim for between 5-9 measures daily. A measure is: 2 tbsp vegetables; small salad; 2 tbsp cooked/tinned fruit; small (100ml) carton fruit juice; a piece of fruit.

Milk, cheese and yoghurt

The major providers of calcium for strong bones, these also provide protein. Aim for between 2-3 measures daily. A measure is: third pint milk; small pot yoghurt; 1.5 oz (40g) cheese (a small matchbox size.)

Meat and others protein alternatives such as poultry, fish,
pulses (beans, lentils and dried beans), eggs and nuts
All provide protein and B vitamins – different foods in the group provide
different vitamins and minerals so eat a variety. Aim for between 2–3
measures daily. A measure is: 2–3 oz (55–85 g) lean meat/poultry (without
skin)/oily fish; 4–5 oz (115–140 g) white fish (not fried); 2 eggs (up to six a
week); 10oz (300g) cooked beans/lentils; 1½ oz (40g) cheese.

Fat, fatty and sugary foods
The tip of the pyramid shows globules that represent the fat in butter,
margarine, low fat spreads, cooking oils and fats. These should be used
sparingly. Limit these foods to no more than 3 measures daily. A measure
is: 1 tsp butter/marg; 2 tsp low-fat spread; 1 tsp oil; 1 tsp mayonnaise/oily
salad dressing.

Fat also appears in other foods such as meat, sausages, chips, crisps,
pies, fatty gravies, luncheon meat, pastries, milk, cakes and biscuits, even
though they're not easily visible.

The crystals at the top of the pyramid represents the sugar found in
sugared drinks, syrups, cakes, puddings and biscuits.

Limit these foods to no more than 1–2 portions daily.

What's important to remember though is that it's essential we all eat a
balanced diet because different food groups play different parts in keeping
our body in peak condition, so don't think in terms of 'good' foods or 'bad'
foods – there's no such thing. No one food can provide everything that we
need, which is why it is vital to eat a varied diet. We need a good mixture of
proteins (fish, meat and cheese; or vegetable sources like pulses and
cereals); complex carbohydrates, or as they used to be called, starchy
foods, such as bread and pasta) plus vegetables and fruit. The other type of
carbohydrate is the refined sort, namely sugar, which experts recommend
we should be cutting back on, see *Sweet Truths*, on page 171.

There's no great secret in getting to grips with the low down on healthy
eating. You simply need to get into the habit of learning how to choose
foods which are high in nutrients and low on energy, so that you feel full,
which means there's less chance of you accumulating surplus calories.

A WORD ABOUT CALORIES . . .

Probably one of the most misused words of the last 30 years! In fact, a
calorie (or, to give it its full name, kilocalorie) is a unit of heat in which

the energy value of food is measured. Incidentally, kilojoules, which is a term often found on food labels, is just the metric measurement for energy but one kilojoule works out at about four times the value of a kilocalorie.

If you think of your body as a petrol tank, then it's easy to see that we need to keep filling up with fuel - or food - to keep us going. Our bodies burn that fuel, and that's where we get the energy to do things. But with no energy, or calories, pretty soon we come to a grinding halt. As proof, just think of the last time you were laid up in bed for a couple of days with, say a virus. By the end of the spell you probably felt weak and wobbly - basically in need of a couple of gallons of four star!

Now if you eat *more* calories than you burn, you end up with a tank full to the brim. And the only place for the excess 'energy' to go is to your fat stores, where it waits patiently for a famine - a time when your tank is more empty than full and so needs to draw on its reserve. Of course, famines being a rarity nowadays, there's not much call on all that stored fat so it stays where it is - and you get bigger.

Obviously it would be complicated to work out exactly what your energy requirements are - in other words exactly how many calories you need to take in before there's enough excess for your body to convert it into fat - although the likelihood is that you know yourself when you're eating too much because, apart from anything else, your clothes get tighter, you feel bloated and, in short, you put on weight.

However, experts suggest that most of us need about 2000 calories a day to maintain our weight - men about an extra 500. Of course this figure will vary, depending on how active as well as how tall you are. A tennis coach, for example, is going to use up a lot more energy than someone who rarely moves away from the TV except, perhaps, to change the channel.

For the sake of this book though, I have tried to keep away from calories as much as possible. If you find it helpful to think in terms of calories when you're trying to decide which foods are high fat ones, that's fine and there's more information on the subject on page 267. However, the idea is not to make you calorie, fat, carbohydrate or anything else obsessed. The point of this book is simply to make you aware enough of what you're eating to be able to make the right sort of choices for you. Your body converts, or metabolizes, its food. After all, when it comes to sitting down to a meal, the pleasure is the enjoyment of the food. No one gets pleasure out of 'eating calories'. Calories are just a unit of measure, not a dietary straightjacket. Calories aren't good or bad. Calories are just calories.

SHORTCUTS TO HEALTHY EATING

To develop healthier eating patterns that will make you feel fitter and help to reduce your excess weight you need to remember four things:

- Eat less fat
- Cut down on sugar
- Increase your fibre and complex carbohydrates
- Eat more fruit and veg.

In theory that shouldn't be too difficult. The problem is that we eat high proportions of processed, and ready-made meals, which means it's not always as simple as looking discerningly at your plate and declaring: 'Ah-ha! I've got an awful lot of fat here but not nearly enough complex carbohydrates!' Let's face it, we eat food, not nutrients, even though many of us may feel we could sit an exam in nutrition because we're bombarded by so many bits of paper on the subject. But, according to the research, while this has all made us painfully aware that we ought to be eating a more nutritious diet, it hasn't actually done much to guide us through a maze of complicated, and at times, contradictory information.

A FAT LOT OF GOOD

There's been an outbreak of low-fat fever amongst some manufacturers and none more so than with the battle of what to spread on our bread. The truth is that whatever our preference, we should be only using a little. The average person's diet in this country is made up of around 42 per cent of energy from fat – recommendations state that fats should be providing no more than 30 to 35 per cent of our intake. The type of fat you use can make a difference but it's easy to lose sight of the fact that all the expert recommendations tell us that our *overall* fat consumption needs cutting. The type of fat you choose is almost a secondary issue. It's also useful to remember that because fat contains over twice as many calories per gram as carbohydrates and protein, it can end up being twice as difficult not to overeat. But, if the majority of your calories come from other nutrients, like complex carbohydrates, then gram for gram, you can actually eat more.

So, bearing that in mind, below is an easy-to-use guide to the different types of fat.

Saturated, or animal fat

Generally thought to be the baddie amongst the fat family because it raises our blood cholesterol level which increases the risk of heart disease. Saturated fat can also be made by hardening vegetable fats (a process known as hydrogenation) which is then used to make processed foods and hard margarines.

Main sources: Any fat that comes from an animal – so meat, chicken, dairy products – or is hard (butter, suet, lard), is saturated, as are palm and coconut oil, which are often used by manufacturers in processed foods like cakes, pastry and biscuits. While it can be easy to spot obvious fat like the layer on your lamb or the skin on your chicken, a high percentage of what are sometimes referred to as 'hidden fats' are contained in foods like salamis, pâtés, pies, pastries, sausages, cakes, crisps, chocolate and salad dressings.

Unsaturated fats

The good guys. There are two types: monounsaturated and polyunsaturated. Both are liquid at room temperature, unless they have been hydrogenated.

Monounsaturates, essential for maintaining a healthy heart and blood vessels. They have also been shown to actually lower blood cholesterol levels, but only when taken as part of a low-fat diet.

Main sources: Olive, rapeseed, groundnut and sesame oils; olives, avocados and peanuts.

Polyunsaturates, also reduces blood cholesterol levels and, used in moderation, are important for the healthy functioning of our bodies.

Main sources: mainly found in vegetable oils such as sunflower, safflower, soya and corn; vegetables and oily fish such as sardines, mackerel, etc.

Trans fatty acids

(also known as hydrogenated fats and oils) – these are produced when manufacturers want to turn vegetable oils into something that can be spread rather than poured. However, although trans fatty acids start life as unsaturated fats, the process of hydrogenation, which hardens edible oils, *trans*-forms them (literally) into behaving like saturated fats when it comes to the effect they have on our body. What this means in layman's terms is that large intakes can significantly increase our risk of developing heart disease. In general, the harder the margarine, the more trans fats it is likely to contain.

Main sources: Cakes, biscuits, etc. Also found in vegetable cooking oils used in restaurants because hydrogenated oils have a longer cooking life. Over the last year there has also been much discussion about the amount of trans fatty acids contained in some margarines. Since the discovery linking these fats with heart disease, some manufacturers have significantly reduced levels in their margarines – notably Flora which means that it now has one of the lowest combined trans and saturated fat levels among leading comparative brands, although other less well-known brands like Vitaquell or Whole Earth's SuperSpread, contain no trans fats.

Whatever your choice, you need to remember that gram for gram, a fat is a fat. Butter – which is 80 per cent fat – contains the same amount of fat and energy, or calories, as margarine. And just because something is high in polyunsaturates doesn't make it low in fat: it's just low in saturated fat.

But what about the 'half-fats', 'reduced fats', 'lows' and 'lowests'?

The variety of labels used on these products is largely down to the fact that legally, if a product doesn't contain at least 80 per cent fat, it can't call itself a margarine – hence we have a variety of alternative low-fat labels that refer to 'spreads'. But, although these spreads contain less fat than butter and margarine, the amounts they contain can vary considerably – anything from 20–25 per cent fat (e.g. Delight Extra Low, Gold Lowest) to 60 per cent (Vitalite Light, for example). So, Light may mean that a product is lighter on fat, and therefore calories, but the term is no indication of *how* light.

It's also worth noting that the higher the fat level in a spread, the more suitable it is for cooking. Spreads that contain less than 60 per cent fat are inappropriate for frying (they splutter all over the place) or baking because they have a high water content.

Obviously taste is a consideration, but as a rule, where you can, opt for a vegetable-based spread which is low in saturates and high in polyunsaturates – for example any low-fat spread labelled sunflower, soya or safflower, or Flora Extra Light, Gold Lowest, etc. If in doubt, check the fat content on the label. Of course doing without butter or margarine is much the better option but if you feel that really would be going too far, then stick to the lower fat alternatives. Your first choice should be an unsaturated low-fat spread, second choice unsaturated margarine.

TRIMMING BACK THE FAT

The more you can reduce the fat in your diet, the more good you'll be doing your heart as well as your waistline – so you don't have to want to lose weight to benefit from cutting back the fat. As we've seen, it's vital to reduce the overall fat content in all our diets and although a staggering 25 per cent of the fat in the average British diet comes from margarine and butter, the remainder comes from a variety of other sources, with: 27 per cent from meat and meat products; 13 per cent from cooking oils and fats; 13 per cent from milk; 6 per cent from biscuits, cakes and pastries; 5 per cent from cheese and cream and 11 per cent from other foods.

Cutting down on any of the above will help considerably in reducing the amount of energy you're consuming. Of course, changing your eating habits involves re-educating your tastebuds and if you've been used to a high-fat diet, you may find it'll take a while before you get used to new tastes and new flavours. You'll also be amazed to find that cutting back on fat means you can actually eat more. As an example, take an average single portion pork pie of, say, 5oz (140 g). It doesn't look particularly big so you may well have it with something else but, just alone, this individual pie can work out at around 600 calories – and that's without adding anything to it. Now, for the same amount of energy, you could actually have a meal of chicken, jacket potato, vegetables, plus fruit for dessert!

Changes that everyone can make though, which will make a huge difference to fat intake are the ways in which you cook and prepare food: grilling your food rather than frying it (one small baked potato works out to around 120 calories while, say, 4oz (115 g) of chips will notch up about 300); using a non-stick pan; using margarines, butters and spreads sparingly; not bothering to pre-brown meat; pre-cooking casseroles and then taking off the fat that has solidified on top. And if you do fry, blot the excess oil off with a little kitchen towel and always fry in unsaturated oil like sunflower, safflower, corn or soya. And if you're frying chips, large, thick, straight cut chips soak up a lot less oil than small thin chips because there's more surface to fry around. And don't forget to drain them on kitchen paper before you serve!

People who gradually change their diet have much more chance of successfully sticking to it than those who make radical changes that leave them left wanting for their former favourites. So, to start with, where possible always opt for a low fat, or reduced fat, alternative. And if you shudder at the thought of 'alternatives', be assured that manufacturers have come a long way from the early low fat days when the foods were a touch tough on the digestion and distinctly poor on the palate! The advances of food technology have meant that low fat is no longer synonymous with low taste and, product for product, it's now difficult to make the distinction between high and low fat.

If there's one product though, that I have heard people consistently complain about, it's skimmed milk – which can be a hard switch to make from the full fat variety. If skimmed is something you really can't stomach, go for semi-skimmed for a while. After a few months, once you're used to it, trying to change to skimmed won't seem quite as drastic.

Other lower fat choices worth considering are:

- Cheeses (from hard to soft, there are now so many options available that many supermarkets are devoting a whole shelf to them)
- Milk and cream
- Mayonnaise, salad creams and dressings
- Dips – most supermarkets offer a variety
- Pâtés – vegetarian as well as meat and fish
- Ready-prepared salads and side salads
- Lean cuts of meat – frozen as well as fresh, joints as well as processed meats, sausages, beefburgers, etc.
- Yoghurts, fromage frais
- fish tinned in brine or, even better, water
- Low-fat drinks, ready prepared foods, etc.

The list is huge – and it's growing all the time. What it shows though is that you can still eat well, even if you're taking in less calories. So, trying to lose weight doesn't mean that you have to sacrifice taste, a love of food – or go hungry. The secret is to understand enough about food to make sure you make the right choices. Looking at the food labels is essential. They now give breakdowns of the type of fat used (saturated or polyunsaturated) but claims can still be made for products that don't tell the whole story.

Take lower fat and reduced fat crisps. Crisp lovers would be forgiven for thinking that they could make a terrific difference to their calorie intake but the 'lower fat' simply means they contain less fat than ordinary crisps – it doesn't mean you're getting a low-fat snack because *all* crisps are fried which means they can't help but be loaded with fat.

SWEET TRUTHS

Unfortunately it isn't only the hidden fats that mask a food's true ingredients. On average, we work our way through almost half a pound of sugar each week – and if you're someone who doesn't even take sugar in your tea or coffee, you may well greet the figure with utter disbelief. But, the reason it's so high is because of the 'hidden' sugars – all those foods we eat that we don't even *realize* contain sugar.

Foods high in natural sugar, like fruit, come bound with fibre which is filling, so there's actually a limit to how much natural sugar we can eat. But once sugar is processed, or refined into sweets, or drinks, it's so easy to eat large amounts of the stuff. The processing strips them of their fibre, as well as vitamin and mineral content, so the danger is that you end up taking in all those calories without any of the essential nutrients that are vital for keeping your body in good health.

So where's our half a pound of sugar coming from? Sugar acts as a preservative and this, with its ability to produce gelling, is responsible for its use in jam. It is also used as a flavour enhancer in canned vegetables and soup and even, in some canned meat and sauces like ketchups.

In The Open University's *Guide to Healthy Eating*, published in 1985, the authors analyzed a number of common foods to see just how much sugar they contained. While you might have a vague idea that a can of Coke has a high level of sugar (seven level teaspoons, actually), as does a glass of Ribena (five), orange squash (two), a Mars bar (five), or even an average portion of tinned peaches in syrup, which contains a staggering *six* teaspoons of sugar, there were some surprises.

A large glass of sweet sherry contains one level teaspoon, a small tin of baked beans, two, a small tin of tomato soup, two to three; two tablespoons of muesli (an average serving), one and a half; one slice of plain cake, three; one tube of Polo mints, two; one glass of orange juice, two and a half and a pot of fruit yoghurt, so often trumpeted as a slimmer's friend, two and a half teaspoons!

As a nation we're eating more manufactured cakes, biscuits, soft drinks, sugary desserts, plus a huge variety of chocolate bars and other sugary snacks and these all give us sugar, as well as fat, in quick and easy forms. Easy to buy, easy to serve, and easy to eat quickly.

Of course now we do have a range of low-fat products on offer, which is good news but it's easy to think low fat automatically equals low sugar – it doesn't. Yoghurts, as we've seen, can contain two and a half teaspoons of sugar, even though their labels proudly trumpet low fat. But, as they are also high in sugar, you could end up losing on the swings what you gain on the roundabouts. To make sure you're opting for yoghurts, or fromage frais for that matter, that are low in fat *and* sugar, look out for the diet or healthy eating ranges. But it is still important to check the labels. Sugar will be under 'carbohydrates' but manufacturers, by law, now have to give a breakdown of the type of carbohydrates included, so you'll be able to see instantly what percentage of the carbohydrate comes from sugar.

And a not insignificant by-product of a diet high in sugar is the higher incidence of dental caries, or tooth decay. Rotten teeth are often caused by a rotten diet so if you want to keep enjoying your food, then be sure to hang on to your teeth – and the best way to do that is check your sugar intake!

A sugar by any other name . . .

There are a variety of different types of sugar (brown, honey, etc.) and sometimes a label will list the name of a manufactured sugar, rather than the terms that we're more familiar with. Names to look out for include: sucrose, fructose, glucose, dextrose, lactose, maltose, sorbitol, mannitol or the more familiar golden syrup, treacle, honey, molasses, malt and corn syrup.

LIQUID COMFORTS

So-called liquid calories that come from drinks can often be a problem for people who are trying to lose weight. I remember talking to several people over the years who couldn't understand why, even though they were being very food-aware, they still found they had put on weight. It turned out to be very simple – they hadn't realized what a difference those drinks make.

While most people don't bat an eyelid over swapping to a low-calorie, diet version of their favourite fizzy drink, they often don't think twice about a bottle of wine at dinner and the gin and tonic in the evening. Alcohol is a truly empty calorie. It contains no nutrients and also lowers any resolve you may have to adopt healthier eating patterns. So, when you're working out what you've eaten in a day – don't forget what you've drunk: alcoholic or otherwise. If it is alcohol, consider adding low-calorie mixtures or topping up your wine with mineral water to make it go further.

HEALTHIER ALTERNATIVES?

Health-food shops have become tempting temples of healthy, nutritious and natural foods. However, many of the foods can contain just as much fat and sugar as the so-called unhealthy snacks bought at your local supermarket. Some health-food bars, for example, may well contain dollops of oats and other cereals but they can also be as high in fat and sugar as a chocolate bar.

Even ten years ago, experts who worked on the BUPA *Manual of Fitness and Well-being* warned consumers to 'beware of "healthy" looking and processed foods in health food stores. Muesli bars, nut crunches, soya mixes and the like may contain as much saturated fat, sugar or salt as a "non-healthy" products bought from an ordinary shop.'

Certainly 'health' snacks like flapjacks, Tropical Fruit, as well as Bombay Mix, are high in fat – a small pack containing the same amount of energy as a packet of crisps. Other health-food goodies like banana chips and yoghurt-coated raisins tell the same story. Carob bars, often bought as a healthy alternative to chocolate, can easily contain more fat and only slightly less sugar than an ordinary plain chocolate. So, check labels and if there isn't one – ask.

VEGETARIAN

A popular misconception these days is that anything bearing a vegetarian flash is healthier than its non-vegetarian counterpart. This comes from the fact that because vegetarians generally ate less saturated fat overall, they had less chance of developing heart disease. Also their diet was thought to be much lower in fat generally as they ate largely meals based on beans and pulses, as well as generous servings of vegetables and starchy foods like pasta, potatoes and rice. While this certainly *was* the case for many years, now, with the emphasis on fast foods, the convenience food sector has caught up with the vegetarian consumer and veggie alternatives now compete for space with non-vegetarian ready-prepared meals.

What all this means is that vegetarian alternatives have become increasingly higher in fat – albeit not animal fat. So a vegetarian cheese and potato pastie is not necessarily lower in fat than the Cornish variety or a lump of Cheddar. In fact, some vegetarian sausages, for example, contain 30 per cent fat, which is higher than many meatier alternatives, and vegetarian cheese, unless it specifically says lower or reduced fat, has as much fat in it as the non-vegetarian variety. Another misconception is that pies, pastries and biscuits made with wholemeal flour are less fatty than the white versions. They do contain more fibre but if you're trying to cut down on your fat content you may need to remind yourself that while fibre contents might differ, fat contents don't.

If it's becoming as easy to have an unhealthy vegetarian diet as it is to have an unhealthy meat-eating one, if you're vegetarian, to get the right balance, eat plenty of iron-rich foods like leafy green vegetables and unrefined cereals, especially wholemeal bread; calcium-rich foods such as any type of wheat, bread, nuts, sesame seeds and green veg, plus make sure you get enough protein by eating a good mixture of beans, soya products and textured vegetable protein, and cereals.

FRESH VERSUS FROZEN

The new advice stresses that we all need to be eating a lot more fruit and vegetables. A variety of fruit is usually available throughout the year, but availability of veg is more tricky. However, the good news is that frozen vegetables have been found to contain the same levels of vitamins as fresh (all contain as much Vitamin C as the fresh varieties, with spinach containing twice as much) although tinned vegetables have slightly less.

ARE YOU GETTING ENOUGH?

Experts views differ on the whole question of whether we need to supplement our diet with vitamins and minerals. Some say if you eat a balanced diet, it's unnecessary, others feel that the chances of any of us, particularly those that are restricting our diets in any way, like slimmers, would be hard pushed to get everything from the daily intake that their body needs to keep in tip top condition. Making sure you eat lots of fruit and vegetables certainly helps but the problem is that while few of us are truly deficient, we might well be performing ever so slightly under par . . . or maybe we're lethargic, or not quite ourselves.

At present, trials are being carried out to see how our vitamin and mineral levels affect our health and until then it's impossible to say what amounts of nutrients we need to stay well. And advice often doesn't take into account the lifestyle factors that can affect our levels of vitamins and minerals – stress, smoking as well as antibiotics, and even the Pill can deplete our vitamin and mineral levels.

Women who have heavy menstrual bleeds have an increased risk of being low in iron. Vegetarians too, need to keep a watch on their iron intake, as well as their calcium levels. Sometimes younger vegetarians may cut out all meat from their diet, without replacing it with other sources of protein. This can cause problems such as vitamin B12, as well as iron, deficiencies. Vegans too may be at a particular risk of deficiencies, including calcium.

If you feel well below par, or you're worried that your diet may not be providing all that you need, have a word with your doctor. He or she may well feel you would benefit from a vitamin and mineral supplement. Don't exceed recommended doses as high intakes of some vitamins and minerals can be dangerous.

EATING FOR YOUR BONES . . .

Dairy products have had a bad press over the last 20 years or so. As research revealed that high-fat diets increased your risk of heart disease – as well as putting on weight – women in particular seemed to ditch dairy products by the fridge load. Dairy equalled fat which equalled fattening. Women drank coffee black and the only cheese that ever passed their lips was the lumpy cottage variety.

The problem, though, with cutting dairy products from your diet is that you're depriving your body of a vital mineral – calcium. Calcium is particularly vital for our bones and if we don't get enough of it, we considerably increase our risk of developing osteoporosis, a condition where our bones become so porous that they break easily, causing painful fractures. Eating dairy foods is an easy way of increasing your calcium intake as it's one of the most readily absorbed forms of calcium.

Affecting one in three women, the disease generally doesn't strike until a woman is past her menopause and so it's often dismissed as a problem that happens to 'older women'. However, our bones grow from childhood through to about the age of 35 when the skeleton achieves its 'peak bone mass' and is at its strongest. After 35 we start to lose some of the calcium that makes the bones strong – which is why the calcium intake in the first half of our lives is so vital. But, we *all* increase our risk of osteoporosis if we:

- have a low intake of calcium, for example by avoiding dairy products
- lose an excessive amount of weight quickly
- have ever suffered from an eating disorder which may mean the body has gone short on calcium
- are deficient in Vitamin D which is needed for the absorption of calcium
- diet after pregnancy or are breast-feeding – a baby's development can deplete the mother's calcium stores at a much faster rate than usual
- live a sedentary life and do no exercise
- are of menopausal or post-menopausal age. In many cases menopausal women are offered HRT as this protects against bone loss, however not everyone can take HRT so, if this affects you, have a word with your doctor.

But the good news is that you can make sure you're feeding your bones properly by eating a calcium-rich diet. And that doesn't have to mean high fat. We've already seen that many manufacturers have risen to the low-fat challenge by introducing lower fat alternatives to traditionally high-fat foods.

So by using foods like skimmed milk and reduced-fat cheese (both of which, incidentally, contain more calcium than their higher fat counterparts), as well as other low-fat dairy products, plus tinned fish such as sardines, pilchards, salmon and so on, as well as calcium-rich dark green leafy vegetables including broccoli, spinach, watercress and spring greens, you can be sure to keep your calcium levels well and truly topped up. The latest thinking also stresses the importance of exercise which helps strengthens our bones – as well as increasing our energy output which means we get to feel fit as well as healthy.

To make sure you're eating a balanced diet, take a look at the menu plans and recipes in chapters sixteen and seventeen. They're proof that you *can* eat well by eating healthier foods and the good news is that all the food is as good for your heart as it is for your waistline!

Chapter Thirteen

Slimmers' Little Helpers

AS WE'VE SEEN, we all eat for different reasons: we have different tastes, cultures, incomes, lifestyles, personalities – and moods. And with so many factors determining what we eat, it's no wonder that we could often do with a little help. But, with so much around that, ostensibly, is there to make our lives easier, what's worth a try and, just as important, what's not worth the bother?

CLUBS

One of the most popular ways of getting support. They used to be very much associated with humiliation and it has to be said that some people still seem to expect to have to stand up and be balled out by a club leader for not reaching the prescribed target – even though this approach is now deemed to be old-fashioned, as well as ineffective.

According to one survey, nearly 900,000 people belong to a slimming club at any one time, which amounts to around 6 per cent of the adult population. Nowadays clubs have received support from some of the most respected quarters. Professor John Garrow, for example, one of Britain's leading experts on obesity, has said that one of the best ways the government can combat obesity is to set up affordable slimming groups, open to the public who want sound advice about dieting . . . Certainly the government could do worse than follow his advice.

All the major clubs now promote a healthy eating philosophy and their diets generally are based on three meals a day, plus a range of snacks and treats. The general format usually includes a weigh-in, a talk by the class leader on a particular aspect of healthy eating and weight control and, in some clubs, a project which involves all members. Some clubs also sell products and magazines.

The club you join can have more to do with convenience as much as anything else. While some 'townies' may be spoilt for choice, if you live in the country there might only be one slimming club within a 20 mile radius. Often held in church halls or community centres, some groups are daytime ones while others only meet in the evening.

Clubs are good for anyone who feels they can benefit from support, as well as advice, when they're trying to lose weight. There's nothing like knowing that there are people who really are in the same position as you. And most sessions are run by people who have previously had a weight problem which reinforces the feeling of 'being in it together'.

Going to a club also means you feel less isolated because you can share your problems with a group of people who are genuinely interested, as well as having the opportunity to discuss any area of concern with the person who is running the club – someone that has usually undergone training, albeit the in-house training devised by the clubs themselves. Many members also talk about how much they enjoy the camaraderie, which shouldn't be under-estimated. Knowing that you're going to enjoy yourself at the weekly meetings is a marvellous motivation when it comes to making sure that you keep going!

If you're unsure whether they're for you, many of the clubs are happy to let potential customers sit in for a meeting, free of charge, before they join, so they can see what they think. Club members meet on a weekly basis and many clubs charge members for missed sessions, unless they have prior warning.

However, clubs aren't for you if you have an eating disorder (many clubs won't take someone with a history of anorexia and bulimia nervosa), are pregnant (unless your doctor is kept informed) or are under 16. If you have diabetes or high blood pressure it is advisable to consult your doctor before joining a club.

Nationwide, the most popular clubs include Weight Watchers, Slimming Magazine Clubs and Slimming World. Scottish Slimmers (known as Weight Management in England) can be found as far north as the Shetlands and have classes that stretch as far south as Doncaster. Other clubs include Slimmer and Rosemary Conley Diet and Fitness Clubs, which are growing all the time.

Slimming Magazine Clubs

Launched in 1971. Nutritionist Dr Elizabeth Evans is their scientific director and she ensures that all diets, as well as the nutritional information given out at the clubs, are sound and that advice reflects the latest thinking and findings in the area. There are around 600 clubs throughout the country.

How it works: Each weekly meeting is taken by a trained club leader. Seventeen diets are on offer to suit different eating habits and food preferences, such as vegan, vegetarian and ethnic. All provide a minimum of 1000 calories a day and members are given an additional calorie allowance of up to 500 for women and 750 for men, to 'spend' how they choose. Emphasis is on calorie counting.

Cost: £6 to join, £2.90 for each visit. Once you reach your goal, the visits are free. There is also a six-week target weight maintenance plan – free if within 7 lbs of target.

Further information: Slimming Magazine Clubs, 9 Kendrick Mews, London SW7 3HG. Tel: 0171 225 1711.

Weight Watchers

Probably the best known slimming club, established in 1963. All diets are devised by nutritionists. There are approximately 5500 clubs.

How it works: Each weekly meeting is taken by a trained club lecturer.

There is basically one diet – the Slim & Trim programme, although a selection of 120 different meals and recipes are available to choose from which are geared towards different tastes and dietary preferences. All contain a minimum of 1200 calories a day for women. Rather than teaching people about calories, the emphasis is on 'portion control' and food groups.

Cost: £9 to join, £3.95 for each meeting. Visits are free once you get down to 7 lbs within your goal. Products are on sale.

Further information: Weight Watchers UK (Ltd), Kidwells Park House, Kidwells Park Drive, Maidenhead, Berkshire SL6 8YT. Tel: 01628 777077.

Slimming World

They have been around since 1969 and although they don't have the publicity machine that's available to Weight Watchers, they still run over 5000 clubs. Diets are approved by a nutritionist.

How it works: Weekly meetings, run by a trained club consultant. There are two basic diets – red and green, the latter for vegetarians. However, within that there is a range of recipes. They don't count calories, although each day's allowance is based on a minimum of 1000 calories. Their emphasis is on choosing from three groups of food – including treats, known to members as 'sins'.
Cost: £6.95 to join, £2.95 a class.
Further information: Slimming World, P.O. Box 55, Alfreton, Derbyshire DE55 4UE. Tel: 01773 521111.

Slimmer Clubs

Launched in 1968, there are 800 classes nationwide. Diets devised by nutritionist.
How it works: Weekly meetings held by trained adviser. Slimmer offer a selection box diet that allows a variety of swaps which cater for different tastes and preferences. Emphasis on calories – nothing lower than 1200 calories.
Cost: £6.50 to join; £3.20 each class.
Further information: Slimmer Clubs UK, Cholswell Court, Cholswell Road, Abingdon, Oxfordshire OX 13 6HW. Tel: 01235 550700

Scottish Slimmers and Weight Management

Launched in 1980, there are around 500 classes, 350 in Scotland. Diets devised by nutritionist.
How it works: Weekly meeting held by trained class manager. No calorie counting. Card system that offers choices for each meal, plus snacks (four for women; six for men). Emphasis on healthy eating.
Cost: Around £6 to join; £3.99 each class.
Further information: Scottish Slimmers and Weight Management, 11 Bonaccord Square, Aberdeen, AB1 2DJ. Tel: Freephone 0800 362636.

Rosemary Conley Diet and Fitness Clubs

Launched in 1993 by Rosemary Conley, there are around 155 clubs. All diets are low fat and are based on Rosemary's *Hip and Thigh* and *Complete Flat Stomach Diet*.
How it works: There are weekly meetings that last for one and a half hours. The first 45 minutes include a weigh-in and chat from instructor whilst the second 45 minutes is a work-out which can be followed 'as gently as you like', which is good news for those who can't remember

the last time they exercised! All instructors are RSA (Royal Society of Arts) qualified. *Cost*: £6 to join; £3.50 each class.

Further information: Quorn House, Meeting Street, Quorn, Loughborough, Leicestershire LE12 8EX. Tel: 01509 62022.

MEAL REPLACEMENTS

Designed to reduce the risk of nutritional inadequacy while helping the dieter achieve the required calorie reduction with the minimum of effort, the main criticism of meal replacements is that they do little to teach anyone about healthy eating. Let's face it, any system that encourages you to substitute a meal for a milkshake isn't going to endear itself to nutritionists and health educators who have worked for years trying to explain what constitutes a healthy diet. It's also worth mentioning that, as yet, it is believed that there are no scientific studies that have looked at the long-term effectiveness of meal replacements.

That said, obviously they work if you keep using them because the replacement drink, bar, biscuit or soup are likely to be lower in calories than what you would eat. The other advantage, claim the manufacturers, is that for people who find they have little time to get all the right nutrients they need in their diet, meal replacements represent a perfect answer because in one packet, you get everything you need for a 'balanced' meal. The only thing you don't get is the inconvenience of having to do any more than rip open a packet or mix up a shake. In theory a perfect answer to a perennial problem – how to get everything you need in one 'hit'.

Other advantages are that they're easy to prepare (some you only need to unwrap), there's no measuring and they're convenient because they're easy to fit in with the busiest lives – most of the replacements can be carried around in the same way that you might have taken a sandwich and a yoghurt.

Who would it suit: someone who doesn't have a lot to lose and someone who wants quick results. Many people complain that the meals are boring. It does certainly take the thought out of what to eat but you need to be pretty steely not to deviate.

Many of these systems are sold through 'counsellors' or even over the counter. The problem with both approaches – and particularly the latter – is that there is no one to give advice when needed. 'Counsellors' are trained by the meal replacement manufacturers and, with the best will in the world, these people may not be experienced in dealing with people who may have very real problems to do with the way they eat. And, if your relationship with food is a source of tension in your life, restricting food even further by relying on ready-prepared packs is not going to ease the relationship.

Which? magazine also found that biscuit meals tended to give you most of your calories from fat and sugar, drinks were high in sugar and some products contained little fibre. And being high in sugar, the sweetness simply establishes a taste for sweet foods, rather than introducing your tastebuds to a variety of tastes and textures. It also gets you used to eating bars and biscuits, which is not necessarily a step forward on the road to healthy eating . . .

Many of the products also don't give advice about who shouldn't use them. Diabetics, for example, may find they have severe problems because several of the meal replacements are high in sugar. The foods can also give the impression of a fast, rapid weight loss . . . something that many unsuccessful slimmers may find is yet another disappointment in their lives.

The other negative is cost. When the Consumer's Association's *Which?* carried out a survey on slimming plans, they discovered that meals with normal food tended to be cheaper than the meal replacements – and some substantially so.

Jane Dunkeld, in *The Good Diet Guide*, feels the main reservation about meal replacements – apart from not doing anything to help re-educate our eating habits into healthier ones – is that many people used the plans badly. Although many of the powders were supposed to be mixed with milk, some users used water instead, in the hope of a quicker weight loss. This, of course, means the body will get far less nutrients than it's supposed to as the vitamins and minerals that you're get from the plan are worked out all very precisely – and mixing the drinks with milk is a central part of that equation.

Another disadvantage is that the replacements contained bulkers and fillers – to help fill you up. This can cause dehydration if you don't increase your fluid intake. Some people had reported feeling so full that they skipped lunch which, once again, is likely to upset the balance of the overall plan. So, if you do use any of these plans, it's vital you follow the instructions to the letter.

Apart from doing little to help us to adopt healthier eating habits, these products are unlikely to cause most people long-term harm. And the length of time most people tend to use them seems to be self-limiting because people get bored with the repetitive daily eating plans. 'Of course you could make yourself a low-calorie breakfast or lunch for much less money than a meal replacement, and in many cases it would be more nutritious too,' believes Jane Dunkeld. 'But if you can't be bothered to count calories yourself, or it is inconvenient to cook, or you want something quickly,' her conclusion is that 'there is no harm in using these products'.

It's worth noting though that while these meal replacements may be useful in the short term, once you've lost the weight you wanted to, you'll go straight back to your old eating habits – the eating habits that helped you to gain weight in the first place.

SLIMMING FOODS

There seems to have been an explosion on the calorie-counted meal front. Nearly all the major stores now have their very own calorie-counted ranges – either flagged up by flashes that declare 'under 300 calories', or described with slimmers' words like 'Lean', 'Healthy', 'Low', 'Light' (or increasingly, 'Lite') or, the rather more traditional, 'Diet'.

While that can be very good news for people who find it hard to assess how much energy is in what they eat, the bad news is that one report, carried out by the Food Commission, claimed that some manufacturers were charging up to a staggering 40 per cent *more* for low-fat versions of their products. While many manufacturers explain this increase as being down to more expensive ingredients being used as well as extra processing costs, it is interesting that some companies, for example Marks and Spencer and Ambrosia, charged no more for their low-fat versions than they did for their regular ready meals and desserts.

The other complaint that has been levelled at 'healthier' and 'calorie-counted' versions of standard meals is the portion size which some slimmers consider 'meagre'. Another problem is that some people find they actually put on weight when they first start using low-fat products – mainly because they think low fat is akin to no fat so they eat as much as they want.

Ready-prepared meals certainly have a place when you're trying to cut down on what you're eating: they're convenient and you at least know how much energy you're taking in. They're also handy to have in the freezer for those times when you don't have the time, or inclination to cook, but don't want to overeat. However, as a regular way of eating they can work out to be extremely costly and they don't necessarily contribute much to the family ambience at meal times if you're tucking into your portion of 'no more than 300 calories' while the rest of the family are working their way through soup, meat, veg, rice and pudding. Surely better for your morale, as well as their health, for you all to eat the same food – all low in fat but equally high in taste? Turn to chapter seventeen for some ideas on recipes to please all the family.

PILLS AND POTIONS

Many of the commercially available products contain appetite suppressants in the form of either methyl cellulose or glucose. However, as they can be bought over the counter they are only licensed to contain a limited amount of these ingredients which, some experts feel, may mean that they have a very limited effect – if any. Also however much they may or may not reduce your appetite, they do nothing to change your eating habits.

DOCTORS, DIETICIANS, CLINICS

Doctors may offer general dietary advice but many will refer you to a dietician for help. Dieticians offer diet sheets and advice and will, where possible, try to devise an eating regime to suit your lifestyle. In some cases of obesity you may be referred to a specialist clinic where treatment will include dietary and psychological advice plus, in some cases, drug treatment. Appetite suppressants and metabolism-enhancing drugs may be used and in cases where all approaches seem to fail, surgical intervention may be suggested, such as stomach stapling.

There are a number of private clinics offering treatment; however many have had a bad press for treating people who are not considered clinically obese – yet the clinics concerned have still charged the customer a hefty fee.

It's worth remembering that treatment and advice is available on the NHS, and if you feel you have a problem, you should ask your doctor for a referral to a clinic. What's on offer will probably vary from area to area, and if there isn't a clinic near you and you're prepared to travel, your doctor can refer you to one further afield.

HELP IN THE FUTURE . . .

American researchers have identified an obesity gene which is responsible for the production of a hormone, leptin, which, when injected into overweight mice, helps to suppress their appetite and speeds up their metabolism. The mice then burn off enough body fat to get them down to a 'normal' weight: the more leptin the mice were given, the more weight they lost.

Apparently leptin is produced by a specific gene and it helps the body control its own weight by telling us when it has had enough food. When our body gets that message, it stops eating. However, the American research suggests that if we're lacking in leptin, then there is nothing to let our body know that it's had enough . . . and the result is we eat too much and end up vastly overweight.

In fact more than one obesity gene has been identified and although the research has exciting potential, some scientists have pointed out that just because something works with mice, it doesn't always follow that the same results will occur in humans. For example, as humans we often have a relatively higher level of leptin in our bloodstream – regardless of our weight. So, although in some cases obesity may be caused by a fault in our system, the experts are by no means certain what – or where – that fault lies.

Obviously research has yet to start on humans but if the results from the mice experiments are repeated on people, it could make a huge difference to the treatments available to those that are obese. Experts believe that in a small number of cases, obesity could be caused by minor genetic defects. But, as Dr Andrew Prentice, from the Medical Research Centre's laboratory in Cambridge concludes, after a massive seven-year research that looked at why we put on weight, 'obesity rates in this country are soaring too fast to blame it all on changes in our genes. Much of the obesity in society has to do with non-genetic factors . . . high-fat diet and our modern sedentary lifestyle'.

Chapter Fourteen

Moving swiftly on . . .

A FUNNY THING happened to me while I was writing this book. Like many journalists, I never seemed to have enough time to finish everything. Those deadlines loom and life becomes one huge panic that involves endless weeks sat upright (with inclinations to slouch as the weeks progress!) at the computer, myopically facing the screen.

While I have sat, cosseted away in purdah, my body has remained largely immobile. Literally. My diet has stayed almost the same as when I go to an outside office to work, possibly with the addition of more teas and coffees. However, the funny thing that has happened is that I've put on weight. Not a huge amount, I'll grant you. But enough for me to feel a tightening of the trousers and notice a swelling of the stomach. The last time I experienced a similar condition, it was known as pregnancy. Now my condition is sedentary.

Interestingly, the *British Medical Journal* carried an article submitted by the Dunn Clinical Nutrition Centre in Cambridge about this very subject – they referred to the evidence that suggests inactivity can be as much a cause of someone's weight problems as overeating.

MODERN TIMES

There's no secret that, as a nation, we're getting fatter but what isn't quite so commonly commented on is that, according to research, as a nation we are also actually eating considerably *less*.

As we've seen, obesity can't be blamed on just one factor, although your genes, your background and generally the life you lead will play a part. However, the one certainty that all the experts do agree on is that people get obese when there is a continuous imbalance between the energy they eat and the energy they use. So, if all the evidence shows that we're eating less and still putting on weight the reason is quite simple – it's our energy output that's at fault: our bodies are just not working hard enough to use up the energy we're feeding them.

When you think about it we shouldn't be too surprised by this observation. Our homes are filled with labour-saving devices, we travel everywhere by car (or bus or train, but rarely walk) and we spend most of the time when we're not working, sitting in front of the television. Apparently, the average person in Britain now watches a minimum of 26 hours of television a week – that's double what it was in the Sixties. If the trend continues, we'll have little time left for anything else. To a certain extent, that's already happened in America where the couch potato syndrome has now been identified as one of the most important causes of childhood and adolescent obesity.

But you don't have to be a telly moron to register as inactive. By day many of us sit in front of computer screens, by night videos. But while we seem to excel at conserving energy, we're pretty pathetic at expending it. One of the most telling reports on the subject was published by the Health Education Authority and the Sports Council and was based on a survey carried out by Allied Dunbar. The survey revealed that:

- Although 80 per cent of the adult population believe that regular exercise is important for health, seven out of ten men and eight out of ten women do not do enough in an average week to keep themselves healthy.
- One third of men and two-thirds of women are unable to continue walking at a reasonable pace up a gentle slope (that's one in 20 . . .) without becoming breathless, finding it physically demanding and having to slow down or stop.
- Among 16 to 24 year-olds, 70 per cent of men and over 90 per cent of women are below the activity levels necessary for a fit and healthy life.
- Sustaining a reasonable walking pace for several minutes on level ground constitutes severe exertion for half the women over 55.

Now if you think none of this applies to you, one last figure from the survey. Eighty per cent of both men and women of all ages believed themselves to be fit and the majority believed that they did enough exercise to keep fit. However, when their activity levels were examined, it was shown that their assumption was actually incorrect – not only were they unfit but the amount of exercise they did wasn't going to make them any fitter.

So, if you've ever felt breathless after running up the stairs at home, stiff when you stretch or find that unexpected exercise has left you feeling as if your body is about to seize up, chances are you're less fit than you think. And if you think that as long as you 'watch' what you eat, your body can take care of itself, you couldn't be more wrong. Experts are increasingly convinced that if you are overweight, you need to be as concerned about what you do as much as what you eat.

Apart from anything else, if we don't make full use of our bodies they start to deteriorate. Our muscles get weaker and our circulation becomes sluggish. Think of your body as a car – if it stands idle for any length of time and you don't give it a regular run around, then eventually the chances are it will refuse to start.

BUT HOW WILL EXERCISE HELP ME?

As we've seen, if you're serious about doing something about your weight, then you need to accept that what you do with your body is as important as what you put into it. But the good news is that research is increasingly showing that exercise can play a large part in helping you keep your weight down.

Studies show that those who run, jog, cycle or go to aerobics weigh less than those who do no exercise. Even regular walking has been shown to keep the weight down. In fact men and women who are physically active are less likely to put on weight than their more sedentary friends and adding exercise to a weight-loss programme means you'll lose more than by simply changing your eating habits – however healthy those changes may be.

Even the *Which? Way to Slim* survey, carried out by the Consumer's Association back in 1978, reported that nearly half of the male slimmers and quarter of the female slimmers who filled in their survey form said they had 'got fat when they stopped taking regular exercise'. And experts have found that even the effect of a small amount of exercise in keeping your weight down makes a difference – as was discovered when people stopped doing it. 'If you drive half a mile to the station every day instead of walking,' the survey revealed, 'at the end of the year you may find yourself nearly half a stone heavier . . .'

So, I'm afraid there's no escape. Thin or fat, it's time for all of us to rise from our chairs, couches and cars – and get moving. As a nation we've moved from being both physically active with a limited choice and availability of food, to being basically sedentary beings with endless access to an unlimited supply and variety of food.

But if exercise can help stop us putting back on the weight that we've lost, it can also be used to increase the metabolic rate and decrease the proportion of fat to muscle. Regular exercise helps to replace fat with muscle. Muscle burns more calories than fat so the leaner you are the higher your metabolic rate. To enthusiasts exercise is becoming something of the elixir of the Nineties. And when you weigh up the evidence, it's easy to see why. Regular physical activity can help reduce our risk of a number of major diseases like high blood pressure, coronary heart disease, diabetes and strokes as well as helping to reduce cholesterol levels and ease circulation problems.

But apart from strengthening our heart, improving our circulation and increasing the capacity and efficiency of our lungs, exercise considerably increases our bone density which means it offers protection against the bone-thinning disease, osteoporosis, which can make the bones brittle and more liable to fracture.

But if all these long-term benefits are hard to grasp, you could think more short term. Exercise reduces stress and makes you *feel* good – and that really is official! Exercise stimulates the release of endorphins, which are the body's natural painkillers, and these produce a general feeling of well-being. In fact, the evidence is so strong that doctors have recommended exercise as a way of relieving depression as well as insomnia. In some parts of the country, doctors are even issuing prescriptions that entitle patients to membership of health and exercise clubs because they're so convinced by the evidence concerning the benefits of regular exercise.

And one last advantage that is worth mentioning. Exercise takes your mind off food – which is not an inconsiderable factor to consider when you're trying to lose weight . . .

THE LEAST YOU CAN GET AWAY WITH . . .

The minimum to aim for is 20 to 30 minutes, at least three times a week. But, it doesn't matter if it takes you some time to get there – any exercise is better than none.

What's more, the good news is that you certainly don't have to attend regular sessions where you're exposed to pulsating music and surrounded by lithe young things clad in lycra from neck to toe! Increasing your level of activity doesn't mean you *have* to take up a sport or even begin a formal programme of exercise.

But it is important to find something you like. The majority of people who take up sport drop out within a short space of time and while practical reasons play a part (can't get back in time to pick the kids up; classes are held at inconvenient times), one of the overriding reasons seems to be boredom. People are taking up exercise because they feel they *should* but they're not actually doing anything they *like*. The result, not too surprisingly, is that they stop doing it.

So, if you're not sure what appeals and, like me, the last time you really thought about exercising was when you played for the school netball team, then be an aerobic butterfly for a couple of months – leaping around from activity to activity, until you find something that you genuinely enjoy. Also try to rope in a friend or partner: if there's a social element to what you do, there's a greater chance that you'll stick with it – and thoroughly enjoy yourself into the bargain.

WHAT'S BEST FOR ME?

Aerobic exercises (walking, jogging, cycling, swimming, etc.) generally do the most good because they work all the large muscle groups (for example the legs and trunk) as well as the heart, lungs and circulatory system. The other form of exercise is known as anaerobic and these involve sharp, short bursts of muscle activity – the sort of movements that are required for squash or tennis.

The Breath Test

For exercise to be really beneficial you need to do it vigorously enough to work up a bit of puff! This means you'll initially feel a little breathless but you should still be able to hold a conversation. If you can't, you're doing too much. The activity should make you feel slightly warm as well but if you're out of breath, you're doing too much.

Be Safe, not Sorry

A word of warning. If you're not used to exercise, it's important to remember that aerobic exercise should be built up slowly. If you're unfit, your muscles may be short of oxygen so you won't get an adequate supply when you exercise.

To be on the safe side, if you really are unused to being active and still have quite a bit of weight to lose, check with your doctor before you undertake any regular exercise, particularly if your newly found enthusiasm ends up making you undertake a schedule which, prior to reading this, would have produced a glazed expression and a quick retreat!

If you have high blood pressure, a heart condition, or suffer with asthma or arthritis, do inform your doctor before undertaking anything and the same applies if you've recently had an operation.

Whatever your state of health, it's always important to start with relatively gentle exercises, then build up to something more strenuous as you become fitter. It's important to spend at least five minutes at the beginning and at the end of each session with gentle stretching routines (the infamous warming-up and winding, or cooling, down), as this gradually increases the supply of energy to your muscles, ensuring that they work at their best, and avoiding the chance of damage such as a tear or strain: they also help reduce after-class stiffness the following day.

New to the Game?

If you are, it's often worth joining some organized group or class that is run by a qualified instructor. That way you can be sure that the amount of physical activity you're undertaking is the right level for you and that all the exercises – whether warm-ups or press-ups – are properly supervised. If you don't feel happy with the idea of going to something organized, or simply can't fit it into your day, then try a video or a sound tape (see Going It Alone, page 197).

PICKING THE EXERCISE TO FIT YOUR STYLE

If you've decided that you are going to give exercise a try, the information below should provide a good starting point. Remember, if you're unsure what you'd enjoy, then try a variety of ways of exercising. Most classes and health centres are happy to let you have a 'try-out'. You might even find that you enjoy several different types of exercise. So, if you want to swim once a week but spend your other 30 minute blocks of exercise walking, or even at an actual exercise class, it's up to you.

No one says you have to lock yourself into, say, jogging three times a week, all alone when you'd rather do something that the rest of the family can join in with. The idea is that you enjoy the increased physical activity, rather than view it as a penance. The more you enjoy it, the more chance there is that you'll stick with it.

And if none of the activities below appeal, bear in mind you can still increase your fitness by putting the physical activity back into your everyday life. Hoovering, cleaning, gardening, even DIY, are all ways to increase your heartbeat and get your body moving – provided they're carried out vigorously.

Walking

You may not think of walking as real exercise but it is. In fact, if you walk an extra mile every day for a year, you could lose 10 lbs, and that's without any form of dieting! Walking is a good starting point for the type of person who rarely exercises as it can be fitted in whenever you have the time. You don't need to book classes or wear special clothes – it's all down to you. That said, a general stroll down your local high street for a touch of window shopping is *not* considered exercise. For walking to have any effect you need to aim to walk briskly, arms swinging as you go, for 20 to 30 minutes, at least three times a week. If you are unfit, though, start with five to ten minutes of brisk walking and build up the time gradually.

Swimming

Probably one of the best all-round activities, particularly if you're over-weight as the water supports your body. Most pools are open at a variety of hours so you can usually fit in a visit to suit your schedule. Check local pools for details. Ultimately you want to aim for 20 to 30 minutes non-stop swimming but you should build this up slowly, particularly if you're not used to exercise. Gentle swimming (any stroke you like) is fine to start with until you feel fit enough to build up to something more vigorous.

Jogging/running

Like walking, running or jogging, is cheap (although it's important to invest in a good pair of running shoes) and you can run when and where you want to. It's also a good exercise for both your heart and lungs and it's easy enough to pace yourself so that you stop when you feel your body has had enough. If you're relatively new to the exercise game, experts recommend that you start walking first and then build up to a jog.

Also the more overweight you are, the more important it is to start slowly as every time your feet hit the ground, you are putting three or four times your body weight on them. Hence the importance of buying a decent pair of trainers that are made specifically to take the weight of these types of activities. Ideally it's also better to jog or run on a soft surface, such as in a park where you can run on grass, as the shock to your body, caused by the pressure of landing on the ground, is partly absorbed by the soft ground.

Cycling

Some people prefer an exercise bike to the real thing and although you could miss out on fresh air and picturesque scenery, if you live near a main road in a busy town, the inside version of cycling may actually do your sensibilities, as well as your lungs, less harm! Obviously the easiest way of working cycling into your lifestyle is to cycle everywhere but the practicalities of doing this depend on where you live. Outdoor cycling can be an activity the whole family can share but if you're not sure it's for you, then try borrowing a bike. Like other exercises, start slowly and build up to longer and more frequent sessions, getting your legs to work harder as you get fitter. If you've opted for an exercise bike, once again build up slowly, although most machines can easily be adjusted so that you set yourself ever-increasing targets.

Aerobic exercise dance/classes

These are organized classes where the aim of the session is to swiftly move from one set of exercises to another, in time, to music. It's important to make sure the teacher is qualified so that she can assess what you can and can't do. Attempting any exercise that is beyond your level of fitness can be dangerous as well as painful, so you need to ensure that your teacher knows exactly what she's doing.

With any class, ensure that you have a five to ten minute warm-up and cool-down period which allows your body to adjust to the sharp change in pace. A good teacher will keep a watch on beginners and will usually suggest that you just do whatever you can – no one expects you to keep up when you've never done it before. The idea is not to be flat on your back in exhaustion within five minutes of starting – the aim is to be slightly out of breath – not totally breathless. And the most important rule is that if it hurts, stop IMMEDIATELY. Ask around for details of local classes, or at your local library.

Skipping

Yes, that old playground favourite offers a wonderful opportunity for cheap and convenient exercise, right on your doorstep. If you get bored, break off for a few minutes running on the spot. Once again start slowly and gradually build up your time.

. . . and the rest

Exercises like tennis and squash are excellent when it comes to overall fitness but as they involve a lot of stopping and starting they can be hard to maintain for any length of time without a break. So, strictly speaking, unless you have the stamina of André Agassi, the chances are you won't be exercising aerobically. And if you are overweight, and unused to exercise of any sort, these types of sports can put quite a strain on your body. In fact, just to sustain a game in something like squash or tennis, you need to be fairly fit in the first place.

Other exercises, like weight training, will also improve your overall strength and although they will probably get you huffing and puffing – which is what you need to improve your overall fitness – exercises like this aim to build up particular muscles, rather than building up your heart and lungs. So, if you really want to lose weight, as well as get fit, you're going to have to move your whole body, not just part of it!

Going It Alone

You may well find it more convenient, and even less embarrassing, to exercise in the privacy of your own home along with a video, or audio tape, for guidance. Tapes are available at most high street stores but whichever one you buy, make sure that the exercises have been put together by a qualified expert who knows what she's doing, or more accurately, what they're getting you to do. At certain times of the year the shops are hit by a rash of 'celebrity' tapes – while some might be safe and sound, others are decidedly dodgy, so do choose carefully. Opt for tapes where the instructor has a background in teaching exercise rather than just a desire to share their exercise secrets with you – read the info on the back of the tape box *before* you buy.

It's also important to make sure that you choose a tape that offers exercises that are at the right level for you. If you really are a beginner, then that's the level you want from a tape. Anything more advanced won't make you fitter. If anything it'll just make you depressed because you won't be able to keep up. There's no point in buying advanced aerobics when you haven't even reached first base! And if you don't like the idea of disembodied voices giving you instructions but you do like dancing, you can always dig out some old records and dance to them – if you've got kids, get them to join in too!

And Exercise for Those That Don't . . .

If the whole idea of exercise really does make you want to lie down in a darkened room, then you need to look at less obtrusive ways of boosting your activity level. If you take up some of the suggestions below then at least it will get you moving until you're ready to tackle something that requires a little more effort . . .

- Always, always use the stairs rather than the lift. The only time you have an excuse is if you have a buggy/baby with you!
- Every time you go up the stairs at home, try running up them.
- If you've taken the car (are you sure you couldn't have walked?) and you're parking in a car park, leave the car as far away from the entrance as possible.
- If you've only a short journey to make, don't wait for the bus – walk. You'll probably get there more quickly anyway.
- Get into the habit of taking a dog for a walk. Puppies are best as they move quickly and can keep going for ages. If you don't have a dog, don't you know someone who does?
- If there's music on the radio, and you're at home, dance.
- Offer to play chase with the kids.
- Hide all remote control boxes.
- If you do have to walk anywhere make sure you do it briskly, striding out, arms swaying to and fro.
- Think before you sink . . . whether it's into your car, an armchair, a park bench . . . think of whether you could be doing something to help burn up some of that excess fat. The more you get into the habit of using your body, the greater the difference it will make to your overall energy output.

At the end of the day, it's down to you to decide how active you want to be. As we've seen, even walking, which is cheap, easy to do and basically risk-free, is considered good news whether you're trying to lose or even simply maintain your weight. Anything that involves increased activity is an advantage – gardening, walking to get a paper, even sex (the more vigorous the better, say the experts!) count as beneficial exercise. The key, though, is to stick to it. Make it part of your routine, part of your life. You'll not only look better and feel better for it, but there's a pretty good chance that you'll also have an awful lot of fun. But don't take my word for it. Try it for yourself and see.

Chapter Fifteen

Dieting For Life

UP TO NOW, you've read an awful lot about why you eat and how you eat, as well as when you eat too much and when you don't eat enough. Hopefully you've also seen how to minimize your weaknesses and make the most of your strengths. So with a strategy firmly established in your mind, you now need to arm yourself with a stock of tactics to make your strategy a success. After all, however much you may understand the psychology of exactly *why* you find it hard to say 'no', at the end of the day you still have to cope with the weekly shopping at your local supermarket and the children's tea.

So what follows is a list of practical advice on what you can do to help yourself, as well as a look at some of the help that's on offer.

If you prefer a structured approach to eating, advice on portions as well as a selections of menu plans, can be found in chapters sixteen and seventeen. However, by adopting an altogether healthier approach to food and eating, you should find the weight starts to fall off, while you start to feel altogether fitter and healthier. But remember . . .

- Eat at least a pound of fresh fruit and vegetables a day. That works out at about eight portions a day - a piece of fruit is one portion but check the healthy eating pyramid on page 163 to remind yourself of exact amounts.
- Eat lots of starchy foods like brown rice, wholemeal pasta, bread, potatoes, beans and pulses, etc. Apart from filling you up, because they release glucose into the bloodstream slowly, you feel better for longer.
- Eat fish at least twice a week - oily fish at least once.
- Restrict red meat to twice a week. Replace it with poultry, fish or non-meat meals (discover lots of new ideas to tempt your tastebuds in chapter seventeen).

■ When you're hungry, eat - and when you're full, stop.
■ Eat breakfast - one piece of research showed that people who missed breakfast ended up eating 600 calories more than people who ate when they woke up.

MAKING THE MOST OF FOOD

You may already be following some of the suggestions but a quick read through may act as a useful reminder.

When you're eating

■ Make an occasion of the meal - whatever you're eating, do it sitting down at the table, with a knife and fork, the food served on a plate. Savour the food - even eating snacks should be an event.
■ Make yourself aware of what you're eating - concentrate on food as absent-minded eating is one of the main reasons that we have such a huge intake of fat. To stop yourself eating when you're doing something else, restrict eating to one room - the kitchen, for example.
■ Put your knife and fork down between mouthfuls so that you give yourself the chance to taste what you're eating rather than just bolting it down.
■ Try to eat more slowly. The more you chew, the more aware you are of what you eat.
■ Leave a gap between courses. Firstly it will give you an opportunity to sit and relax but secondly it gives you a chance to feel full: it takes around 15 to 20 minutes for us to feel full after we start eating and for the brain to sense how much food has been eaten, so the longer you can leave between one course and the next the better!
■ Don't leave serving dishes on the table. That way they're less easy to dip into and nibble at when you've finished eating. If the food isn't staring you in the face, there's less chance of you eating seconds - unless you actually want it.
■ Say no when you want to - and don't let anyone persuade you otherwise!
■ If food is left over, get it out of sight as soon as you can. Plates full of leftovers are just asking to be nibbled at . . . !
■ If you're hungry, head for carbohydrate-based foods rather than fatty ones. Apart from the fact that they'll do you more good,

research has shown that carbohydrates are more satisfying to eat than fat so they not only fill you up but you remain fuller for longer. So, say yes to rice, potatoes, pasta and bread which have fewer calories than foods which contain fat. But, remember to be wary of creamy sauces, rich toppings and thick spreads – all of which are high in fat.

- If you know you have a tendency to overeat, drink a glass of water about 20 minutes before a meal as it reduces your appetite. It's also an effective way of taking the edge off your hunger as well as quelling cravings which may have more to do with thirst than anything else.
- Try to have soup as a starter as high-fibre low-fat varieties (like vegetable or lentil) appease the appetite so you'll end up eating less.

When you're shopping

- Write a list – and stick to it. That way you won't 'impulse' buy what you don't need or don't really want.
- Don't shop when you're hungry.
- If possible, don't shop with children. You may intend to stick to your list but I've yet to meet a mother who can do it with a child in tow!
- Don't be sucked in by 'two for the price of one' promotions. If you wouldn't normally have bought it, then however cheap two of the same products are, it's even cheaper when you buy neither.
- Check labels – particularly when it comes to margarines and spreads. Reduced fat can mean reduced by five or 25 plus per cent so always look at the label before you buy.
- Lower sugar doesn't mean low sugar. Once again check. The higher up the ingredient is on the label, the more there is in the product. And look out for words like glucose, sucrose, fructose, malt extract, syrup and so on. The names may not be so familiar but it still means sugar.
- Don't assume low fat means low energy – and that's particularly true of non-savoury foods. Many average 5oz (150ml) pots of low-fat yoghurt can notch up 160 calories.
- Always opt for leaner cuts of meat or, even better, fish.
- Try to avoid processed foods but if you do like to eat sausages and beefburgers occasionally, check out the lower fat varieties first.

There's about 21g of fat in two ordinary sausages (and remember experts recommend we should eat no more than 30g in a whole day!) but about half that in lower fat varieties.

■ Whenever possible switch to skimmed milk. If you don't like the taste, go for semi-skimmed.

When you're cooking

■ If you're using pastry, try to use filo (available from most supermarkets). It contains less fat than other pastry although it still needs brushing with oil or butter, so do so sparingly.

■ Try to fry as little as possible. The oil alone can double your energy intake.

■ If you need to fry, put a little oil on some kitchen towel and rub round the pan. Alternately, use a spray oil which squirts out minute amounts at a time.

■ Grill whenever you can, but without adding fat. By marinating food (strips of chicken, or meat) beforehand, you get a tasty meal, full of flavour. If you worry that the food may dry out, either brush with a little oil or lemon juice.

■ Try steaming or baking rather than frying.

■ If you like thick soups and casseroles, try thickening them with puréed vegetables or natural yoghurt rather than cream.

■ Use less meat when you're cooking. Bulk out meals with pulses, beans and veg.

■ Always remove visible fat from meat.

■ Try to use mashed potato rather than pastry when you're making savoury pies.

■ When casseroling make it a day ahead. That way you have time to let the casserole get cold and the fat will float to the top of the saucepan so you can simply skim it off.

■ If casseroling chicken, remove skin first as most of the fat is found under the skin.

■ If roasting, use a trivet or a rack so that the fat drips into the pan. Cover food with greaseproof paper or foil and baste regularly to stop meat drying out.

■ It can be hard to tell how much fat there is in mince - even the fairly red looking sort can be quite fatty. Either buy extra lean mince or place the mince in a pan, covered with water and bring to the boil. After five minutes or so, remove from the heat and let the pan cool. As it cools, the fat will rise to the top of the pan making it easy to skim off or pour away.

- If you want to reduce the fat in your gravy, as with the mince, let it get cold, then skim off the fat before you re-heat and serve.
- If you like cheese, opt for lower or reduced fat versions. Low fat no longer just means cottage cheese. Low-fat hard cheeses are available from Cheddar to Red Leicester.
- Spice up your meals – spicy food quells the appetite more than blander foods, so you eat less.

When you're eating out

- Avoid buffets – unless you can resist temptation!
- Avoid anything fried or sautéed or deep fried. Go for roast, grilled, steamed, poached, baked or cooked 'in own juice'.
- Reserve fatty foods like duck or goose for special occasions.
- Cream sauces are high in fat so if there's an alternative, opt for that.
- Take advantage of the variety of vegetables on offer. They're filling, high in nutrients and low in calories. And even better – you haven't had to wash, scrub, peel, chop or slice them!
- If you know you have a tendency to graze, make sure the rolls and bread sticks are placed under someone else's nose.
- If a main meal is served with something you'd rather not have, ask the waiter to swap it for something else.
- For starters opt for melons and clear or vegetable soups rather than pâtés or fried food like whitebait or fried mushrooms.
- Go for jacket or new potatoes rather than chips or roast.
- If you've opted for a low-fat salad, don't turn it into a high-fat side dish by adding dressing. Try a squeeze of lemon juice instead.
- If you like dessert, opt for sorbets, ice-cream, strawberries or fresh fruit salad.
- Try to avoid foods flavoured with monosodium glutamate which can end up stimulating your appetite rather than suppressing it.
- Above all, remember you are the customer. You have every right to ask the waiter to explain how food is cooked, or what a dish is served with. And if you end up with something that you really don't like, say so. It's your stomach, your health and, on a more practical note, it's also your bill!

ARE YOU GETTING ENOUGH?

Sometimes slimmers skip meals rather than risk the overeating that may come from facing a full dish of food. But the truth is the more you reduce the energy content of your diet, the more chance there is that your body is going short of essential nutrients. Also the more you cut down on what you eat, the more hungry you get and the more chance there is that you will dive into the first available food you can find – regardless of its nutritional content. Simply cutting down on the food you eat is not the successful way to lose weight – not if means you're always hungry. So:

- don't skip meals – it's better to eat a little of something than nothing at all.
- And don't skip breakfast! It's tempting, particularly when you're in a hurry, but evidence shows that eating a high-fibre breakfast can help you to cut down on food because it makes you feel full for longer. This means it helps beat the urge to snack – and that's official! One recent study revealed that over a period of three months, slimmers who ate a low-fat, high-carbohydrate breakfast (a high-fibre cereal and toast), lost an average of 4 lbs (1.8kg) more than those who didn't.
- Get your biological clock into a regular eating pattern. Slimmers tend to be chaotic eaters and this means they're more likely to impulse eat. By getting into the habit of eating regular meals, your body gets used to being fed at certain times – rather than throughout the day.

SMALLER APPETITE, BETTER HEALTH

Experts stress that it's important to eat a variety of different foods – but not all at the same time! It seems our appetite goes into overdrive when it's presented with a larger than normal choice of tastes. For example, one study revealed that when a group were presented with plates of just cheese sandwiches, they tended to eat what they wanted, and left the rest: there was a limit to how much of the same they could stomach. However, when another group were presented with a selection of sandwiches – all different tastes and textures – considerably more were eaten.

In prehistoric times this self-limiting ability was probably very useful. It meant that we only ate what we needed of a particular food, while our bodies instinctively knew that they had to leave space for other foods, containing different essential nutrients. However, when we transport this ability to the Nineties, the result is that we are able to stuff ourselves silly with a main course, only to discover that we still have 'room' for pudding. So, to stop your body going into taste overload, particularly when you're presented with a 'help-yourself' invitation, stick with two to three types of foods, rather than tasting everything you can see. And eat just enough rather than too much. That way you don't get left with a nasty aftertaste that needs to be superseded by another taste before it will go away . . .

So, if you do feel you eat far too much, how do you get yourself to eat less? 'Hunger is all to do with what your stomach expects,' says Professor John Garrow, so teach it to expect less, and you'll no longer want to keep eating more. But, practically speaking, there *are* steps you can take to help yourself.

- Remove temptations – particularly if you're someone whose appetite is stimulated by the sight or smell of food.
- Keep a diary so that you learn to recognize your triggers.
- Take the edge off your appetite by drinking a glass of water 20 minutes or so before you eat – it'll mean there's less chance of you pigging out.
- If you're peckish, snack on fruit or pieces of vegetable. Or have a cup of low-calorie soup, or even try one of the low-calorie chocolate drinks like Options. Once again it'll take the edge off your appetite but it also treats your body to something warm and comforting.

And when you feel you want to eat but suspect that you're not actually hungry, try the 'the Five Step Hunger Test' below. All you need to do is:

Stop . . . before you eat

Look . . . at what you're about to eat

Listen . . . to your hunger – is it emotional or is it physical?

Think . . . about what you really want. And if you're not sure try to put off the decision to eat, until you are.

Do . . . something else that will take your mind off food. Have a bath, phone a friend, curl up with a book, or magazine, strip a wall . . . it doesn't matter what it is as long as it's something YOU want to do.

FORBIDDEN FRUITS

Remember there's no such thing as a bad food and no foods should be forbidden. Putting a ban on any food is like raising a red rag to your appetite. And like the bull, your appetite will just go for it . . . regardless of what else you've eaten during the day. So, if you don't want your deprivation to lead to depravity, try to wean yourself off your favourites rather than going cold turkey. So, if you do like your piece of chocolate – fine. But limit how much of it you eat.

Staying in control . . .

One effective way of doing this comes from psychologist Dr Peter Honey. He suggests you take whatever it is that you find really irresistible, for example chocolate, then cut, or break, a small piece off and put it on a plate. Next, sit, relax and savour – every last bit of it. Think about how much you enjoyed it and think about how terrific it was to be in so much control of your appetite that you could eat a little – rather than all. Then get up, clear away the plate and leave the room. Do something completely different. If possible, something that'll keep your hands busy.

Do this whenever you feel like a treat over say, a week or two. Try to restrict it to no more than once a day. Be sure to savour the feeling of self-control as much as the enjoyment of the food.

The next stage of the exercise involves taking the treat and halving it. Wrap the other half well and place in the back of a cupboard. Then, sit, savour and enjoy the treat, in the same way that you did when you were having twice as much. Once again, congratulate yourself for being so in control and, once again, as soon as you've finished, move away swiftly and do something completely different.

On the following week, cut the treat in half but keep both in front of you. Eat one half and then wrap up the other one and put it away for another day. Did you do it? Once you have you're going to, quite rightly, feel proud of yourself for having such tremendous self-control. Again, once eaten, clear away the plate and go and do something else.

Finally, put your broken or cut treat, place on the plate and ask yourself whether you actually want it at all. If you do, then just cut off only what you want. Try to think about your hunger – what is it you really want – is it even this at all?

Eventually you'll stop even getting the treat out of the wrapper because suddenly it won't be that important. But as soon as it does become important *have it*. Once you realize that no one is stopping you from eating what you want you'll realize that you're the one in control and you have the power to say no to something as much as you might have said yes.

One other thing worth remembering. The actual stress of worrying about what you eat can actually cause you to overeat. So, it helps to find ways to relieve the stress – that way you stop worrying about food. Some experts recommend yoga, but other tried and tested relaxation methods include meditation, walking, aromatherapy treatments, going to the hairdresser (really!), running and almost any form of exercise – turn to Chapter Fourteen to find out the best exercise for you.

TREATING YOURSELF

If you do like chocolate, sweets and snacks you'll find that your desire for them will start to wane as you fill up on other more nutritious foods. The idea of developing a healthier approach to food is working out a diet full of foods that you enjoy – that way you'll stick with it. Cutting back on the fat in your diet doesn't mean you can't have treats anymore, but to stop you overindulging, what about some of the following?

Fun-size bars are good news because you get to finish a pack, or bar, and other self-limiting treats include Lo Bars, sachets of low-fat, low-calorie drinks and soups, diet chocolate mousse, portion of Chocolate

Flavour Bird's Angel Delight with No Added Sugar, Chocolate mini roll, chocolate muffin, two fingers of Kit Kat . . .

If you prefer savoury snacks, go for the lower fat options. *Twiglets* are a good choice or try *salted popcorn* rather than the toffee variety. A *hot crumpet or muffin* is always a real treat, or if you're peckish have a *slice of toast or a small seeded roll* which is filling, has great crunch appeal and tastes good too.

BE REALISTIC

Changing the eating habits of a lifetime isn't going to happen overnight. Make changes gradually - people who do are a lot more successful than people who attempt to make their 'new' way of eating radically different from the old way.

- Don't set yourself rigid goals that are inflexible. Start off by trying to maintain your weight. Once you've done that, you know you're on the right track.
- Remember you're aiming to lose one to two pounds a week. If you're doing that, you're doing brilliantly and the chances are the weight that's come off will stay off.
- Don't think in terms of a diet. A new way of eating is not like a course of antibiotics. Like a dog bought at Christmas, a healthier diet is a diet for life.
- Part of a healthier diet is a healthier lifestyle and that means introducing exercise into your life. Increasingly experts are discovering that revving up your output is becoming as important as re-assessing your input. Read more about upping your output in Chapter Fourteen.
- Don't think of food as threatening and something to fear. It's part of your life. Your aim is not to avoid it, just to re-think the way you eat and start to understand what you're eating and why.

The more you learn about food - what it contains and what it doesn't - the more you're in the position to make choices about what you eat as well as how you eat. And when that happens, you really are truly in control. Remember that although the process of eating can be a joy in itself, there's an unnatural balance in your life if it's the only joy. Discover new ways to indulge yourself. Let food play a part in your life . . . just make sure it isn't the major part.

PART THREE
The Diets

Chapter Sixteen

Eating for your Health

The last few chapters have concentrated on the theory of healthy eating along with suggestions and tips to help you buy, cook and eat in an altogether healthier way. I have tried to make realistic suggestions for cutting back both fat and sugar in your diet, although, as we've seen, the main problems often stem from eating too much fat. But don't forget it's essential we get some fat - albeit only a small amount.

Below are a selection of ideas, recipes and menu plans which, hopefully, show how easy it is to eat well by applying some of the basic principles of healthy eating. Eating healthily is about making as much use as possible of the variety of foods available. Remember it's all a question of balance, getting the mix right. So, eat what you enjoy, but go easy on foods that are as tough on your heart as they are on your waistline. With a little imagination, and the right information, you'll find that in no time at all you'll be eating your way to a fitter, leaner and healthier you.

ABOUT THE EATING PLANS

Below are a list of breakfast, lunch and supper ideas. The main meals are split into seven sections, each containing seven meals. I have done this because I hope it will show that there are no restrictions to eating well. Everyone can do it - whether you live alone, with a family or are vegetarian or even like to entertain.

All recipes can be adapted to suit your tastes so if you don't like chilli, leave it out, and if you prefer baked beans to kidney beans, then simply swap them. As long as you stay loosely within the food groups (vegetables, meat, beans and pulses, etc.) swapping like for like shouldn't make any difference to the overall taste of the recipe. The key is to experiment. What's important is that you end up with something you like, you eat – and you've enjoyed enough to make again.

With the suppers, or main meals, I deliberately haven't specified amounts of food like rice, pasta or vegetables because getting a fair proportion of your intake from vegetables and starchy foods is what you should be aiming for. Also, getting hung up on portion sizes and amounts can mean you end up developing an unnatural attitude to food – which is the last thing you want.

Quantities have been given in the recipes where, if you're not specific, you'll find the balance of foods will be affected and the recipes just won't work. That said, for vegetables I've given the number you need, rather than the weight. No one, but no one, should be wasting their time worrying about whether they should eat four or six ounces of an onion. Life is most definitely too short! Food is there to be eaten – not unnecessarily weighed and measured. If you're looking for guidance, though, stick with the amounts given in the healthy eating pyramid in chapter twelve.

Remember though, the first step is simply to adopt some of the basic principles of healthy eating which means eating a varied diet, with less fat and sugar and more starch and fibre. So, when it comes to vegetables with your meal, generally there's no reason why you shouldn't eat as much as you like – as long, of course, as the veg aren't fried or smothered in high-fat sauces!

I have also given a selection of starters as well as puddings. For many people, two courses are adequate but, if you prefer one to the other, I thought it useful to provide a selection of recipes for both. That way it's up to you to choose. Certainly having fruit as a dessert a couple of times a week is good news for increasing your fruit and fibre intake and a pot of low-fat, low-sugar yoghurt will give you a healthy dollop of calcium. There are plenty more tips about what are good news foods earlier in the book, but if in doubt, just flick back to the pyramid on page 163.

Overall I hope that the recipes and suggestions below will help you to devise a healthier way of eating to suit your mood, your tastebuds and your lifestyle. The suggestions under Lunches are lighter meals, mainly because most of us eat our main meal in the evening. However, if that doesn't fit in with your day, then swap them around. As long as only one meal is a main one, that's fine.

One final word – about calories. I deliberately *haven't* included calorie counts. This is because long term, the only way to really understand about a healthier way to eat is to get to know about the food you're eating. To decide against eating something because it's high in fat is a lot more useful than deciding against something because you may think it's too high in calories. Clearly some foods will contain more calories than others but, as we've seen, calories are only what you get when you add a bunch of nutrients together – what matters is what those nutrients are. So, a plate of pasta may have more calories in it than a bar of chocolate, but there's no prize for guessing which one is better for your health! The secret is to go for foods that are packed full of vitamins and minerals. Foods that will make you feel full, and nourished, for longer.

All the recipes given are low in fat and, if you do want to lose weight, as long as you eat no more than the portions suggested, you should find that the weight will start to drop off – slowly but surely. It will also make a difference if you opt for fruit and yoghurts at the end of a meal, rather than puddings, and up your fish intake as fish dishes tend to contain less fat than meat dishes. The same is true of bean and vegetable-based meals.

So, if it's weight loss you're after, follow these simple rules:

- Cut out puds
- Up your fish and vegetables
- Cut back on meat
- Watch your fat (even low-fat spreads *still* contain fat)
- Snack on fruit
- Fill up on fibre
- Get moving – remember, the greater your output, the less you need to worry about your input

And when you have those days when whatever you do, all roads seem to lead to your mouth – regardless of how much you've already eaten, then simply follow these five simple steps to eating when you really want to.

Stop . . . before you eat

Look . . . at what you're about to eat

Listen . . . to your hunger – is it emotional or is it physical?

Think . . . about what you really want. And if you're not sure try to put off the decision to eat, until you are.

Do . . . something else that will take your mind off food. Have a bath, phone a friend, curl up with a book, or magazine, strip a wall . . . it doesn't matter what it is as long as it's something YOU want to do.

And if you end up feeling that you really are hungering for food, always make sure you make the most of what you're eating.

Eating should always be an occasion so:

- Whatever you're eating, do it sitting down at the table, with a knife and fork, the food served on a plate. Enjoy and savour the food – even snacks should be an occasion.
- Concentrate on food. Absent-minded eating is one of the main reasons that we have such a huge intake of fat. To stop yourself eating when you're doing something else, restrict eating to one room – preferably the kitchen.
- Put your knife and fork down between mouthfuls so that you give yourself the chance to taste what you're eating rather than just bolt it down so that you make room for the next mouthful that's already loaded onto the fork before you've swallowed the one before.
- Try to eat more slowly. The more you chew, the more aware you are of what you eat.
- Try to leave a gap between courses. Firstly it will give you a chance to sit and relax but secondly it will give you a chance to feel full: it takes around 15 to 20 minutes for us to feel full after we start eating and for the brain to sense how much food has been eaten, so the longer you can leave between one course and the next, the better!

- Eat when you're hungry, stop when you've had enough.
- Don't leave serving dishes on the table. That way they're less easy to dip into and nibble at when you've finished eating. If the food isn't staring you in the face, there's less chance of you eating seconds – unless you actually want it.
- Say no when you want to – and don't let anyone persuade you otherwise!
- If food is left over, get it out of sight as soon as you can. Plates full of leftovers are just asking to be nibbled at . . .
- If you're hungry, head for carbohydrate-based foods rather than fatty ones. Apart from the fact that they'll do you more good, research has shown that carbohydrates are more satisfying to eat than fat so they not only fill you up but you remain fuller for longer. So, say yes to rice, potatoes, pasta and bread which fill your stomach up with fewer calories than foods which contain fat. But, remember to beware of creamy sauces, rich toppings and thick spreads – all of which are high in fat.
- If you know you have a tendency to overeat, drink a glass of water about 20 minutes before a meal as it can reduce your appetite. It's also an effective remedy for taking the edge off your hunger as well as quelling cravings which may have more to do with thirst than hunger.
- Try to have soup as a starter as high-fibre, low-fat soups (like vegetable or lentil) appease the appetite which reduces the chance of you overeating.

BREAKFAST IS A MUST

We tend not to give breakfast the respect it deserves. From the days our mothers told us we couldn't go out in the morning without 'something inside us', we've been fairly dismissive of a meal that we've generally squeezed in between getting up and getting out. But the advantages of breakfast are worth considering – whether you're interested in losing weight or simply just staying healthy.

- It affects your willpower as well as your brainpower. As well as being more likely to nibble, studies have revealed office workers found it more difficult to concentrate and worked at a slower rate without breakfast.

- Breakfast skippers have lower intakes of vitamins and minerals. A cereal breakfast, in particular, has been shown to result in significantly higher intakes of vitamins B1, B2, niacin, folate, B12, vitamin D, calcium and iron. Women who didn't start the day with a cereal were actually found to be lacking in folate and calcium to the extent that their levels were lower than those recommended.
- Studies in the USA have shown that breakfast skippers tend to have lower energy and nutrient intakes than those who eat breakfast.
- Drivers who go without have more accidents.
- During the morning at school, children who've skipped are slower, less creative and make more mistakes and are less able at PE. *But* . . .
- Lower fat and cholesterol intakes have also been reported in people who eat breakfast cereals.
- Cereals, in particular, provide a major source of fibre in our diet.
- Eating a cereal (particularly those fortified with vitamins and minerals) with skimmed milk provides a hefty dose of essential nutrients.
- In Australia it was reported that breakfast cereals contribute significantly to the trace elements that we consume – so they could play a role in our overall diet.
- Cereals in particular are low in fat, often rich in carbohydrate as well as high in fibre which means they conform perfectly to government recommendations regarding the sort of food we should be eating. And lastly, recent research seems to suggest that eating starch-rich foods like breakfast cereals leads to a lower overall intake of fat.
- High-fibre breakfasts means you're less likely to overeat at lunch. In other words, you feel full for longer and when the next meal comes along, you're not as hungry, so you eat less . . .

So breakfast really can help you lose weight!

SIMPLE WAYS TO EAT HEALTHILY

Breakfast menus

Most people agree that breakfast is the most rushed meal of the day and lack of time is the most frequently quoted reason given for skimping on, or even skipping, breakfast. So, whether you like a hearty start to the day or you tend to favour a quick re-fuel before you leave the house, below is a healthy selection of suggestions for breakfast. All are served with tea or coffee but use skimmed milk if possible. Also, if liked, have a small glass of orange juice. When having bread, or toast, opt for thickly sliced wholemeal.

- Thick slice of wholemeal bread, low-fat spread, topping of choice. Try reduced-sugar jams and marmalade, Marmite, peanut butter or reduced-fat cheeses.
- One or two Weetabix (depending on appetite!) with skimmed milk and a little sliced banana.
- Small bowl of no added sugar muesli (an average portion is about 1½ to 2oz/40 to 55g), with skimmed milk, add a dollop of low-fat plain yoghurt if liked. Beware though as muesli can end up an energy dense start to the day – even without added sugar. It still contains nuts, which are high in fat, and dried fruit, which contain sugar.
- Small bowl of any of the high-fibre breakfast cereals, e.g. bran flakes or bran sticks, skimmed milk, little sliced banana and kiwi.
- One poached, boiled or scrambled egg on slice wholemeal toast with low-fat spread.
- Bowl of porridge, add a little dried fruit if liked. If it needs sweetening, add artificial sweetener.
- Low-fat traditional breakfast: one well-grilled low-fat sausage, slice grilled best back bacon, grilled tomato and mushrooms. Small wholemeal roll.
- Poached haddock (small fillet is about 4oz/115 g), with grilled tomato or mushrooms, slice of wholemeal toast.
- Florida cocktail (segments of orange and grapefruit – use fresh or tins canned in own juice); slice of wholemeal toast, or wholemeal roll, with low-fat spread.
- Small bowl of fruit compote. Make up a large dish in advance, and keep in fridge. Choose an assortment of dried fruit (apricots, prunes, apples, pears, etc.) and after soaking, simmer according to instructions. Add artificial liquid sweetener, if liked.

Lunches and Light Meals Menus

For many of us lunch is a filler, something to plug the hunger gap until we eat our dinner in the evening. But however little time you designate for lunch, it's still important you have something that is nutritious and filling.

If you don't, then pretty quickly you're going to be thinking about food. So stave off mid-afternoon nibbling by eating a nourishing midday snack. And don't forget wherever you're eating it, make it as much of an occasion as possible. Set the table (or clear the desk!), sit down and take a little time to enjoy what you're eating, however modest. Enjoy the meal from beginning to end, clear away and then get on with the rest of the day.

Below are a variety of suggestions for lunch but what you eat will obviously depend on where you are at the time. Remember they are just recommendations and individual tastes will make a difference to what you will, and won't, want to eat. The plan is to give you an idea of just how much choice you have.

If you're at work and the shops near by don't seem to offer anything that fits in with your new healthier eating regime, take home-made sandwiches with you, using thickly cut slices of wholemeal bread. Failing that, if you're out and about, try to buy sandwiches from one of the supermarkets, or stores like Boots, where each pack is labelled. Just about every store now has a healthier option/low-fat range – if you can't find it, ask. And if they *don't* have one, ask why not!

Follow your sandwich, salad or cooked lunch with some fruit and a pot of low-fat diet yoghurt or fromage frais and a hot drink if liked. If you're looking for a quick, filling drink that will also fill you up, try one of the reduced-calorie cuppa soups – most supermarkets stock a variety of flavours. If you're vegetarian, all the following recipes work well using vegetarian cheese.

Croque-monsieur
2 slices of wholemeal bread
1 slice of reduced-fat sliced cheese
1oz (25g) ham
little mustard, if liked
lightly toasted bread

Cover one slice with cheese, the other with a little mustard, then ham. Place bread with cheese under grill until cheese is bubbling. Then sandwich together and serve with a little home-made coleslaw, made from shredded cabbage, carrots and a little reduced-fat mayonnaise to bind.

Poached haddock, topped with poached egg
Poach fish until cooked – about 10–15 minutes. Remove with slotted spoon and place on plate. Meanwhile, poach one egg in boiling water and

when cooked place on top of fish. Add a couple of slices of tomato and black pepper.

Cheese and pickle
Take 2 slices of wholemeal bread and cover one slice with 1½oz (40g) grated reduced-fat hard cheese. Add one tbsp of pickle and top with other slice of bread.

Scrambled eggs
1 or 2 eggs
2 tbsp skimmed milk
seasoning
To serve: snipped chives and slices of tomato.
Mix egg(s), milk and seasoning. Pour into non-stick pan and cook over a gentle heat, stirring frequently. When cooked, pile onto one slice of unbuttered toast. Top with chives and, if liked, thin slices of tomato.

Tuna sandwich
Make with two slices of wholemeal bread, around 2oz (55g) tuna, canned in brine, mixed with a little reduced fat mayonnaise, black pepper and as much cucumber, tomato, lettuce, spring onion, etc. as you want. If liked, mix in a spoonful of sweetcorn.

Egg mayonnaise sandwich
Make with two slices of wholemeal bread, one egg mashed with a little reduced-fat mayonnaise, black pepper and chives. Add lots of salad to add crunch to the smoothness of the mashed egg.

Beanie baked potato
The humble potato is often underrated but a baked potato with beans is positively packed with nutrients!
Bake a medium size potato in its skin (about 4–6oz/115–175g), and when cooked add reduced-sugar, reduced-salt baked beans. (For other fillings, see page 236)

Baked beans on toast
Use a small tin of baked beans (reduced sugar and salt). Warm through and pour on wholemeal toast.

Sardines on toast

Can (4oz/125g) of sardines, pilchards or mackerel in brine or tomato sauce, mashed. Add squeeze of lemon juice and black pepper if liked. Either serve on warm toast or sandwich between two slices of wholemeal bread, with salad.

Egg on toast

1 boiled or poached egg on toast.

Pitta pockets

1 wholemeal pitta, spread with humous then stuffed with sliced cabbage and salad. Alternatively, substitute thin slices of smoked turkey, chicken, ham or pastrami for the humous.

Soup and roll

Bowl (or two!) of soup – anything stock-based, as long as it doesn't include thickening ingredients like cream or full-fat milk. Check labels if using tins. Alternatively, make your own using 1-1½ lbs (450-675g) of vegetables (e.g. a mixture of carrots, leeks, onions, parsnips, turnips, courgettes, swede, tomatoes) plus 2-2½ pints (1.2-1.4l) stock, and seasoning. (See next chapter for ideas.) There's no need to brown the vegetables first. Place ingredients in a large saucepan, bring to the boil, then simmer until veg are soft. Liquidize if preferred. If you like thicker soups, add potatoes, or pulses like butter beans. Serve with crusty roll.

Banana sandwich

Mash one banana and sandwich between two slices of wholemeal bread spread with a little low-fat spread.

Pulse bowl

This is one, as they say, that can be made earlier! Use a selection of pulses (many supermarkets sell packs of mixed beans and pulses) and soak and cook according to instructions. For lunch mix a bowl of beans with celery, spring onion and apple. Add a little oil-free dressing. You could also add a little tuna to the beans instead of the celery and apple.

Quick pulses

As above but instead of having to soak and simmer, buy canned beans (e.g. kidney, cannellini, butter, etc.) which are ready to use in the time that it takes to open the can!

Fish fingers

Two fish fingers, grilled, served with grilled tomato and some baked beans.

Pizza roll

One soft wholemeal bap, cut in half. Spread both halves with a little tomato purée or tomato sauce. Sprinkle with some mixed herbs then cover with a little grated low-fat cheese, or use a low-fat cheese slice. Pop under grill until bubbling.

Stuffed sandwich

Two slices of wholemeal bread, filled with thinly sliced lean chicken, turkey, lamb, beef, prawns or grated low-fat cheese, plus lots of crunchy salad.

Fruit platter

Variety of fresh fruit, chopped, piled on to crunchy lettuce and cucumber. If liked, top with spoonfuls of cottage cheese, either plain or with pineapple.

Mixed salad bowl

Slice, chop and cut up as many vegetables and as much salad as you like. Try to include crunchy veg like cabbage and carrot. Then add up to 3oz (85g) of sliced, lean meat and/or grated low-fat cheese. Top with a dollop of one of the low-fat dressings, mix and serve with wholemeal roll.

Chicken salad

Small joint of chicken, skin removed, plus as much salad as you like or, dice lean, cooked chicken, a fresh peach, or mango, and serve on a bed of shredded lettuce.

Lemon prawn platter

Bowl of prawns, served on sliced lettuce. Top with juice of half lemon and black pepper. Serve with roll, if liked.

Dinners/Main Meal Menus

Below are a selection of dishes that will, hopefully, suit your tastebuds as much as your health. I have divided them up into seven sections (Eating for One, Family Eating, etc.) but this by no means is meant to provide a rigid structure to the meals that you eat. The idea is simply to show an example of just some of the dishes that look good, taste good – and will most certainly do you good, too! So, if you're cooking for a family, there's nothing to stop you flicking through the vegetarian menu plans in case you feel like whipping up a non-meat meal for a change.

However, if you do choose from, say, the Food for two menus, and there's four in your family, simply adapt the ingredients accordingly. I have also included a selection of starters and desserts. Most people nowadays seem to have either one or the other so by providing both, it's up to you to choose which you prefer. You'll notice, too, that there's a separate section called Desserts for Friends. While these are slightly more impressive, they are still, nonetheless, low fat. Of course you may decide not to have dessert at all, or would prefer to have some fruit or a yoghurt. That's fine. But if you have a family who are used to pudding, having a few healthier options up your sleeve may just come in handy!

Once again I haven't included calorie counts for the dishes. The idea is for you to enjoy what you're eating rather than worry about the calories. That said, if you are trying to lose weight, simply follow the recommended portion sizes where specified. As a rule, for an accompaniment to a main meal, have around 1½ to 2oz (40g–55g) rice or pasta (uncooked – remember it swells to just under double). However, it's worth saying that if you're used to eating a low-fibre, higher fat, sugary diet that's also high in energy and calories, you'll find that by following a healthier way of eating, you'll automatically start to lose some of the excess weight. Also by structuring your day so that you're having three filling and nutritious meals, the chances of you *wanting* to eat anything else are reduced considerably.

And if you do binge, overeat, have that bar of chocolate that's 'had its eye on you for ages' . . .? Remember, it doesn't much matter. Eating a little of what you fancy is no big deal. It's only a problem when what you fancy is high in fat and you don't stop at a little. At the end of the day what's important is the way in which you eat and the way you feel about eating. A healthy attitude is more likely to mean a healthy appetite.

Family meals (recipes start on page 227)
Turkey Burgers
Curry
Roasted Herb Chicken
Chicken Livers Supreme
Fish Mornay
Beef and Bean Tagine
Chicken Pilaf
Stir Fry
Basic Ragù
Shepherd's Pie
Tasty Lamb Hot Pot
Bean and Bacon Bake
Pasta and Tuna Sauce
Fish Cakes
Satay Style Chicken

Food for One
Gammon Steak
Speedy Stir Fry
Sweet and Sour Fillet
Turkey Chow Mein
Scrambled Egg with Salmon
Cornets of Cooked Meat
Solo Spirals
Haddock topped with Poached
   Egg
Fish Pizza
Tuna Pasta
Smoked Chicken Salad
Lamb Chops
Stuffed Jackets
Turkey Escalope with Orange
   Sauce
Chicken Kebab

Food for Two
Chicken Dijon
Gammon Steaks
Pork Glaze
Glazed Lamb
Speedy Stir Fry
Meatballs
Cajun Turkey
Tuna Patties
Fish Parcels
Mackerel in a Flash
Chicken with Barbecue Sauce
Chilli
Eggs Florentine
Cheese Ribbons

Vegetarian
Meatless Meatballs
Bean Quartet Casserole
Stuffed Aubergines
Hot 'n' Spicy Pasta Sauce
Spinach Pie
Crispy Quorn Pancakes
Vegetable Moussaka
Roots with Crunch Crust
Lentil Lasagne
Chickpea Curry
Stuffed Cabbage Parcels
Broccoli, Leek and Fennel Bake
Cheese and Mushroom Soufflé
Smoked Tofu Fingers
Mushroom Stroganoff
Lentil Burgers

Food for Friends

*Starters
Fresh Sardines
Melon and Mint
Grapefruit and Orange Segments
Carrot and Coriander Soup
Onion Soup
Lemon Prawns
Tuna and Beans
Marinated Mushrooms
Tomato Soup
Crudités
Pâté
Courgette Soup
Watercress Soup
Pea and Mint Soup

*Main Course
Turkey Escalopes with Orange
  Sauce
Fish Creole
Chilli
Tropical Chicken
Pork and Prune Casserole
Cheat's Tandoori Chicken
Kedgeree
Pasta with Pepper sauce
Trout Parcels
Salmon or Salmon Trout
Surf 'n' Turf Kebabs
Turkey Rondelles with
  Watercress Sauce
Redcurrant Lamb
Beef and Bean Tagine

*Desserts
Zabaglione
Fruit Fool
Lemon Cloud
Rhubarb Fool
Berry Brûlée
Exotic Fruit Platter
Filo Fruit Tarts
Meringue Nests
Berry Jelly
Gingered Fruit
Weight Watchers Dessert Bombe
Mint Coffee Cream
Hot Spiced Peaches
Pears in Red Wine

Family Puddings
Fruit Jelly
Fruit Kebabs
Berry Jelly
Fresh Fruit Platter
Stewed Rhubarb and Raisins
Baked Apples
Stewed Apples
Baked Bananas
Fruit Compote
Dieter's Ice-cream
Berry Bowl
Slices of Fresh Pinapple
Fresh Fruit Salad
Green Ginger

Chapter Seventeen

The Recipes

FAMILY MEALS (Each recipe serves four)

 **Turkey burgers**

---

*1lb (450g) turkey breasts, skin
  removed, minced*
1 onion, finely chopped
1 clove garlic, crushed

*1 tbsp fresh thyme or half tsp
  dried*
*1oz (25g) wholemeal
  breadcrumbs*

Blend ingredients well in large bowl and divide into four equal portions, shaped as burgers. Place under preheated grill for around 15 minutes, turning once, until evenly browned. If burgers look as if they are drying out, brush with a little oil. Alternatively, dry fry burgers in non-stick frying pan. If burgers start to stick add a little water – about 1 tbsp.

Curry

---

*1lb (450g) of either white fish,
  skinless chicken fillets or lean
  beef*
a little oil
1 onion
1 green/red pepper;
*1 tbsp curry powder of choice
  (e.g. hot or mild)*

1 tbsp flour
½ pint (300ml) stock
1 tsp lemon juice
1 apple, peeled and chopped
1 tbsp sultanas

Heat oil in pan and fry onion and pepper for five minutes. Stir in flour and curry powder and cook for one minute. Gradually blend in stock and lemon juice. Add apple, sultanas and fish or meat. Season. Cover and simmer for 25 minutes. Serve with rice and a dollop of low-fat plain yoghurt.

❦ Roasted herb chicken

1 medium size chicken	2 garlic cloves, crushed
1 tbsp fresh thyme (half tsp dried)	seasoning to taste
	1 tbsp honey
1 lemon	
1 onion	

Place chicken in roasting pan. Add chopped onion and garlic and add a little water. Place half lemon inside cavity. Brush chicken with a little warmed honey mixed with lemon juice from the remaining half of lemon. Add thyme and seasoning. Roast in medium oven, 180°C/340°F/Gas 4, for about one and a half hours, until chicken is cooked and juices run clear. If necessary, cover chicken for last half hour of cooking. If liked, add cut potatoes, carrots and parsnips to the pan.

❦ Chicken livers supreme

8oz (225g) chicken livers	1 tbsp fresh parsley or sage
2 tbsp dry white wine or sherry	(1 tsp if dried)
1 onion, sliced	1 tsp coarse grain mustard

Chop livers roughly, removing any fibrous threads, then rinse well until the water runs clear. Dry fry onions over a high heat, stirring frequently, for five minutes then add herbs and livers. Seal, then add wine or sherry, plus mustard. Lower heat and cook for five to ten minutes until livers are cooked through. When cooked thoroughly, serve with rice.

👻 Fish mornay

---

4 fillets of chunky fish (around
   6oz (175g) each)
1 tsp dried parsley
½ pint (300ml) skimmed milk
1 tbsp cornflour

2oz (55g) reduced-fat hard
   cheese, grated
1 tsp dried mustard
1oz (25g) wholemeal
   breadcrumbs

Place fish in large pan. Add milk and parsley and place on medium light. When simmering, cover and cook for around 20 minutes. When cooked, pour milk into a jug and make up to half a pint (275ml) with water. Pour into a saucepan. Mix cornflour with cold water to make smooth paste, then gradually add to milk and place over low light, stirring all the time. Bring to boil, then simmer for two minutes. Add 1oz (25g) cheese and cook until cheese is melted. Add seasoning and mustard. Mix well then pour over fish. Sprinkle with remaining cheese plus breadcrumbs and place in oven or under grill until the cheese is bubbling.

👻 Beef and bean tagine

12oz (350g) lean stewing beef,
   cubed
1 large onion, chopped
1 red pepper, sliced
14oz (400g) can kidney or
   butter beans
quarter pint beef stock

¼ pint/(125ml) red wine
1 tbsp flour
1 tbsp paprika
1 tsp cumin
seasoning to taste

Trim all visible fat from meat, dry fry until sealed. Remove from pan and set aside. Dry fry onion and pepper for five to ten minutes, then add meat. Sprinkle on flour and coat meat and onions thoroughly. Cook for one or two minutes then add stock, wine, seasoning and beans. Bring to boil and simmer for 1½ hours, until meat is tender.

🍏 Chicken pilaf

12oz (350g) cooked chicken, diced	1 leek, sliced
6oz (175g) mushrooms, sliced	1 garlic clove, crushed
4 tomatoes, skinned and roughly chopped	quarter tsp allspice
1 red pepper, deseeded and chopped	1 tsp ground or grated root ginger
1 onion, sliced	1 pint (600ml) chicken stock
	8oz (225g) rice

Dry fry onion and garlic for five to ten minutes, until onion becomes transparent. Add stock. Bring to boil and add rice, vegetables and seasoning. Fifteen minutes before rice is ready, add cooked chicken. Leave to simmer until rice is cooked through and chicken is hot. Add a little water if pan becomes dry.

🍏 Stir fry

1lb (450g) chicken skin removed, cut into strips (could also use lean beef)	4oz (115g) mangetout
a little oil	4oz (115g) beansprouts
1 green and red pepper, cut into strips	2 tbsp soy sauce

Pour oil into pan. When hot, add peppers and cook for a couple of minutes, stirring frequently. Add chicken and cook for five minutes, then add vegetables and soy sauce. Cook for a further five minutes, until chicken is tender. Serve.

👟 Basic ragù

1lb (450g) lean minced beef
1 onion, chopped
1 garlic clove, chopped
14oz (397g) can of plum
  tomatoes
2-4oz (55-115g) grated carrots

1 tsp oregano
2 tbsp passata or tomato purée
1 tsp paprika
black pepper

Dry fry the meat in a non-stick pan. Add other ingredients and simmer for 40 minutes. Use as basic for bolognaise sauce. If liked, add mushrooms, red and green peppers.

Shepherd's pie

Use basic ragù recipe, omitting tomatoes and passata. If liked, add peas and a little stock if mixture seems dry. Pour into ovenproof dish and top with 1 lb mashed potato. Dot top with half ounce (15g) low fat spread or brush with milk. Place in oven 200°C/400°F/Gas 6 for 30 minutes or so, until potato starts to brown.

👟 Tasty lamb hot pot

1½ lbs (675g) lean lamb, cut
  into pieces
1 onion, sliced
2 garlic cloves, chopped
6fl oz (175ml) passata
1 tbsp Worcestershire sauce

1 tsp rosemary
black pepper
around 4 medium size
  potatoes, sliced

Place all ingredients, except potatoes, in casserole dish. Add thin layer of scrubbed sliced potatoes, with sprinkle of rosemary on top. Place in oven on 200°C/400°F/Gas 6 for approximately one hour, until meat is tender.

❦ Bean and bacon bake

---

1 onion chopped
4 carrots, sliced
3 potatoes, diced
14oz (400g) can kidney beans
in spicy sauce
6oz (175g) smoked bacon,
chopped
¾ pint (425ml) stock

1 tsp Worcestershire sauce
2 slices wholemeal bread
quarter tsp marjoram
1 tsp paprika
seasoning to taste
1oz (25g) reduced-fat cheddar,
grated

Fry onion, carrots and potatoes in non-stick pan, stirring frequently, until onion is transparent. If pan dries out add a little water. Add bacon, cook for another five minutes. Add stock, bring to boil and simmer until potatoes and carrots are tender – about 20 mins – then stir in pulses, Worcestershire sauce and seasoning. Simmer for five minutes, then spoon into ovenproof dish. Meanwhile put bread, herbs and spices in food processor. Process until bread turns into breadcrumbs. Stir in grated cheese. Pour evenly on bean mixture and place under preheated grill until breadcrumbs are toasted and cheese is bubbling. Serve with salad.

❦ Pasta and tuna sauce

---

2 × 7oz (200g) can tuna in
brine
1 14oz (397g) can plum
tomatoes
2 tbsp tomato puree
1 tbsp oregano

black pepper
6oz (175g) sliced mushrooms
2oz (50g) pitted black olives,
halved, if liked

Place ingredients in saucepan. Mix well and break tomatoes up roughly with wooden spoon. Heat gently and simmer for 15 minutes, stirring occasionally. Serve with pasta.

🍅 Fish cakes

*1lb (450g) filleted and skinned
  cod or haddock
1 tbsp lemon juice
1 tsp grated lemon rind
1 tbsp horseradish sauce*

*4 fl oz (100 ml) skimmed milk
1 tbsp fresh parsley
12oz (750g) mashed potatoes
2 tbsp (approx) sesame seeds*

Put first seven ingredients in blender. Mix thoroughly. Shape into either four large or eight smaller fishcakes. Sprinkle top with sesame seeds, pat in and oven bake until golden, on 200°C/400°F/Gas 6, for around 25 minutes. Serve with salad.

🍅 Satay style chicken

*4 chicken portions (4-6oz/115-
  175g)
2 tbsps peanut butter (smooth is
  easier for coating)
2 tsp lemon juice*

*couple drops of soy sauce
pinch of chilli powder,
  coriander and cumin*

Mix ingredients thoroughly. Skin chicken and cut through chicken meat with sharp knife then spread sauce over chicken, ensuring evenly coated. Grill on a piece of foil, turning and basting frequently. When juices run clear, the chicken is cooked.

FOOD FOR ONE

Gammon steak

Grilled. If liked, top with one pineapple ring, taken from tin of pineapple canned in own juice or fresh peach half.

Speedy stir fry

In large pan stir fry as many vegetables as you can cope with peeling, slicing or chopping. Add 1 tbsp soy sauce, a little grated fresh ginger (or use half tsp). If ingredients dry out, add a splash of water. When vegetables start to soften, add 4oz (115g) cooked chicken, turkey or beef. Cook until chicken is hot.

Sweet and sour fillet

4oz (115g) pork fillet or chicken or turkey breast, seasoned. Grill with a little lemon juice for five to ten minutes each side, until cooked through. Meanwhile, in small saucepan heat 1½ tsp of marmalade, wine vinegar (or wine if easier!) orange juice and demarara sugar. Continue cooking until sauce becomes thick and syrupy then serve with meat.

🍏 Turkey chow mein

4oz (115g) cooked turkey (or chicken), diced	1 tbsp soy sauce
	pinch of chilli powder
3oz (85g) cooked noodles	1 tsp ground ginger
2 tbsp cooked petits pois	1 tbsp fresh coriander leaves
1 tbsp sweetcorn	black pepper
4 mushrooms, sliced	¼ pint stock

Place all ingredients in large saucepan. Bring to boil, stirring occasionally. Simmer for 15 minutes until meat is cooked through thoroughly.

🍏 Scrambled egg with salmon

1 egg	1oz (25g) smoked salmon, cut into slivers
2 tbsp skimmed milk	
seasoning	

Mix first three ingredients and pour into non-stick pan. Cook over gentle heat, stirring frequently to stop eggs sticking. Add spread and when melted add salmon pieces. When cooked pile on one slice of wholemeal toast.

❦ Cornets of cooked meat

4oz (115g) lean meat of your choice with all visible fat removed (choose from chicken, beef, lamb, ham, etc.)

Small baked potato plus steamed vegetables

Slice meat thinly, then gently place a finger on corner of a slice and roll it into a cornet. Repeat until all the slices are used up. Arrange the cornets on plate and, if liked, serve with a baked potato, and either a salad or lightly steamed vegetables of your choice.

❦ Solo spirals

1½-2oz (40-55g) pasta spirals
10oz (280g) can ratatouille

1 tbsp parmesan cheese or grated reduced-fat cheddar

Cook pasta. Meanwhile, warm through ratatouille. Add a little water if too thick. When piping hot, pour over cooked pasta and top with cheese.

❦ Haddock topped with poached egg

---

1 fillet (about 4-6oz/115-175g) of white fish e.g. cod or haddock

1 egg
1 tomato, sliced

Poach fish fillet until cooked – about 10-15 minutes. Remove with slotted spoon and place on plate. Meanwhile, poach one egg in boiling water and when cooked place on top of fish. Garnish with sliced tomato.

🍎 Fish pizza

---

1 cod fillet (about 4-6oz/115-175g), frozen if liked	*pinch dried basil*
spoonful or so of passata	*1 1oz slice of low-fat cheese*
	1 tomato, sliced

Grill fish on both side, for about five minutes. When cooked, spread with a little passata and basil. Top with cheese slice, plus slices of tomato and put back under the grill under cheese bubbles.

Tuna pasta

(See recipe for four on page 232 but use only 3½oz/90g tuna)

🍎 Smoked chicken salad

---

*Small smoked chicken breast
  (about 4oz/115g) sliced
half a mango (or could use
1 peach), sliced
little oil-free dressing*

Place chicken and mango on bed of green salad (watercress, shredded lettuce, etc.) and beansprouts. Drizzle over dressing before serving.

Lamb chops

Mix a little fresh rosemary, 2 tbsp orange juice, 1 tbsp soy sauce and brush over chops (approx 4oz/115g total weight). Grill until cooked through, spooning over sauce frequently to keep chops moist.

Stuffed jackets

Medium-sized jacket potato (about 6oz/175g), filled with either 4oz (115g) baked beans, sweetcorn, half tin of ratatouille, small tin of tuna, low-fat soft cheese (try 'light' garlic and herbs variety), a little grated reduced-fat hard cheese . . . the fillings are infinite, just make sure you opt for the low-fat ones though!

🐝 Turkey escalope with orange sauce

---

1 6oz (75g) turkey escalope
Sauce: half tbsp cornflour
*   blended with 1 tbsp water half*
*   tsp brown sugar; rind and*
*   juice of half an orange; half*
*   tsp ginger; seasoning*

Grill turkey, for five to ten minutes on each side, until cooked. While cooking, mix blended cornflour, juice, rind, sugar and ginger in a bowl. Heat sauce gently in saucepan for several minutes until it begins to thicken. Stir, then simmer for several minutes, check seasoning and serve with escalope.

🐝 Chicken kebab

4oz (115g) chicken breast,   *1 tsp oil*
*   cubed, marinated for 30*   *1 garlic clove, crushed*
*   minutes in 1 tbsp soy sauce,*
*   grated rind of 1 orange or*
*   lemon, ¼ tsp ground ginger*
*   powder, or tsp grated root*
*   ginger*

Place chicken on skewer, alternatively threading with vegetables of choice (choose from mushrooms, courgettes, onions, peppers, etc.) Place under hot grill, turn and baste frequently.

FOOD FOR TWO

😽 Chicken Dijon

8oz (225g) chicken breasts (all
   skin and visible fat removed)
1 orange - rind and juice
1 tbsp olive oil

4 tsp mild mustard (e.g. Dijon)
2 tbsp wine vinegar
1 tbsp honey
seasoning

Mix all ingredients well. Place chicken in shallow ovenproof dish. Spoon over marinade. Cover and leave in fridge overnight. Remove from fridge, uncover. Coat chicken in marinade and bake in oven (190°C/375°F/ Gas 5) until cooked through, around 45 minutes, frequently basting during cooking.

Gammon steaks

(See recipe on page 233 and double the quantities.)

😽 Pork glaze

About 8oz (225g) lean pork
   chops
1 tsp chopped sage
1 tbsp honey

4 fl oz (125ml) apple juice
seasoning

Mix sage, honey, juice and seasoning. Warm through and brush over chops. Grill, for approximately ten minutes, occasionally brushing with glaze.

😽 Glazed lamb

---

about 8oz (225g) lean lamb
   chops
2 tbsp redcurrant jelly

1 tsp fresh chopped mint or
half tsp dried

Mix redcurrant jelly and mint. Warm through and brush over chops. Place under grill until cooked through, basting regularly.

Speedy stir fry

(See recipe on page 233 and double the quantities.)

Meatballs

Use basic ragù sauce from page 231, using ½lb mince and omitting tinned tomatoes and passata. Instead add to raw ingredients 1 tsp dry mustard, 1 egg and 2oz wholemeal breadcrumbs. Mix well and form into tablespoonful-sized meatballs. Chill for 30 minutes then dry fry in non-stick pan to seal. Transfer to casserole and, if liked add 14oz (400g) can of tomatoes and herbs to make a sauce. Cook on 180°C/ 350°F/Gas 4 for 45–50 minutes until meatballs are cooked through.

🍒 Cajun turkey

1 onion	14oz (397g) can plum
1 lb (450g) turkey meat	tomatoes
(breasts, preferably) cut into	4oz (115g) green beans
strips.	4oz (115g) okra
a little spray oil	2 large carrots, cut into sticks
1" (2.5cm) root ginger, peeled	4 sticks celery, cut into sticks
and grated	quarter tsp chilli powder
2 cloves garlic	

Fry onion and turkey strips for around ten minutes, stirring frequently, until sealed. Add ginger, garlic, tomatoes and seasonings. Bring to boil, cover and cook until turkey is cooked through (about five to ten minutes). Stir in vegetables. Cook over high heat until soft. Serve with rice and green salad.

❦ Tuna patties

14oz (400g) can tuna drained	*1 tsp parsley*
4oz (100g) mashed potatoes	*2 tsp soy sauce*
half an onion, finely chopped	*2 tbsp plain low-fat yoghurt or*
1 tbsp chives	*low-fat fromage frais*

Mix all ingredients thoroughly and shape into four fish cakes. Place in fridge for 30 minutes so the mixture firms up. Top with a thin layer of rolled oats or a sprinkling of sesame seeds and bake for 20 minutes on 200°C/400°F/Gas 6 until golden brown.

❦ Fish parcels

2 6oz (175g) halibut steaks	*1 tbsp herbs – either tarragon,*
grated rind and juice of one	*dill or oregano*
lemon or lime	*seasoning to taste*

Mix rind, juice, herbs and seasoning. Take each fish steak and place on piece of foil (large enough to wrap fish in) and spoon over some juice. Wrap foil around fish loosely and place in shallow dish and cook for 20 minutes on 200°C/400°F/Gas 6.

❦ Mackerel in a flash

2 small mackerels per person,	*1 tsp ground coriander*
cleaned and filleted, or 4	*pinch of chilli powder, if liked*
mackerel fillets	*juice and rind of 1 orange,*
Black pepper	*1 lemon or lime*
1 tsp ground ginger	

Cut mackerel in half to make two fillets. Mix together pepper, ginger, coriander and chilli powder and rub onto flesh of each fillet. Heat a non-stick frying pan and fry fish, spice-side down for three to four minutes. Turn over and fry for another four minutes. Add rinds and juice and cook for several more minutes. To serve, lift fillets onto plates and spoon over juices.

❦ Chicken with barbecue sauce

---

8 chicken drumsticks or thighs
1 clove garlic, crushed
2 tbsp wine vinegar
1 tbsp soy sauce
1 tbsp Worcestershire sauce

1 tbs brown sauce
1 tbsp honey
1 tsp dry mustard
2 tbsp tomato ketchup

Take skin off chicken and use a sharp knife to make slashes at regular intervals in the chicken. Place chicken in shallow dish. Mix other ingredients together and pour over chicken. Leave to marinate, preferably overnight. Turn occasionally. Then either grill chicken, basting with sauce, or bake for one hour, on 200°C/400°F/Gas 6, until tender.

Chilli

Make ragù sauce as on page 231, adding either 1 tbsp chilli powder or one fresh chilli pepper, chopped, at start of cooking, plus 1 tsp cumin and 1 small tin kidney beans, drained.

❦ Eggs Florentine

---

1 lb (450g) fresh spinach
¼ pint semi-skimmed milk
1 bay leaf
2½ tsp cornflour
1 tsp vinegar

2 eggs
seasoning plus pinch of nutmeg
1oz (25g) grated half-fat
    cheddar cheese

Heat milk and bay leaf until almost boiling then remove from heat and leave to cool slightly. Meanwhile remove all stalks from spinach and wash leaves thoroughly. Cook spinach in large pan, without any extra water, for eight to ten minutes, stirring frequently until wilted. Increase heat to evaporate excess water. Drain in colander. Press firmly with plate to squeeze out any remaining water then spoon into flameproof shallow dish. Season with pepper and nutmeg. Remove bay leaf from milk, mix a little cooled milk with cornflour until smooth. Stir in remaining milk then cook, stirring over medium heat until thickened and smooth. Season. Half fill a frying pan with water. Add vinegar and bring to boil. Reduce heat to simmering and add eggs. Gently swirl water to help eggs keep their shape. Poach for three to four minutes, until just set. Lift out with slotted spoon and place on top of spinach. Spoon over sauce and sprinkle over cheddar. Cook under hot grill for five minutes or until sauce is bubbling.

 Cheese ribbons

---

3oz (70g) 'light' garlic and herb
  cream cheese
¼ pint (150ml) skimmed milk
2oz (50g) chopped walnuts or
  toasted almonds

black pepper
12oz (350g) cooked coloured
  pasta ribbons (e.g. spinach or
  tomato)

Melt cream cheese over low light. When it begins to melt, add other ingredients and leave on low light for five minutes, stirring – until ingredients are mixed thoroughly and form a creamy sauce.

VEGETARIAN

Meatless meatballs

4oz (115g) yellow split peas and
  2oz (55g) red lentils, soaked
  overnight
1oz (25g) blanched almonds,
  toasted
half tsp coriander seeds
grated rind of small lemon
1 garlic clove, crushed
2 tbsp wholemeal flour

quarter tsp bicarbonate of soda
seasoning
Sauce: 14oz (397g) can
  chopped tomatoes; 1 tbsp
  tomato purée; 1 small onion,
  chopped; 1 garlic clove,
  crushed; half bunch fresh
  basil leaves.

Boil peas and lentils in fresh water for 20–25 minutes, then drain and place in food processor. Blend until finely ground. Add almonds and coriander seeds and blend. Stir in lemon rind, garlic, flour, bicarbonate of soda and season well. Using wetted hands, shape into 12 equal-size balls and dust lightly with flour to coat. Place on lightly greased baking sheet and chill for 30 minutes. Cook in oven 200°C/400°F/Gas 6 for 25 minutes or until crisp and cooked through. Meanwhile, put chopped tomatoes, purée, onion and garlic into a pan and simmer for ten minutes. Pour into food processor and add basil leaves. Blend briefly. Season and serve hot with meatless meatballs.

🐛 Bean quartet casserole

---

1 onion	8oz (225g) French beans
1 garlic cloves, chopped finely	1 tsp cumin
14oz (397g) can tomatoes	1lb (450g) potatoes, mashed
14oz (400g) can kidney beans	2 carrots, mashed
14oz (400g) can butter beans	seasoning to taste
14oz (400g) can borlotti beans	2 tbsp grated low-fat vegetarian
1 tbsp Worcestershire sauce	cheese

Dry fry onions and garlic until onion becomes transparent – about ten minutes. Add tin tomatoes, beans and seasoning. Mix well and turn into ovenproof dish. Stir grated cheese and mashed carrot into mashed potato and cover beans. Place in oven for around 30 minutes on 190°C/375°F/Gas 5.

🐛 Stuffed aubergines

---

2 aubergines, cut in half	1oz (25g) dried fruit
8oz (225g) couscous	1 tsp ground coriander
1 onion, finely chopped	½ pint (300ml) veg stock
2 red peppers, deseeded and	seasoning
roughly chopped	

Cover couscous with stock and leave for around 30 minutes. Meanwhile blanch aubergines and peppers in hot water for a couple of minutes. Scoop out insides of aubergines then toss filling plus peppers, onions and fruit in a little olive oil. Add couscous and seasoning. Mix well and pile into aubergine shells. Place in ovenproof dish, cover with foil, then pop in oven on 190°C/375°F/Gas 5 for ten minutes.

♨ Hot 'n' spicy pasta sauce

---

1 clove garlic, crushed
1 onion, chopped
1 small chilli, chopped finely
2 tbsp capers
2oz (50g) pitted black olives,
    sliced

14oz (400g) can chopped
    tomatoes with herbs
black pepper

Fry onion and garlic in non-stick pan, until onion is transparent – five to ten minutes. Add remaining ingredients, stir well and simmer for ten minutes. If you like thicker sauce, add a tablespoon of tomato purée or passata. Serve with egg pasta noodles.

♨ Spinach pie

1lb (450g) spinach (frozen or
    fresh)
2 onions, sliced thinly
2 cloves garlic, crushed
1 tsp cumin
pinch of chilli powder if liked
seasoning

8oz (225g) low-fat soft cheese
    (either cottage cheese or
    low-fat curd)
2-3 tbsp passata
filo pastry (about 7 sheets)
2 tbsp melted half-fat butter

Dry fry onions and garlic until onion becomes transparent. Add cumin, chilli if liked, seasoning, spinach and cook through. Stir in cheese. Line baking dish with one sheet of filo pastry, brush lightly with half-fat butter. Repeat process with another two sheets of pastry. Roughly spread a thin layer of passata over pastry then spoon over spinach mixture. Top with another three layers of filo pastry, each one spread thinly with low fat butter. Take another sheet of filo and 'scrunch' it up and arrange on top of pie. Dab with a little melted butter. Place in oven 200°C/400°F/Gas 5 for 35 minutes – until pastry is browned.

✌ Crispy quorn pancakes

1lb (450g) Quorn, sliced (4oz/
  115g per person)
packet of thin pancakes
plum sauce
cucumber and spring onion, cut
  into fine strips

Marinade: 3 tbsp soy sauce; 1
  tbsp dry sherry; 2 tbsp hoisin
  sauce

Marinate Quorn strips for around 30 minutes in the sherry and soy and hoisin sauce, occasionally stirring. Stir fry Quorn strips for a few minutes – just to heat through. Serve with thin pancakes, plum sauce and strips of cucumber and spring onion.

✌ Vegetable moussaka

1½ lb (675g) potatoes, sliced
1 aubergine, sliced
1lb (450g) courgettes, sliced
1 onion, sliced
2 garlic cloves, crushed

14oz (397g) can of plum
  tomatoes
2 tbsp tomato purée
1 tsp basil
black pepper

Boil potatoes for ten minutes, then cool and slice thickly. Meanwhile, dry fry onion and garlic until onion becomes transparent, about five minutes. Then add tomatoes, purée, basil and pepper. Let mixture simmer for five to ten minutes. Meanwhile place layer of potatoes in baking dish, followed by layer of aubergines and then courgettes. Add half tomato mixture, then layers of vegetables, as before. Mix two eggs with half pint skimmed milk, add pepper and 1 tsp parmesan cheese and pour over vegetables. Bake for about 45 minutes on 200°C/400°F/Gas 6, until vegetables are soft and topping is golden.

Roots with crunch crust

---

2 lbs (900g) of mixed root
   vegetables, scrubbed, chopped
   and sliced
½ pint/300ml skimmed milk
bay leaf
1 onion, sliced
1 garlic clove, crushed

½ tsp marjoram
seasoning
4 tsp cornflour
pinch nutmeg
2 tbsp wholemeal breadcrumbs
1 tbsp parmesan
quarter tsp mixed herbs

Infuse bay leaf in ½ pint (300ml) hot milk for 30 minutes. Spray a little oil
into a non-stick pan, then fry onion and garlic until onion becomes
transparent. Add rest of vegetables plus marjoram and seasoning. Stir and
cook for five minutes. Pour vegetables into ovenproof dish. Remove bay
leaf from the milk, then mix cornflour with 2 tbsp milk and stir cornflour
mix into rest of milk in small saucepan, add nutmeg. Cook, stirring over
low heat until thickened and smooth. Pour on vegetables, mix thoroughly. Mix breadcrumbs with parmesan and seasoning plus quarter tsp
mixed herbs. Arrange evenly on top of vegetables – should be enough to
form a 'crust'. Cook in oven on 190°C/375°F/Gas 5 for 35 minutes.

Lentil lasagne

12oz (350g) red lentils (could
   use other coloured lentils but
   you'll need to pre-soak first)
pack of lasagne (go for ones that
   don't need pre-cooking)
14oz (397g) can of tomatoes
½ pint (300ml) vegetable stock
1 onion, chopped

1 garlic clove, crushed
½ tsp mixed herbs
1 pint (568ml) milk
2½oz (70g) half-fat butter
2½oz (70g) flour
2oz (55g) reduced-fat hard
   cheese, grated

Cook red lentils according to instructions. Then, add to a saucepan with
tomatoes, stock, onion, garlic and herbs. Simmer for ten minutes.
Meanwhile line an oven-proof dish with sheets of lasagne. Pour on half
of lentil mixture. Top with more pasta sheets, more lentils, then finish off
with a layer of pasta. Set aside. Melt half-fat butter in small saucepan, add

flour, stir well and cook for two minutes. Gradually add milk, stirring continuously until a smooth sauce has formed. Simmer for a couple of minutes, then pour sauce over pasta dish. Top with grated cheese and pop in oven for 25 minutes on 190°C/375°F/Gas 5, until bubbling.

😈 Chickpea curry

---

1 aubergine, cubed	½ pint (300ml) stock
1 onion, sliced	1 tsp curry (more if liked!)
2 crushed cloves garlic	1 tsp cumin
14oz (397g) can tomatoes	2 tbsp fresh coriander leaves
2 14oz (400g) cans chickpeas	

Fry aubergine, onion and garlic in a little spray oil, for around five minutes. Add tomatoes and stir well. Add chickpeas, tomatoes and spices and simmer for 45 minutes, until aubergines and chickpeas are soft.

😈 Stuffed cabbage parcels

---

1 Savoy cabbage	1-2oz (25-55g) currants, if liked
1 onion, sliced	
1 garlic clove, crushed	1-2 tbsp pinenuts
1lb (450g) cooked rice (either brown or wild)	red pepper coulis: 3 large red peppers, ¼ pint (150ml) stock,
½ pint (300ml) stock	1 garlic clove, crushed and chives
¼ tsp of ground coriander, cumin, turmeric	

Fry onion and garlic in a little spray oil until onion is transparent. Add stock, seasoning and cook for ten minutes. Add rice, and currants if liked, plus pinenuts. Stir well. Cool. Take eight large trimmed and blanched cabbage leaves and divide mixture between leaves, making sure to spoon into middle of leaves, leaving enough to wrap round mixture. 'Parcel' up each filled cabbage leaf, then place on lightly greased baking sheet and pop in oven for 15 minutes or so to heat through, on 190°C/375°F/Gas 5. Meanwhile, deseed red peppers and blanch in boiling water for a couple of minutes. Place in food processor and blend with stock and garlic. When smooth, pour into small saucepan and re-heat. Just before serving, add some snipped chives. Serve with cabbage parcels.

❦ Broccoli, leek and fennel bake

1lb (450g) broccoli, trimmed and cut into florets	2 eggs
1 large head of fennel, trimmed and thinly sliced	2 tbsp cornflour
2 medium leeks, trimmed and sliced	seasoning
	quarter tsp ground mace
1 pint (600ml) plain yoghurt	1oz (25g) parmesan cheese, grated
	1oz (25g) granary breadcrumbs

Wash vegetables well and steam for around ten minutes. Arrange in ovenproof dish. Mix together yoghurt, eggs and cornflour. Season well and add mace. Pour over vegetables and sprinkle with cheese and breadcrumbs. Cook in oven set at 190°C/375°F/Gas 5 for 35–40 minutes or until mixture is set and golden brown.

❦ Cheese and mushroom soufflé

1oz (25g) half-fat butter	½ tsp mustard powder
1½oz plain flour	black pepper
½ pint (300ml) skimmed milk	2 oz (55g) grated reduced-fat hard cheese
4 eggs, separated	
8oz (225g) mushrooms, sliced	

Melt half-fat butter and sauté mushrooms for a couple of minutes. Remove with slotted spoon, and set aside. Add flour and cook for one minute. Add milk, slowly, stirring constantly. Bring to boil and simmer for a few minutes until sauce thickens. Remove from heat and mix in yolks, mushrooms, mustard, cheese plus seasoning. Whisk whites until stiff then gently fold into custard mixture. Put in 2 pint soufflé dish and cook for 25 minutes, 190°C/375°F/Gas 5, until soufflé has risen and is brown.

😺 Smoked tofu fingers

---

*8oz (225g) smoked tofu, cut into
   equal fingers
1 egg, beaten*

*3oz (85g) wholemeal crumbs
1 tbsp sesame seeds*

Coat tofu fingers in egg, crumbs and seeds. Chill for 15 minutes. Place on lightly greased baking tray and oven bake for 20 minutes or so, on 200°C/ 400°F/Gas 6, until golden and crisp.

😺 Mushroom stroganoff

---

*1½lbs mushrooms, sliced
2 onions, sliced
1 clove of garlic, crushed
1 leek, sliced
1 tsp paprika*

*¼ tsp grated nutmeg
½ pint (300ml) vegetable stock
seasoning to taste
5oz (140g) pot low-fat plain
   yoghurt*

Lightly coat large frying pan with spray oil. Fry onions and leek. Add sliced mushrooms, ½ pint (300ml) vegetable stock and seasoning to taste. Simmer for 10-15 minutes, until mushrooms are tender. Remove from heat and stir in yoghurt.

😺 Lentil burgers

---

*4oz (115g) of both green and
   red lentils, soaked overnight
1 heaped tbsp crunchy peanut
   butter
3oz (85g) wholemeal
   breadcrumbs
1 tsp each ground cumin and
   coriander*

*pinch chilli powder
1-2 tbsp coriander leaves
1 garlic clove, crushed
1 tbsp wholemeal flour
1 egg, beaten
seasoning*

Drain lentils and place in food processor. Blend until finely ground then stir in peanut butter, 2oz (55g) breadcrumbs, cumin, coriander, chilli, coriander leaves, garlic, flour and seasoning. Put remaining breadcrumbs on one plate, beaten egg on another. Using wetted hands shape lentil mixture into four equal-sized burgers. Coat in egg and breadcrumbs then place on baking sheet and chill for 20 minutes. Spray oil into a large non-stick frying pan and cook burgers over a medium heat for 15 minutes, turning twice until crisp and cooked through.

FOOD FOR FRIENDS

Starters

Fresh sardines

(2–3 each), grilled with a little lemon juice.

Melon and mint

Melon balls served with sprigs of mint and 1 tbsp apple juice. Chilled.

Grapefruit and orange segments

Using pink grapefruits and large juicy oranges.

❦ Carrot and coriander soup

---

1 onion, peeled and sliced
1 potato, peeled and quartered
2 pints (1.2l) stock

1½ lbs (650g) carrots, sliced
2 tsp ground coriander

Bring ingredients to boil and simmer for about 30 minutes, until carrots are tender. Cool then liquidize soup until smooth.

❦ Onion soup

---

a little spray oil
1½lbs (675g) onions (preferably Spanish), peeled and sliced

1 tbsp flour
2 pints (1.2l) beef stock

Cook onions in oil until transparent, then add flour. Stir well. Add stock plus seasoning and simmer for about 30 minutes – until onion is soft.

Lemon prawns

Prawns, drizzled with fresh lemon juice served on shredded lettuce with bread sticks.

Tuna and beans

Can of tuna in brine, drained and mixed with can of cannellini beans, drained. Dress with a little oil-free dressing, mix well. Divide between four side plates. Top with thinly sliced onions and serve.

Marinated mushrooms

About 1lb (450g) button mushrooms, wiped, and sliced, marinated overnight in 4fl oz (100ml) wine, 1 tbsp olive oil; 1-2 garlic cloves, crushed; and 2 tbsps fresh parsley.

☘ Tomato soup

1 onion, sliced	*1 14oz (397g) can tomatoes*
1lb (450g) fresh tomatoes,	*1½ pints (850ml) stock*
* skinned*	*1 tsp fresh basil, chopped*

Place all ingredients in pan. Bring to boil, add seasoning and simmer for about 25 minutes. Cool, then roughly purée.

Crudités

Selection of stick size veg served with low fat dips.

Pâté

7oz (200g) canned smoked tuna or mackerel, mixed with 2oz (55g) low-fat cheese, 2 tsp lemon juice, little tomato purée and seasoning.

☘ Courgette soup

1 onion, sliced	*1½ lbs (675g) courgettes, sliced*
2 tomatoes, skinned and	*2 pints (1.2l) stock*
* chopped*	*pinch turmeric and seasoning*

Put all ingredients in pan, bring to boil and simmer for 25 minutes, until courgettes are soft. Cool, then purée.

Watercress soup

2 packs watercress, washed and chopped	*1 pint (568ml) skimmed milk*
1 onion, peeled and sliced	*1 pint (600ml) stock*
2 medium-size potatoes, peeled and quartered	*pinch of nutmeg*
	seasoning

Put all ingredients in pan (reserving some watercress for serving), bring to boil and simmer for about 25 minutes. Cool then liquidize.

🍎 Pea and mint soup

1lb (450g) frozen minted peas	*1½ pints (850ml) stock*
1 onion sliced	*seasoning*

Put all ingredients in pan, bring to boil and simmer for about ten minutes. Cool, liquidize, then, if necessary, sieve.

Main courses

🍎 Turkey escalopes with orange sauce

4 turkey breast steaks (about 6oz (175g) each)	*1 tbsp white wine vinegar*
1 tsp olive oil	*½ pint (300ml) chicken stock*
1 orange	*5 tsp cornflour*
	seasoning

One at a time place turkey steaks in polybag and flatten with rolling pin. Brush each lightly with a little oil. Heat a non-stick frying pan and cook turkey over a high heat for 5 minutes each side until golden. Meanwhile using a vegetable peeler, pare rind from orange and cut into fine strips. Halve and squeeze out juice. Remove turkey from pan and add vinegar and stock. Bring to boil, stirring and scraping base of pan to remove sediment. Mix juice and cornflour together until smooth and stir into pan. Stir over medium heat until thickened and smooth. Season well and stir in orange strips. Add turkey and spoon over sauce. Simmer for five minutes, stirring occasionally. Serve.

🥄 Fish creole

1½lbs (675g) fresh fish or 2lb
(900g) bag of frozen seafood
cocktail, available at
supermarkets
1 garlic clove, crushed
1 onion, chopped
2 peppers (red or yellow) cut
into strips

3 sliced tomatoes
¼ pint (150ml) dry white wine
¼ pint (150ml) stock
2 to 3 dashes of Tabasco sauce
seasoning, to taste

Dry fry onions and garlic in non-stick pan, stirring frequently. If onions start to stick, add a little water. When onions are transparent, add peppers and cook for five minutes. Add rest of ingredients, bring to boil and simmer for approximately 25 minutes, until fish is thoroughly cooked.

Chilli

Make meat sauce for ragù recipe, as on page 231, adding ¼ tsp chilli powder, ¼ tsp sweet paprika, half tsp cumin and 14oz (400g) can kidney beans, drained.

🥄 Tropical chicken (could also use lamb or lean gammon)

---

1 chicken, cut into portions
1 red pepper, sliced
1 tsp cumin
1 tsp paprika

seasoning
1 7oz (200g) tin of pineapple
pieces, canned in own juice
8fl oz (250 ml) chicken stock

Place chicken in casserole with pepper, spices and seasoning. Cover and cook for about one hour on 180°C/350°F/Gas 4. Add pineapple pieces and juice and cook for a further 25 minutes, until chicken is tender.

🍒 Pork and prune casserole

---

4 boneless pork loin chops,
  trimmed (around 6oz/475g
  each)
1 tbsp olive oil
2 leeks, washed, trimmed and
  sliced
1 tbsp plain flour

½ pint (300ml) stock
¼ pint (150ml) dry cider
4oz (115g) ready-to-eat pitted
  prunes
1 tbsp fresh chopped sage or
  1 tsp dried seasoning

Heat olive oil in large flameproof casserole. Cook chops over high heat for ten minutes, turning frequently until golden. Remove from pan. Add leeks and cook over low heat for five minutes until softened. Stir in flour and cook for one minute. Gradually stir in stock and cider. Stir over medium heat until thickened slightly and boiling. Add prunes, sage, chops and season well. Cover and cook in oven at 180°C/350°F/Gas 4 for around one hour. To serve, place chops on plates and spoon over sauce and garnish with fresh sage.

🍒 Cheat's tandoori chicken

---

1 medium-size chicken, cut into
  portions
1 onion
1 garlic clove
2 tbsp lemon juice
½ tsp paprika

½ tsp coriander
¼ tsp cayenne
pinch turmeric
2-3 tbsps Tandoori paste
2 × 5oz (150g) pots of plain
  low-fat yoghurt

Remove skin from chicken and make slashes deep into meat, at around half inch intervals. Place in dish. Put other ingredients in mixture, and mix until roughly puréed. Pour sauce over chicken, making sure it seeps into meat. Place in fridge to marinate – preferably overnight. Ensuring chicken is fully covered with sauce, place in oven, for first ten minutes on 220°C/425°F/Gas 7, then turn down to 180°C/350°F/Gas 4 for around one and a half hours.

✾ Kedgeree

12oz (350g) smoked haddock	*1 tsp curry paste*
4oz (115g) rice	*1 tsp turmeric*
8oz (225g) peas	*2-3 tbsps fresh parsley*
½ onion, chopped	
2 hard-boiled eggs, cut into	
quarters	

Poach fish until tender – about 15 minutes. Drain and flake. Cook rice and peas and dry fry onion for five to eight minutes until transparent. Add fish, peas, onion, curry paste, turmeric and seasoning to rice. Mix and heat thoroughly. Add hard-boiled eggs, parsley and serve.

✾ Pasta with pepper sauce

---

1 onion, sliced	*1 5oz (140g) pot of plain low-*
2 cloves garlic, crushed	*fat yoghurt*
half bunch fresh basil	*basil leaves, to serve*
black pepper	*pasta of choice*
4-6 peppers (depending on size):	
ideally red, yellow or orange;	
deseeded and sliced	

Fry onion and garlic in a little spray oil, until onion becomes transparent. Then add peppers, basil and seasonings. Cook until peppers are soft, add a little passata if sauce becomes dry. Leave to cool, then purée. Warm through and add small pot of plain low-fat yoghurt and serve with pasta. Garnish with basil leaves.

❦ Trout parcels

4 trout	*little sunflower oil for greasing*
1 tbsp fresh tarragon	*small knob of half-fat butter*
lemon juice	*(about ½ oz/15g or 1 tsp)*
black pepper	

Clean fish under cold running water. Dry with kitchen roll. Place each trout on a large piece of greased, greaseproof paper. Mix tarragon, juice and pepper and spoon into cavity. Add small knob of half-fat butter. Wrap fish loosely and place in shallow dish. Cook for 25 minutes in oven at 180 °C/350 °F/Gas 4. Serve with salad and rice.

❦ Salmon or salmon trout

1 large salmon or salmon trout	*seasoning*
(about 3½ lbs/1½kg), cleaned	*a little oil for cooking*
1 lemon	

Place whole fish in large piece of foil that has been brushed lightly with a little oil or melted half-fat butter. Place slices of lemon on top of fish and season. Wrap foil loosely around fish. Place wrapped fish in large roasting dish and cook in oven at 190 °C/375 °F/Gas 5 for 20 minutes per lb. When cooked, remove from oven and leave to cool. Serve with salad and new potatoes.

❦ Surf 'n' Turf Kebabs

8oz (225g) meaty white fish e.g.	*2oz (55g) button mushrooms*
monkfish, cod, halibut	*1 lime or lemon*
8oz (225g) rump steak	*1 tbsp chopped dill*
4oz (115g) cucumber	*4 fl oz (125ml) vinaigrette*

Cut fish and meat into one inch (2.5 cm) cubes. Cut cucumber lengthways and slice into chunks. Peel prawns, halve mushrooms. Thread skewer alternatively with fish, meat, cucumber, lime (or lemon), prawns and mushrooms. Place on grill pan and cover with vinaigrette and dill. Grill, turning frequently to ensure kebabs are cooked evenly – ten minutes approximately.

✿ Turkey rondelles with watercress sauce

1½ lbs (675g) turkey mince
1 onion, finely chopped
½ tsp dried marjoram or
  oregano
1 egg
3 oz (85g) wholemeal
  breadcrumbs
seasoning
pinch grated nutmeg

Sauce: 1 spring onion, trimmed
  and finely chopped; 1 bunch
  watercress, washed and
  stalks removed; ½ pint
  skimmed or semi-skimmed
  milk; ¼ pint (150ml) yoghurt,
  2 tbsp cornflour, 3-4 tbsp
  fresh parsley

Put mince in bowl and stir in onion, marjoram or oregano, egg and half the breadcrumbs. Season well and add nutmeg. Using slightly wetted hands, divide mixture equally into eight portions and shape into rounds. Pat remaining breadcrumbs onto rondelles to coat lightly then place on baking sheet. Chill for 30 minutes. Cook in oven at 200 °C/400 °F/Gas 6 for 25 minutes or until cooked through. Meanwhile put spring onion, watercress leaves and milk into a pan. Heat until almost boiling. Mix yoghurt and cornflour together and stir in. Stir over medium heat until thickened and smooth. Simmer for three minutes. Blend sauce briefly in food processor then return to pan and reheat. Season well. Add nutmeg, stir in parsley and serve.

✿ Redcurrant lamb

---

8 × 3oz (75g) loin lamb chops
3 tbsp redcurrant jelly
4 tbsps cranberry or orange
  juice

2 crushed garlic cloves
1 tbsp mint
½ pint (300ml) vegetable stock

Trim away excess fat and place chops in shallow dish. In saucepan mix jelly, garlic, juice and herbs. Stir over low heat until jelly melts. Pour over chops and set aside for at least 30 minutes. Remove chops, reserving sauce. Grill meat for five minutes, each side, until cooked through. Return sauce to saucepan, bring to boil and reduce liquid until it is syrupy - about ten minutes. Stir in stock and return to boil. Add seasoning to taste. Place chops on plate and serve with redcurrant gravy, plus vegetables of your choice.

DESSERTS (FOR ENTERTAINING)

🦃 Zabaglione

---

4 egg yolks   *4fl oz (125ml) Marsala wine*
1½oz (40g) caster sugar

In a large bowl, beat egg yolks and sugar together. Mix in Marsala. Put bowl over saucepan of simmering water and gently heat, whisking until mixture is thick and creamy. Pour into six ramekins, or glasses, top with slices of kiwi and chill until ready to serve.

Fruit fool

8oz (225g) puréed strawberries, raspberries or blackberries (could use frozen berries, but make sure they're well drained): reserve some for decoration.

Mix puréed fruit with ½ pint custard (use low-fat varieties – sachets will do), mixed with ½ tsp vanilla extract, plus ½ pint (300ml) plain, unsweetened yoghurt. Artificial sweetener to taste. Pour into serving dishes. Place reserved berries on top. Chill until ready to serve.

🦃 Lemon cloud

3oz (75g) caster sugar   *3 egg whites, whisked into stiff*
3 lemons – rind and juice   *peaks*
½oz (15g) gelatine

Put juice in jug and make up to 4fl oz (125ml) with water. Place in saucepan, bring gently to boil and add rind. Remove from heat and cool. Strain (keeping some of the rind) and place in pan with sugar. Heat until sugar has dissolved. Once again leave to cool. Meanwhile, stand a small basin in a pan of simmering water and place gelatine with 4 tbsp of cooled mixture. Leave to dissolve over low heat. Stir in lemon mixture and ½ pint (300ml) of water. Leave for around 30 minutes, until almost set. Whisk until frothy and then fold into whisked egg whites. Spoon into glasses, decorate with some of the reserved rind and chill for at least one hour.

🍎 Rhubarb fool

---

1 lb (500g) rhubarb
grated rind and juice of 1 orange
½ pt (300ml) custard
½ pt (300ml) diet yoghurt –
* plain or fruity if you have a*
* sweet tooth!*

½ tsp ginger, or, if you prefer,
* mixed spice*
artificial sweetener to taste

Cook rhubarb, orange juice and spices on a low heat until fruit is soft. Cool, then purée. Mix together custard and yoghurt. Fold in rhubarb, then spoon into serving dish.

🍎 Berry brûlée

---

1 lb (450g) berries
6oz (175g) low-fat fromage frais
pinch cinnamon

2–3 tbsp skimmed milk
granulated sweetener
2 tbsp demarara sugar

Place fruit in heatproof dish. Beat milk with fromage frais until frothy – add sweetener if wished. Spoon over fruit. Chill. Sprinkle with sugar, making thin layer, then place under grill until golden. Chill.

Exotic fruit platter

Selection of seasonal fruit, sliced or quartered. Include melon, berries, figs, kiwi, pineapple, grapes, etc.

🍎 Filo fruit tarts

---

3 large sheets filo pastry
1oz (25g) half-fat butter, melted
2 tbsp sugar-free strawberry
* preserve*

4oz (115g) prepared chopped
* mixed fruit e.g. strawberries,*
* apples, plums, etc.*
icing sugar for dusting

Set oven at 190°C/375°F/Gas 5. Lay the filo pastry sheets on a flat surface, one on top of the other. Using scissors cut into 12 equal-size squares about three inches large.

Lightly grease a 12 section patty tin with half-fat butter. Place a single layer of pastry into each section. Brush with butter. Arrange the next two layers of pastry on top, position the corners of each to the centre of the next to create a star-shaped pastry basket. Divide preserve between each basket then top with fruit. Brush pastry edges with a little butter then cook for approximately 25 minutes or until golden brown. Turn tin in oven if necessary. Serve warm with icing sugar.

Meringue nests

Use bought meringue nests and serve with fresh berries and virtually fat-free fromage frais, sweetened if liked.

Gingered fruit

2 kiwis (sliced and halved), 2 bananas (sliced), 2 oranges (segmented – pith removed), 8 green grapes (seedless, halved). Small bottle (around 8fl oz) low-calorie ginger ale, squeeze of lemon juice. Place fruit in bowl and toss in lemon juice. Add ginger ale and mix. Place in fridge for two hours or so to allow the ginger to seep into fruit.

Weight watchers dessert bombe

Available from supermarkets.

Berry jelly

---

1 lb (450g) berries (use frozen if
  liked)
¼ pint (150ml) water
½ pint (300ml) orange juice
6 tsp gelatine (or vegetarian
  equivalent if preferred)

3 tbsp white wine
artificial sweetener equivalent
  to 1 tbsp sugar

Put almost all berries in pan, reserving some for decoration. Simmer until soft and mushy. When cool, purée and stir in juice. (If a clearer jelly is preferred, strain before adding gelatine.) Dissolve gelatine in wine and stir into mixture. Pour into jelly mould and chill until set. Scatter reserved berries just before serving.

Passion dessert

Seed and slice a melon, arrange on flat serving plate and spoon over seeds of passion fruit. Chill before serving

❦ Hot Spiced Peaches

---

6 peaches skinned
1 tbsp caster sugar
pinch allspice
2 pinches of ground cloves

1 tsp lemon rind
½ tsp nutmeg
½ tsp ginger

Mix ingredients and roll peaches in mix until covered completely. Place each peach on a piece of silver foil and parcel up, dividing any remaining spiced sugar between the peaches. Place in shallow dish, in oven, for 20 minutes, on 190°C/375°F/Gas 5. Serve each peach separately with sauce made from 8oz (225g) cooked berries (eg. raspberries) that have been puréed.

❦ Pears in Red Wine

---

4 pears
1 pint (600ml) full bodied red
   wine e.g. Claret or Burgundy
rind and juice of 1 lemon

1 cinnamon stick
1 tsp nutmeg
1 oz (25g) dark brown sugar

Peel pears, slice bottom so they will stand in dish. Put wine in saucepan with rest of ingredients. Bring to boil, add pears, then simmer for 30–40 minutes, frequently spooning sauce over pears so they cook evenly. When tender lift pears from pan and place in serving dish. Boil liquid rapidly until it is reduced to a syrup. Spoon over pears, then chill until ready to serve.

Family puddings

 ### Fruit Jelly

---

1 sachet strawberry sugar-free
  jelly
1 12oz (350 g) can of fruit,
  canned in own juice (e.g. fruit
  cocktail, peaches)

Make up jelly according to instructions, using half pint of boiling water.
When jelly is dissolved, add juice from tinned fruit. Make up to just under
a pint (about 18fl oz/500ml) with water. Add fruit and pour into serving
dish. Refrigerate until set.

Fruit Kebabs

Cut a selection of fruit into one-inch chunks: use melon, apples, pears,
bananas, grapes, pineapple, satsumas, etc. Thread through skewers. Mix
lemon juice with warmed honey then brush lightly over kebabs. Place kebabs
under a preheated grill, turning and basting, until fruit starts to brown.

Berry Jelly

---

1 lb (450g) berries (use frozen if   6 tsp gelatine
  liked)   3 tbsp white wine
¼ pint (150ml) water   artificial sweetener to taste
½ pint (300ml) orange juice

Put almost all berries in pan, reserving some for decoration. Simmer until
soft and mushy. When cool, purée and stir in juice. Dissolve gelatine in
wine and stir into mixture. Pour into jelly mould and chill until set.
Scatter reserved berries just before serving.

Fresh Fruit Platter

Make up either an autumn platter (apples, pears, plums, tangerines, etc.)
or tropical platter which would include paw paw, kiwi, pineapple,
mango, etc.

Stewed Rhubarb and Raisins

Stew rhubarb with a little fruit juice, 1 tsp ginger and 1 tbsp raisins, artificial sweetener to taste.

Baked Apples

Using cooking apples, artificial sweetener and 5 tbsps water or fruit juice and a little reduced-sugar jam and raisins, plus dot of half-fat butter. Core apples and score round with sharp knife. Place in ovenproof dish, fill cavities with jam and raisins, if liked. Place small knob of butter on each apple and put water or juice in dish. Place in oven 190°C/375°F/Gas 5 for 35–45 minutes.

Stewed Apples

1½ to 2 lbs (675g–900g) cooking apples, cored, peeled and sliced, stewed in a little fruit juice and 1 tsp mixed cinnamon plus artificial sweetener to taste.

Passion dessert

(See recipe on page 261.)

Baked bananas

Take four bananas, in skins, and place in baking dish for 20–30 minutes on 200°C/400°F/Gas 6 or until skins have turned black. 'Unzip' and serve with yoghurt or ice cream.

❦ Fruit compote

9oz (250g) dried fruit
2 bags of fruit tea (e.g. passion
fruit and mango)

½ pint (300ml) water

Place teabags in jug and pour over pint boiling water. Leave to infuse. Remove bags and place fruit in a shallow dish and pour over tea. Leave to soak overnight, then cook according to manufacturer's instructions.

Dieter's ice-cream

Bought from supermarket.

Berry bowl

Bowl of mixed berries, sprinkled with a little fruit juice and icing sugar, if liked, chilled.

Slices of fresh pineapple

Sprinkled with a either a little Cointreau, Amaretto or Kirsch. Chill for at least one hour.

Fresh fruit salad

Make up bowl of fresh fruit and let everyone dig in! It couldn't be easier *or* healthier!

Green ginger

Selection of green fruit (e.g. green apples, kiwi, green grapes) sliced or halved drizzled with 1 tbsp syrup from stem ginger jar. Chill before serving.

Appendix

As I hope has been shown over the chapters, food is something that you should feel at ease with, rather than threatened by. Fundamentally, it's food that keeps us going - not calories - so it's vital that food becomes a natural part of everyone's life. Working on the basis that information is knowledge and knowledge is power, the more we understand about the food we eat, the happier we are going to feel about it.

As chapter twelve has shown, one of the greatest barriers that we have about food is based on our lack of knowledge and understanding of the nutrients that are used to make up the type of everyday supermarket foods that we're all familiar with. So, to give you some idea of just how the amounts of energy can differ from one food to another, I've listed below a variety of foods - all containing varying amounts of calories. The reason I have used calories, rather than fat, protein or carbohydrate is that a calorie is the measurement which we're most familiar with. But remember, calories just give you an indication of how much energy a food contains - you shouldn't allow them to dictate what you eat. The whole process of eating is about food, not about calories consumed.

To give an indication of how foods differ, I've included low-energy foods as well as high ones. Also, where possible, I have given amounts for whole, or portions, of foods. Since the way food is cooked, or processed, significantly alters the calorie content I have not included meats, fish, chicken, canned food, etc. For general advice on a balanced diet, use the healthy eating pyramid on page 163 to guide you.

Fruit and vegetables
Apples - 50 cals (approx)
Apricots - 10 cals
Bananas - 60-80 cals (approx - depending on size)
Dates - 15 cals
Grapes - 50-60 cals a portion (about 4 ounces)

Grapefruit - 25 cals per half
Mandarins, tangerines, satsumas - 20 cals
Oranges - 60 cals
Peach - 50 cals
Pears - 40-50 cals
Plums - 15 cals
Cucumber - 4 cals for a chuncky slice
Avocado (half) - 130 cals
Carrot - 10 cals approx per carrot
Greens (broccoli, brussel sprouts, cabbage, spring greens - 5-10 cals a serving
Potatoes:
   Jacket - 150-180 cals (average size potato for baking)
   New (boiled) - per serving (about 4 small new potatoes) - 85 cals approx
   Chips - 250-400 cals per serving
Tomatoes - 10 cals

Rice and pasta
Portion of rice (plain, boiled, about 2-3oz is considered a portion) - 70-105 cals (approx)
Pasta - 60-90 cals per serving (a serving is usually about 2-3oz)

Bread
Rolls - 120-140 cals
Bap - 130 cals
Slice - 60-70 cals
Crumpet - 75 cals
Scone - 150 cals
Fruit scone - 200 cals

Cheese
Portion of cheddar (about 2oz) - 240 cals
Portion of low-fat cheddar - 150 cals
Portion of Leicester or Double Gloucester - 210 cals
Portion of Brie, camembert or processed cheese - 180 cals
Portion of Edam (about 2oz) - 180 cals
Portion of Cottage cheese (a small pot - about 4oz) - 108 cals

Drinks
Apple juice - 60 cals per glass (approx)
Orange juice - 50 cals per glass (approx)
Wine (red or dry white) - 100 cals a glass
Can of Fizzy Drink - 120-160 cals
Can Diet Drinks - 0-5 cals

Chocolates cakes and snacks
Fudge finger - 120 cals
Kit Kat (two finger bar) - 115 cals
Chocolate (50g) bar - 250 cals
Cereal bar - 150 cals
Crisps - 150 cals a pack
   Low-fat varieties - 100-120 cals per pack
Jam tart or cup cake - 130 cals
Mince pie - 200-250 cals (approx)
Iced bun - 215 cals
Jam doughnut - 180 cals
Average slice fruit cake - 300 cals
Nuts - 150-190 cals per ounce
Chocolate Brazil nuts - 55 cals each
Biscuits (will differ slightly, depending on manufacturer):
   Custard creams - 60 cals approx
   Digestive - 70 cals
   Chocolate digestive - 90 cals
   Bourbon - 65 cals
   Hob-Nob - 70-80 cals
   Jaffa cake - 50 cals
   Gingernut - 50 cals
   Maryland cookie - 50 cals
   Chocolate fingers - 30 cals
   Garibaldi - 40 cals
   Chocolate biscuit bars - 110-150 cals

Index

INDEX OF RECIPES AND MENUS

PUBLISHER'S CREDITS

The extract from *Fat Chance* by Jane Ogden (Routledge, 1992) is reproduced by permission of Routledge Ltd.
Extracts from *Tomorrow I'll be Slim* by Sara Gilbert (Routledge, 1989) are reproduced by permission of Routledge Ltd.
Extracts from *The Sensible Person's Guide to Weight Control* are reproduced by permission of Smith Gordon.